# *To Be in England*

*Tintern Abbey, Monmouthshire*

*Richard D. Altick*

---

# TO BE

# IN

# ENGLAND

W · W · NORTON & COMPANY · INC ·

*New York*

ALSO BY RICHARD D. ALTICK

*Preface to Critical Reading*
*The Cowden Clarkes*
*The Scholar Adventurers*
*The English Common Reader*
*The Art of Literary Research*
*Lives and Letters*
*Browning's Roman Murder Story* (with James F. Loucks II)

Copyright © 1969 by Richard D. Altick
*First Edition*
Library of Congress Catalog Card No. 68-20813
All Rights Reserved
Published simultaneously in Canada by
George J. McLeod Limited, Toronto

"Thank you, Mrs. Porter" by A. P. Herbert is reprinted by permission of Sir Alan Herbert and Methuen & Co. Ltd.

*Summoned by Bells* by John Betjeman is reprinted by permission of the author, Houghton Mifflin Company, and John Murray (Publishers) Ltd.

"The Arrest of Oscar Wilde at the Cadogan Hotel," from *Collected Poems* by John Betjeman is reprinted by permission of the author and John Murray (Publishers) Ltd.

From "Burnt Norton" and "East Coker" in *Four Quartets,* copyright 1943 by T. S. Eliot. Reprinted by permission of Harcourt, Brace & World, Inc. and Faber and Faber Ltd.

Printed in the United States of America
1  2  3  4  5  6  7  8  9  0

To
LOUISE AND JIM WILSON
*archetypal Anglophiles*

# Contents

# List of Illustrations

# Preface

*To the reading American a first visit to England is not so much one of discovery as of recognition. Everything, not merely literary shrines, seems and is familiar. The thatched and stone houses, the hedges, the soft summer sky, the speech, clipped, musical, and precise, the top hats, the school ties, the pounds, shillings, and pence. . . . The literary American is early and oddly nostalgic for England. Or, at any rate, so was the author of these pages. I can hardly remember when I first longed to go to England or when I for the first time met an Englishman. But by the time I was a senior in college, the image of England as a green and pleasant land was fixed in my imagination, and fixed, too, was the picture of Englishmen as human paragons, fair-spoken, clean-limbed, polite and poetic—above all quiet paragons.*

—*Irwin Edman,* Philosopher's Holiday (*New York,* 1938) .

I copied down those sentences soon after they were printed, because the latter ones then fitted my case exactly. Perhaps even so early I was subconsciously hoping that some day there could be a book which I might begin with them. Here, thirty years later, it is.

It is a very personal book, written for others because I have reason to believe that the record it contains—a chronicle of delighted recognition, of exploration and fresh discovery, of constantly renewed pleasure in the English scene—is not mine alone. Years of hungry ranging through English books, from Chaucer all the way down, breed in many people a special, if second-hand, familiarity with English names, English places, English customs, English idioms. Things English acquire a special flavour—even the English spelling of certain words. The locales of English films beheld in movie houses three thousand miles away; the accents of English speakers heard on television or in the lecture hall; the curious magic of words like "Piccadilly" and "Charing Cross" which exert a power over the susceptible like that which the evangelist George Whitefield's sonorous utterance of "Mesopotamia" had over the swooning females in his audience—these fugitive suggestions of a land so far away, yet so intimately known through one's reading of Fielding and Dickens and Trollope, feed an insatiable appetite for the reality.

The longer one's first trip to England is delayed, the greater the seeming peril of disappointment. Life's little revenges being what they are, expectations accumulated over the years that separate one from his childhood are in danger of being climaxed not by happy realization but by a dissolution as complete and irreparable as the bursting of a bubble. But somehow this does not happen. Even to the middle-aged, a long-term infatuation with the imagined turns into an unabashed love affair with the actual. Once achieved, the experience of England, unlike most human attempts to find the dream in the reality, results in no disenchantment. The real may not match the dream in every respect, but it turns out to have a charm of its own which more than atones for the occasional discrepancy. That is why a seasoned Anglophile-by-bookish-upbringing can assure every acquaintance who is about to embark for England for the first time that he envies him the unrepeatable experience. "No day in an American's recollection," wrote the Boston man of letters Thomas Wentworth Higginson seventy years ago, "can easily be more cheerful than that in which he first found himself within reach of London, prepared, as [Nathaniel Parker] Willis said half a century ago, to see whole shelves of his library walking about in coats and gowns."

These chapters have been written for all who hope to know, or have already known, the delectable *déjà vu* of literary experience relived in the very presence of wet streets and Portland stone office buildings and country lanes screened by high hedgerows—and people speaking English with English accents. Although, my predilections being what they are, there will be considerable talk of scenes with literary associations, there will be at least as much of matters suggested simply by the Anglophile's acute sense of place and race. For English literature, the miraculous product of a tight little island, has always been marked by a peculiarly strong awareness and use of locale; and that is why readers come to its native soil desiring not only to meet the people from the books on their shelves walking about in coats and gowns but, even more, to savor as intimately as possible the whole world in which those characters live. An American's sensibilities and curiosity, nurtured in the first instance by the English books he has read, soon broaden to an interest in all things English, proceeding quite independently of literary overtones.

It possibly should be added that the following pages are not for those who seek to be directed to where the action is or warned against tourist traps, exorbitant nightclub bills, gouging cab drivers, and all the other hazards that are reputed to beset the innocent abroad who presumably has never had to cope with them at home. Nor are they for people who want to do England on the cheap, because I do not think that anybody who has a reasonable American regard for creature comforts can do England on the cheap. They will prove to contain no potted history, least of all any allusions to those medieval monarchs whom it is so hard, and perhaps in the long run not very important, to distinguish from one another; and such guidebook sites as do appear here will be seen from an unconventional angle. No instruction is contemplated; I have assumed readers who are better informed than the American businessman who asked me one day

in Chester Cathedral whether this was "an Anglican church."
Some of the remarks on driving and the quality of hotels and
food may prove to have a certain practical interest to the reader
who has not yet been in England. But they are included not from
any utilitarian motive but just because they are often part of
Americans' conversation when it turns to England, and I enjoy
talking about them.

Although I have had the first-time visitor particularly in mind,
I have not forgotten Nathaniel Hawthorne's words: "In truth, I
believe that the chief delight and advantage of this kind of literature is not for any real information that it supplies to un-
travelled people, but for reviving the recollections and reawaken-
ing the emotions of persons already acquainted with the scenes
described." Such people will find much in these pages to stir their
affectionate memories and, quite possibly, to kindle their ambition to return. It is they in particular who will, I think, recognize
and concur in the spirit in which I have written, which is not one
of indiscriminate adulation of all things English but—a much
higher tribute to the enduring charm of one's host—of appreciation tempered by candor.

R. D. A.

*I will envy you a little your delightful two months in England—and a picture rises before me of long slopes washed with a cool lustre of watery sunshine—a swan-silenced reach of sallow-fringed river—great humps of foliage contrasting taper spires—cathedral closes, gray Gothic fronts elbowed by red-brick deaneries—broad downs clouded with cumulous sheep—nay, even a misty, moisty morning in London, and the boy with the pots of porter, and the hansom cab just losing itself in the universal gray—even these sights I envy you.*

—James Russell Lowell to Miss Jane Norton, September 9, 1856.

*Thackeray's last home, 2 Palace Green, Kensington*

---

*1*

---

# *Arrival*

IF THE initial experience of England, the first realization of the land of book-bred visions before one's eyes, is potentially so happy a moment, how is it best arranged? Long-anticipated events must be planned with the utmost care.

There is a wrong way, and there is a right way. Take the wrong way first. It begins more or less auspiciously, but ends in anticlimax. Unfortunately, for Americans it has become the most usual approach, and within a few years it may become the only one available. The night jet from the East Coast flies into the dawn in russet mantle clad. The russet reflects from the cloud banks that have hidden the ocean all the way across, and inside the plane there is a general stirring from unrestorative sleep, an attempt to unkink cramped muscles, the work-to-rule serving of breakfast only a few hours after last night's dinner. The occupants of aisle seats lean over their neighbors, ready to glimpse the first landfall, and the inevitable cameras are primed, however unpropitious the light and the distance. The clouds break first, perhaps, over Ireland: not truly England, this, but unmistakably English in its early-morning aspect from the air, the tight alternation of dark brown cultivated fields and lush emerald woods

divided by hedgerows. Then more water—the Irish Sea or St.
George's Channel—and, if the clouds continue to absent themselves, first Wales and then England—England!—lie below.

As the aircraft begins its descent, the ground can be seen in
clearer detail: more woods and fields, marked off by the stone
walls of the Cotswolds; little towns with smoke rising from chimneys and little cars beginning to creep along the winding roads;
the square Norman tower of many a rural church rising above
the trees; more towns, some of them quite large, with dense terra
cotta rows and crescents of Victorian dwellings that look more
agreeable from the air than they will prove on the ground; long
straight stretches of "motorway" (super-highways: have we come
all the way from the New World to see *these?*) ; and the activity
of a nation rousing itself to a prosaic new day, the low-spirited
drivers of the cars and lorries and buses down below going about
their business in a world quite detached from that of a Boeing
capsule in which more than a hundred people have vaulted the
Atlantic at thirty thousand feet in six hours. No matter what the
mode of transportation, the traveler never ceases to feel the psychological distance that separates him, an alien on high adventure, from the utterly routine activity into which he has arrived
—activity that is totally oblivious of him, whose own pattern of
life has been so radically changed for the occasion.

The distance narrows as the aircraft glides down over Windsor
Castle and Eton College chapel; soon one is perforce absorbed
into the routine of the country he is entering. If this is a typical
London morning, the clouds are low and ashen when the aircraft
touches ground and roars down the runway, its engines reversed
for braking. There are patches of water from last night's rain on
the tarmac where huge planes of El Al, Qantas, Swissair, Ethi-
opian Airlines, Air India, and a dozen other exotic companies
graze in international amity. Keeping rendezvous with the jet as
it comes to a halt somewhere in the remoter acreage of this airport
is a bus which conveys the passengers to the terminal.

And the terminal is where the trouble begins, the reason why no approach by air really suits the sentimental expectations and desires of the first-time visitor to England. What he wants is an entrance uniquely expressive of the country, one that will immediately assure him that this is long-sought England and no other possible nation. What he gets instead is an experience just as readily available at Hong Kong, Rome, Karachi, or Sydney: the architecture, sounds, and movements of international airports the world over. Oh, there are a few minor indigenous touches. Stuffed in the pocket of the bored employee who drives the bus from plane to terminal is a copy of a London tabloid; the lettering of the direction signs is in a spare modern style native to England (I shall speak of it later in another connection) ; and the quiet men at the desks at immigration control and customs— their perfunctory inspections and inquiries constitute a welcome threshold to their country—wear British insignia and, with their starched detachable collars, look English. But the language that pours from the loudspeakers is not a distinctive mark of London Airport, the gateway to England. It is the standardized one-world English uttered by airport staff everywhere, and there is no special thrill in hearing it spoken on its native ground. Furthermore, the glossy bare functionalism of air terminal design and appointments is no more expressive of England than it is of Istanbul. One would, of course, scarcely desire an arrival area done in the cozy manner of an Olde Englysshe Inne or anything of that sort. Yet it is ironical to reflect that a similar mismatching of form and purpose, the Gothic style adopted for nineteenth-century railway termini, today is looked upon, and in some quarters increasingly respected, as a peculiarly English phenomenon.

Even after the airport with its homogenized atmosphere has been left behind, the route into London is no picturesque pilgrim's way, not with the English headquarters of firms like Firestone, Black and Decker, and Honeywell punctuating the landscape. The remaining Middlesex meadows have lost such pastoral character as they once possessed and doubtless will soon be replaced by rows of jerry-built housing as ugly in their way as the

present ones along the road, which date, I suppose, from the un-
inspired 1920's. That an airport motel is named the Ariel gives
momentary assurance that one has indeed alighted on Shakespeare's "precious stone set in the silver sea," and to the already
initiate there is further assurance in the fact that the M4
motorway perversely narrows as it approaches the city and the
volume of traffic increases. This is England—the same England
that spent years building a complicated system of underpasses
and walkways under Hyde Park Corner, the busiest traffic confluence in London, with the sole result (as a newspaper pointed
out at the time) of moving the bottleneck a few hundred yards
west, into Knightsbridge. This is also the nation that until recent
years coped with cold weather not by installing central heating
but by sagaciously placing its drainpipes on the outside walls of
houses so that when they froze and burst they would not do any
damage.

Before the M4 climbs onto the "flyover" that will conduct it
over Hammersmith and past the unlovely concrete-and-glass
office buildings that dot the West London skyline, it passes one
site which, if recognized, will authenticate the locale. On the
right side of the "dual carriageway" (divided highway) in Chiswick is a red brick house with a prominent bow window, wedged
between the Cherry Blossom Shoe Polish factory and a laundry.
The name of the laundry is the giveaway: it is "Hogarth," and
the house next door, now a museum, was the artist's country residence from 1749 until his death. But not one in ten thousand of
the passengers who speed past it in a day knows it is even there.

London (Heathrow) Airport and the general drabness of West
London do not, then, offer the arriving visitor the characteristic
scenes and atmosphere that he has expected. Whatever thrill of
recognition he may feel will be strictly minimal. The alternate
means of arrival, the more decidedly English way of entering the
country of one's dream, is the old-fashioned way. So long as England can be reached by passenger liner, I recommend the experience.

Suppose the liner has first called at Le Havre, thus affording the traveler a little preliminary contrast. The train of heavy SNCF passenger coaches waiting at the pier to load for its swift Paris run, the blue-bloused *ouvriers* unloading mail from the ship or lunching with a bottle of wine, the red-tiled roofs of the town—these are decidedly not English, and the delicious impact of the true Englishness shortly to come is made all the sharper because of this brief intrusion of the Continent. Then the ship proceeds back past the breakwater and into the Channel; and, on this sunlit afternoon, its English landfall is a stretch of the coast of Hampshire, a continuous narrow strip of white beach backed by rolling fields. As it crosses Spithead, it passes to port the wooded Isle of Wight, on which the visitor sees his first Stately Homes of England, including, as a helpful railside Briton will point out, Queen Victoria's summer home. Cowes, on the northern side of the island, is gay with bunting and pennants, for this is regatta week, with a host of yachts at anchor in the harbor and a covey of excursion boats that come out to let their passengers inspect a tall liner which was so lately in fabulous New York. As the ship proceeds up Southampton Water to her wharf she passes an Esso refinery among whose gigantic round tanks brown cattle browse: a foretaste of the intimate mingling of the industrial and the bucolic that is modern Britain.

It is true that the Ocean Terminal where transatlantic passengers debark is as modern as London Airport; it was built following the war, when Southampton, like the other south coast ports, reestablished herself on her bombed sites. But in the terminal there is immediate, irrefutable evidence that this is England: the helmeted young policemen standing with arms folded, the bright W. H. Smith & Son bookstall (one's first glimpse of a link in the great chain of shops and stalls whose displays of paperbacks and other books in every town are an added amenity to travel in England) , even the English telephones, which sometimes bring one surprisingly into contact with a male operator. In the American's imagination the voice conjures up memories of pictures he saw

years ago of operators, men and boys, in the days of Alexander
Graham Bell, standing before fearsome tangles of cords connected to a primitive switchboard, shouting into their mouth-
pieces and giving their exasperated subscribers as good as they
got by way of insults. But the voice at the end of this wire is
decorous, and unmistakably British.

The boat train waits at dockside, a long string of cherry-red
coaches bearing the British Railways insignia and labeled "Waterloo": as positive a mark of England as one has yet encountered, and one that is immediately substantiated by the interior
of the compartment, which recalls scenes in Sherlock Holmes
stories. Inspector Bradstreet, accompanied by Holmes, Watson,
and the newly thumbless hydraulic engineer, draws a circle
with his compasses on an ordnance map of Berkshire he has laid
out on the seat; Holmes dampens Watson's admiration of the
sunlit Hampshire scenery outside the carriage window by observing, "It is my belief, Watson, founded upon my experience, that
the lowest and vilest alleys in London do not present a more
dreadful record of sin than does the smiling and beautiful countryside." As the train fills, one watches the comings and goings of
railway workmen *on bicycles.* Eventually, in the watery June twilight with the sun only fitfully visible, the train creeps through
Southampton on the *left side* of the line. On sidings are strings of
absurdly tiny four-wheeled "goods wagons" (freight cars), no
bigger than they were when railways were invented a hundred
and forty years ago. (The reason is that many old sidings have
too sharp curves and too narrow clearances for larger cars. Moreover, the little ones can be shifted by hand if a locomotive is not
around.)

Uninspiring as Southampton is from the railway—though no
more so than any other city—it is, beyond denial, English: corner
pubs with their company signs, doubledecker buses lumbering
along the streets, small English cars, workers' tenements which
are probably cramped, cluttered, damp, cooking-odored, and depressing inside but each of which nevertheless has its tiny plot of

flowers and a television antenna on the roof. The Hampshire countryside, once it is achieved, suggests eastern Pennsylvania with its farms and woods, an occasional town with a modern industrial plant or two, herds of cattle, and flocks of sheep. The rhododendrons in riotous bloom along the right of way are, however, England's own touch. Tea is served as the train rushes along, its shrill self-important whistle echoed by locomotives that tear past in the other direction, on (one cannot help worrying about it) the wrong side of the line.

And thus into the suburbs of London on a misty evening. Alongside the priority boat train from Southampton, as it slows, rumble green suburban trains with a few lonely passengers reading evening papers in the smoking compartments. The incidence of neon signs, red buses, and housing blocks and factories increases; and then one sees his first instantly identifiable landmark, the lighted tower of Big Ben across the river. The River Thames. This is England. It is, in fact, London.

Waterloo Station: big, bustling, not sepulchral like today's American termini. Numerous stalls for magazines, flowers, tea, and every other railway-station vendible; direction signs everywhere, plain, explicit, always helpful—no traveler who can read is in danger of being misled in Britain. To the taxi stand, and another gratifyingly authentic touch of London, the high-slung, dignified taxi with its pipe-smoking, tweed-jacketed, cloth-capped driver. The cab weaves into the busy London night-time streets, traffic moving more swiftly than in the New York one has left, seemingly with much greater smoothness and certainly with less cacophony of horns. Across Westminster Bridge into Parliament Square, policemen with luminous white sleevelets on traffic duty, clots of red buses, "zebras" (pedestrian crossings marked by white stripes on the pavement and blinking yellow lights at the curbs; pronounced with a short *e*), the immediate sense of cleanliness, briskness, a modern city at its evening best. A dizzying movement from one street to another, the momentary glimpse of a sign reading "Ebury Street": memories of George Moore, *Con-*

*versations in Ebury Street.* A sudden glimpse of Buckingham Palace guarded by soldiers in red uniforms and towering bearskins. And so to one's first hotel in England.

This is not quite the London that you grew to know so well—you thought—from Dickens; your great expectations have been fulfilled, but in a curious, almost paradoxical, way. It is London's modernity, its very lack of picturesqueness at night, that pleases you: an English version, much quieter, air-washed, of the more sightly parts of a large American city. And this discovery, unanticipated though it is, is wholly satisfying. You are prepared to accept London on its own terms; and these, you will discover, are very generous.

*Old London and the new: the Blewcoat School (1709), Westminster*

# 2

## Survey of London

It is well that someone visiting London for the first time can be pleased initially by the city's very modernity, because sentimental expectations nurtured exclusively through pre-twentieth-century literature and its accompanying topographical art are bound to be in some measure disappointed. This is not, after all, the Thames-side town described in John Stow's classic *Survey of London* (1598) and illustrated in Visscher's often reproduced panoramic engraving of 1616—the wood-built, cramped London that Shakespeare and Ben Jonson knew intimately; it disappeared in flames in the summer of 1666. Nor is it now the renewed London that figures in subsequent English literature from Defoe's time to Dickens'. Most of that London has gradually vanished through demolition and reconstruction, and, more recently, through the catastrophic action of war.

But until thirty years ago enough of it remained, in essential profile, to recall the London which Sir Christopher Wren admired from across the Thames as the rebuilding he supervised was completed after the Great Fire, and which moved Wordsworth as he rode on a coach crossing Westminster Bridge a century later. The dome of St. Paul's Cathedral, topped by its

golden cross, dominated the City—the square mile constituting
the original area of medieval London—from Ludgate Hill.
Thickly surrounding it, like acolytes, were the spires and towers
of the City churches, mostly by Wren. The other fixed points of
reference, upstream in Westminster, were the Houses of Parliament and Westminster Abbey. These were the chief landmarks
visible from the green elevations beyond the city, Highgate Hill
and Hampstead Heath to the north and the nearest knolls of
Surrey to the south. Between them, and far outward in all directions as it grew, London clung to the ground, the level square
miles, compact of dwellings and shops, punctuated only by stee-
ples and, from the early Victorian era onward, by occasional gas
holders and factory chimneys. Until after the Second World War
the prevailing London dimension was the horizontal. In its basic
character the view from the top of the Monument near Pudding
Lane when it was opened in 1617 (marking the spot where the
Great Fire had begun) and that from the swaying basket of a
Victorian balloonist was—allowing for immense expansion—the
same.

But now, as one takes one's measure of London from the top
of the spindly General Post Office Tower newly rooted in the
London clay just off Tottenham Court Road, London's electronic-
age answer to the Eiffel Tower, or from a jet plane arriving from
the Continent on a fine summer afternoon, the flatness of the great
city below is repeatedly punctuated, as far as one can look, by
white and yellow cube-shaped excrescences: tall hotels along Park
Lane, office towers in Victoria Street and Holborn and Notting
Hill Gate, clusters of vertical housing blocks in every direction.
In the City the ancient supremacy of St. Paul's is challenged by
acres of stone and ferro-concrete office slabs. Perhaps it is only a
matter of time before the dome is totally obscured by the growth
of surrounding structures.

But the aspect of London from aloft is deceptive. If one drastically shortens one's perspective and returns to ground level, one
discovers that the transformation actually has been much less strik-

ing or sweeping, and that much of the London portrayed in engravings and photographs of the last century or so—the London embodied in literature—still survives. For every mini-skyscraper there remain ten thousand London buildings, three to six stories tall, complete with dignified façades, clustered chimney pots, railed areaways, and complicated systems of drainpipes clinging to the walls, which preserve the flavor of the older city. The brave new world of "improvements," as the signboards term the process of eradication and construction (often with justice), though it is evolving more rapidly now than at any previous time in recent history, is still far from overwhelming the London one has come to see. Apprehension over that city's imminent total disappearance is as premature as Henry James's comment that "London is fast becoming an American city" was in 1886.

Yes, Piccadilly perhaps, and Oxford Street and Regent Street, with their up-to-date shops and department stores, and the scores of smaller retail centers in the Greater London that sprawls out fifteen miles in every direction from Charing Cross. The theatrical Shaftesbury Avenue is an inadequate imitation of a typical street near Times Square except for the lower incidence of pornography shops, and at the street's southern end Piccadilly Circus, with its hordes of youthful vagrants encamped around the Eros statue, its advertising signs and traffic jams and bored but vigilant young policemen, is an inadequate imitation of Times Square itself. But the supreme charm of today's "Americanized" London (as disparaging Englishmen choose always to call it) is the persistent, indeed near-universal, availability of the past. To adapt Mark Twain's observation about the New England weather, if you don't like the London present, walk but a hundred yards in any direction, preferably into a narrow court or alley, and you will find yourself in some fragment of the desired past.

One moment you are in noisy, congested Parliament Square; a minute's walk south across Broad Sanctuary and through the precincts of Westminster Abbey and you are in a world removed from that of the outlanders aiming their perpetual Kodaks at Big Ben: whole streets of Georgian dwellings, as placid and snug as the close of a provincial cathedral. Or if you wander from Parliament Square in another direction, into Great George Street which leads to Birdcage Walk—such names!—again the traffic and the crowds abruptly vanish, and you find yourself in little enclaves of eighteenth-century houses such as Petty France (where Milton once lived) and Queen Anne's Gate. Farther on, a few steps from Victoria Street with its big office buildings, all gray polished granite and glass—the *new* New Scotland Yard, Mobil House, Westminster City Hall, and Roebuck House, headquarters of the Watney brewing business—are well-kept little dwellings with gladioli blooming in their areaways.

Recollection of these recurrent juxtapositions of the present instant and some span of yesterday—the era of the Napoleonic Wars, say, or the confident years of the Prince Consort—is among the most dependable pleasures the old London hand (as he likes to think of himself) derives from the maps he pores over, three thousand miles from the locales they record. The affection they evoke is by no means solely a matter of literary association, for sometimes the tie is remote at best. The mere fact that they are part of London automatically endows them with a certain aura. To the devout explorer, a mean slum street, a railway marshaling yard, a half-abandoned canal is picturesque just because it is where it is—in London. The magic name is enough to offset all ugliness or mediocrity.

Superimposed on the real map, then, is the informal atlas of accumulated memory, an intimate mingling of literary predilections and sympathies with sheer delight in physical and sociological topography for its own, not necessarily esthetic, sake. The hue of the compilation constantly alters as experience grows, and the London learned from literature is ever more thoroughly assimilated into the London of today.

Let the well-traveled map, still serviceable after countless unfoldings, stir impressions once again. Here near the center, for in-

stance, is Mayfair. Surrounded by brisk shopping streets (Piccadilly, Oxford Street, and Regent Street) and by the West End's
luxury hotel row (Park Lane, overlooking Hyde Park), and
shabbily commercial at its northeastern fringes, where workshops and small warehouses support the Oxford and Regent
Street retail trade, in its interior western reaches Mayfair still has
something of the atmosphere it grew up with in the eighteenth
century. One would not really be surprised to meet a gilded
sedan chair coming down the street, borne by two liveried servants in powdered wigs and preceded at night by a linkboy.
(Some of the houses still bear, alongside the front door, an iron
ring where a torch could be placed.) These thoroughfares—
Grosvenor Street, Mount Street, Dover Street, Upper Brook
Street, Sackville Street, Berkeley Street, Audley Street—were
fashionable addresses more than two centuries ago, and some
remain so. Both Lord Chesterfield and Horace Walpole had town
houses in Mayfair; Boswell, on his frequent visits to London,
usually stayed in lodgings at one location or another, none of
which survive; Smollett lived in Curzon Street, and Sterne died
in New Bond Street, just off Piccadilly. In these streets, too, and
the broad green squares to which they lead, were the residences
in a later day of Byron and his friends, and still later of Thackeray's friends and many of his well-to-do fictional characters as
well. Today some of their red brick Georgian houses are still
lived in, by people of the same class. Others have been converted
into captivating little shops, specialized and expensive, with
immaculate trim, colorful hanging signboards, fanlights, and,
sometimes, small-paned show windows: the whole conveying the
impression that the business has been in the hands of the same
family since the Regency, which in some cases it has.

With the disappearance of horses, coaches, and stablemen, the
mews behind the houses have been transformed into rows of tiny,
dainty, high-rent dwellings. Even in Dickens' time, mews houses
that were just around the corner from a fashionable square com-
manded extravagant rents, despite the pervasive odor of horse;

Mr. Tite Barnacle, permanent adviser in the science of How Not to Do It to the successive titled heads of the Circumlocution Office, lived in such an ambiguous situation off Grosvenor Square. But Dickens tended to locate his affluent families north of Mayfair, across Oxford Street in Marylebone. Mr. Dombey's unhappy mansion was between Portland Place and Bryanston Square, the Podsnaps lived in Portman Square, and the Merdles and Noddy Boffin, who made his fortune in the garbage, trash, and sewage trade, were near Cavendish Square.

On the southern edge of Mayfair, likewise, despite the encroachment of modern offices and shops, "clubland"—St. James's Street and Pall Mall—retains much of the appearance and flavor it had when Thackeray's men of leisure sat in their clubs' windows. Trollope methodically wrote installments of his novels at the Athenaeum before breakfast, and Phileas Fogg set out from the Reform Club on his eighty-day trip around the world. Clubland, with its elegant traditional façades, is where barristers, bishops, actors, scientists, and editors foregather for lunch in the dining room, drinks at the bar, and *The Times,* the *Guardian,* and the *Economist* in the library. A great deal of the serious political and cultural business of Britain has been informally transacted within these walls in the last century and a half.

Move the reminiscent finger southwest of Mayfair and Hyde Park Corner. Here is stately Belgravia, in whose streets and broad squares the earls and duchesses of Victorian fiction lived, as do some of their descendants—and particularly lucky commoners—today. For although many of the imposing mansions, especially in Belgrave Square itself, have become the headquarters of diplomatic missions and learned societies, many more are still residences or have been converted into luxury flats. The long rows of tall, porticoed houses, painted in shades of cream with brightly colored trim, exude the same air of wealth and luxury in the age of the welfare state that they did at the peak of Gladstone's—or Ouida's—career. On spring evenings, before the curtains are drawn, the stroller in Belgrave or Eaton Square

gains glimpses of high bookshelves, crystal chandeliers, oil paintings, and fine furniture: all the appurtenances of the good life in
or out of fiction.

Directly west of Belgravia, across Cadogan Place and Sloane
Street, lies Chelsea. *Plus ça change* . . . : for all I know to the
contrary (having reliable sources in neither sector) Dickens' description of the delicate social distinction between the two regions is as valid today as when it was written in 1839 (*Nicholas
Nickleby,* Chapter 21) :

> *Cadogan Place [where the ambitious Mr. and Mrs. Witit-
> terly live] is the one slight bond that joins two great ex-
> tremes; it is the connecting link between the aristocratic
> pavements of Belgrave Square, and the barbarism of Chel-
> sea. It is in Sloane Street, but not of it. The people in
> Cadogan Place look down upon Sloane Street, and think
> Brompton [a neighborhood farther west] low.* . . . *Not that
> they claim to be on precisely the same footing as the high
> folks of Belgrave Square and Grosvenor Place, but that they
> stand with reference to them rather in the light of those
> illegitimate children of the great who are content to boast of
> their connexions, although their connexions disavow them.
> Wearing as much as they can of the airs and semblances of
> loftiest rank, the people of Cadogan Place have the realities
> of middle station. It is the conductor which communicates to
> the inhabitants of regions beyond its limit, the shock of
> pride of birth and rank, which it has not within itself, but
> derives from a fountain-head beyond.* . . .

What Dickens does not mention, because the tendency had not
yet begun, was the artistic-literary flavor that eventually set Chelsea apart from other middle-class London neighborhoods. Carlyle
and Leigh Hunt already lived there, and so, after 1846, did
J. M. W. Turner, though incognito. But Chelsea achieved promi-
nence as an artists' and writers' quarter only with the founding

of the Rossetti-Swinburne-Meredith ménage in Cheyne Walk in the early 1860's, an animated episode in Chelsea's literary and zoological history which will appear on a later page. At the same time, Whistler, and later Sargent and Oscar Wilde, and still later Henry James in his last years lived in these quiet streets not far from the river. Their successors are still there today: writers, editors, artists, actors, museum curators, career government officials.

Together, of course, with the newest wave of avant-garde youth, who make the sidewalks of Chelsea's main street, the King's Road, a perpetual Peacock Alley—a parade of the latest bizarre fashions in human plumage which are displayed, however, in a slouch rather than a strut. This and kindred phenomena of what the world has come to know as Swinging London may be studied *in extenso* in all the "media," from *Time-Life,* whose discovery it seems to have been, to the latest film about life and morals among the trendy. Their London is not the London of the present book.

Beyond Chelsea and the perennially more or less fashionable Knightsbridge, presided over by Harrods, the aristocrat of department stores, lies South Kensington. This wide area, mile upon mile, square upon crescent upon terrace of solid masonry— much of it built by Galsworthy's "Superior Dosset" Forsyte and his fellow entrepreneurs—is *par excellence* the Victorian part of London. Its nucleus was Kensington Palace in the eighteenth century: hence the title of *The Old Court Suburb,* a history and appreciation by Leigh Hunt, who after his Chelsea phase lived here and westward in Hammersmith. The outward aspect of South Kensington is one of portentous respectability, Philistine rather than Dionysian. If Mayfair recalls sedan chairs and linkboys, South Kensington suggests hansom cabs, large families on the way to church (Pugin Gothic in design, staunchly Anglican in doctrine), and maidservants lugging cans of bath water up four flights of stairs. Its comfortable virtues as a place of residence attracted Thackeray, who lived most of his mature life at a succession of Kensington addresses, Browning and Henry James, who were neighbors in DeVere Gardens, and W. S. Gilbert.

The tone of the whole area is increasingly influenced by the presence, south of Hyde Park, of the complex of institutes and museums that began when it was decided to apply the considerable profits of the Great Exhibition of 1851 to educational uses. The vast Victoria and Albert, the Science, Geological, and Natural History Museums, and numerous technical institutions and schools of fine and applied arts make this the center of specialized higher education for the whole British Commonwealth. As a result, South Kensington abounds with the polyglot and multi-hued, and in many streets the former upper middle-class homes, tall, uniform, and stuccoed, now tend toward the condition of rooming houses, hostels, and cheap hotels. In these sections Kensington is not especially inviting, and farther west, in Earl's Court, it degenerates into outright seediness. These prospective slums may today be the obscure breeding grounds of important new intellectual and artistic movements, which are as likely to come to eventual bloom in Africa or India as in London, but whatever shape they take will not owe much to the residuary influence of such old Kensingtonians as Thackeray and Walter Pater.

Back in the center of the city, east across Regent Street from Mayfair, is another cosmopolitan section of London, indeed its oldest one. Soho, as such street names as Poland and Greek imply, was a foreign quarter when South Kensington was still mostly acres of market gardens. Although it once was a dignified neighborhood—Dryden's last years were spent at 43 Gerrard Street, and later Edmund Burke lived down the street at number 37—most of Soho's literary connections are with the young and the transient. It was here that seventeen-year-old Thomas De Quincey, having quit his school and drifted, penniless, to London, was succored by the golden-hearted prostitute Ann, in circumstances memorably described in *Confessions of an English Opium-Eater*. Shelley, also a dropout (in his case, by order of his Oxford college), found lodgings for some months in Poland

Street. Hazlitt lived here, too, as a journalist and miscellaneous writer, and was buried in the yard of the now bomb-ravaged church of St. Anne. In this period—the beginning of the nine-teenth century—Soho had already begun to decline into the heterogeneous region of edge-of-poverty trades, shabby lodging houses, and street markets that it remains, in part, today. But in our own century its principal occupation has long been catering to the sundry appetites of the flesh. Some of its famous restau-rants are as good as they are touted to be; some are not. This literary tourist is unable to report on the quality of the night-clubs, strip-tease establishments, peep shows, and other enter-tainments advertised by the yellowing come-on photographs at their portals. Soho's tawdriness and (beneath all the neon entice-ments to be gay) its essential squalor make it, to my taste, one of London's most expendable areas.

Still farther east, beyond Charing Cross Road and Leicester Square, is Covent Garden, richer in literary associations than Soho but scarcely more picturesque. It has been rendered falsely romantic by the old wholesale fruit, vegetable, and flower mar-ket, now slated for removal, the opera house crowded against it, and the fact that Eliza Doolittle had her flower-selling pitch under the east portico of St. Paul's church. (It is not often ob-served, by the way, that this world-famous portico affords no entry into the church; it is a false front, or, more precisely, rear, and the actual entrance is at the other end.) Covent Garden is prominent in the annals of seventeenth- and eighteenth-century literature chiefly as the site of several coffee houses frequented by the age's literati, the talented and gregarious progenitors of mod-ern café society: Will's (Dryden, Congreve, Vanbrugh, Wycher-ley, and later Addison, Steele, Swift, and Gay), Button's (to which Addison and Steele moved from Will's, to be joined by Pope and Swift), and the Bedford (Fielding, Garrick, and Hogarth). But no trace remains of the coffee houses; the nearest approach to them, and a remote one it is, is represented by the unappetizing pubs and lunchrooms for the market workers.

The house in Russell Street, then a bookshop run by Tom Davies, where Boswell first met Dr. Johnson in 1763, has been swallowed up in the general dilapidation. A touch of literature remains, in that the Covent Garden–Long Acre neighborhood contains a number of publishers' warehouses. Print among the produce: the books and magazines of Odhams Press are wholesaled side by side with Tasmanian apples and Israeli melons. Bow Street is still the site of the chief London police court, as it was over two hundred years ago when Henry Fielding and his blind half-brother were its energetic and innovative magistrates. The blue-uniformed policemen who attend it are the descendants of the famous Bow Street runners, a corps of writ-servers and detectives, instituted in the Fieldings' time, which was supplanted by the first Metropolitan Police in 1829.

And, of course, Covent Garden still has its two venerable theaters. Although the one bearing the region's name has long been England's foremost opera house, for most of its career it was a home of the legitimate drama, locked since the mid-eighteenth century in rivalry with the nearby Drury Lane. But neither of the present buildings dates back to the beginning or even the zenith of that famous rivalry. Today's Royal Opera House, Covent Garden (to use its official title) is little more than a hundred years old, succeeding three former buildings on the same site, two of which burned down. Nor is the Drury Lane Theatre the same one that witnessed the managerial and acting triumphs of Garrick, Kemble, and Sheridan, though it was the scene of Macready's: it was built only in 1821, likewise on the site of former theaters. The two houses' competition, indeed, was not confined to the stage. In the late eighteenth and early nineteenth centuries they seem to have vied to see which could burn down oftener.

The literary echoes of Covent Garden, then, while numerous, are more than ordinarily elusive. Just as "Hudibras" Butler's and William Wycherley's graves in St. Paul's churchyard have disappeared, so the memories of Addison and Steele, Pope and Swift, Boswell and Johnson, all of whom knew Covent Garden well, are

lost in the crush of unloading lorries and porters' hand carts and
the litter of wilted cabbage leaves, broken crates, and discarded
tissue wrappings of oranges.

Bloomsbury, to the north of Covent Garden across New Oxford Street and Holborn, is the only London district to have
given its name to a literary movement or coterie. It should not be
over-rated on that account. The Bloomsbury Group has been excessively anatomized in recent years—"what a set!" as Matthew
Arnold exclaimed of the Shelley circle—and anyway the influence of place upon the writings of Lytton Strachey, Clive Bell,
Roger Fry, Bertrand Russell, and John Maynard Keynes has yet
to be demonstrated. (The unique art of Virginia Woolf, which
was constantly inspired and colored by the London, though not
necessarily the Bloomsburian, atmosphere, is another matter.) If
one wishes to see where the Bloomsbury Group lived, this is the
place to come. When they held their intellectual parties here in
the century's first decades, the elegance of the eighteenth-century
residential streets and squares was largely intact. But Bloomsbury began to decline in the 1930's under the inroads of business
and the needs of the burgeoning University of London, and it
received more than its share of punishment during the Blitz.

Although some of its former architectural distinction is preserved, it is not the favored region it once was. Many of the
former houses have been taken over by institutes, departments,
and other annexes and divisions of the university, various student
and professional societies associated with it, and cheap hotels and
lodging houses. I should think that the pursuit of knowledge in
Bloomsbury must be attended by a fair amount of inconvenience
and discomfort. Like American urban universities which year
after year must make do with quarters improvised from whatever
the nature of the adjacent real estate affords, the Bloomsbury
complex, though comparable to the South Kensington one in
importance, is no more calculated than the latter to induce
much nostalgia in the souls of former students once they
have won their degrees and gone back to wherever they came

from. Among other things, the Bloomsbury atmosphere is polluted by the traffic heading to and from the main railway stations and the road exits to the North.

Of course there is the British Museum, a major literary landmark—or the library portion thereof, at any rate. Not only does it contain one of the two greatest collections of books in the English-speaking world: its vast domed reading room has housed countless writers gathering material, and a number of not unimportant books, such as Butler's *The Way of All Flesh,* were actually written at these desks. There is a bare chance that Dickens and Karl Marx may have read together in the forerunner of the present reading room. Dickens, we know, had a ticket and often used it, and Marx spent most of his time there after he settled in London, a political refugee, in 1849. The ironic imagination, recalling Bernard Shaw's dictum that *"Little Dorrit* is a more seditious book than *Das Kapital,"* likes to believe there was such an encounter.

Marx seems to have been immune to the Museum's distractions, but Thomas Carlyle was not so lucky. When he was assembling information for his life of Cromwell, he complained, with a frantic eloquence all his own, of the noise and smell of the place— this again was the predecessor of the present quiet and well-ventilated reading room—and most particularly about the custom respectable families had of parking their dimwitted brothers and sons in the library day after day to keep them out of trouble. Among other reader-lunatics, Carlyle alleged, was one who blew his nose punctually every half hour. Finally Carlyle and a group of sympathizing friends formed their own subscription library— no eccentrics admitted—which still flourishes and serves: the London Library in St. James's Square.

Although the visitor may catch a glimpse of the reading room past the guard at the door, he cannot enter without a reader's card such as bona fide students obtain at the library office. Another literary shrine (of sorts) is, however, freely accessible to roughly one-half of the people who enter the British Museum.

This is the gentlemen's lavatory, reached down a flight of stairs outside the reading room entrance. Any reader of George Gissing must pay it a sentimental visit. Gissing, the longtime inhabitant and bitter portrayer of London's New Grub Street, like so many other men of hand-to-mouth literary occupation made the British Museum his daytime home. In *The Private Papers of Henry Ryecroft* he recalled how, "on going down into the lavatory to wash my hands, I became aware of a notice newly set up above the row of basins. It ran somehow thus: 'Readers are requested to bear in mind that these basins are to be used only for casual ablutions.' Oh, the significance of that inscription!" continued Gissing. "Had I not myself, more than once, been glad to use this soap and water more largely than the sense of the authorities contemplated? And there were poor fellows working under the great dome whose need, in this respect, was greater than mine. I laughed heartily at the notice, but it meant so much." The sign is no longer there, but the facilities remain, and no male book-lover visiting London should fail to go down and have a casual ablution in sympathetic memory of George Gissing.

The City (capitalized to distinguish it from the metropolis represented by the lower-case word) is, as I have suggested, the historic heart of London, once enclosed by the Roman-medieval wall, a few fragments of which can still be seen and the sites of whose portals are recalled by such names as Bishopsgate, Ludgate, Aldgate, Newgate, and Moorgate. Thus it has older associations with literature than any other part of what is now modern London. Not only is this the ground that Shakespeare knew: it was the habitation of almost all the Elizabethan and Jacobean dramatists, though their precise haunts usually are impossible to ascertain. John Donne was rector of St. Dunstan's, Fleet Street, and dean of St. Paul's Cathedral (his effigy in the present building is the only one to have escaped the fire that destroyed its predecessor). Izaak Walton had an ironmonger's shop near Chancery Lane. Milton was born in Bread Street and during his life resided in several houses in the City, all of them now gone.

Samuel Richardson, master printer, did business in Fleet Street and the now vanished Salisbury Court. At Christ's Hospital, then in Newgate Street, Charles Lamb, Samuel Taylor Coleridge, and a little later Leigh Hunt studied Latin and endured the birching of the master. John Keats was born over a livery stable in Moorfields, a topographical accident that eventually resulted in the youth's being ridiculed as a "Cockney poet" by critics belonging to the literary establishment. At the East India House in Leadenhall Street, a site now occupied by Lloyd's insurance firm, worked Lamb, John Stuart Mill, and Thomas Love Peacock, "City men" all in the modern acceptance of the term. Dickens, though neither a native of the City nor a resident there, knew its every court, lane, and alley. He used it time after time for his settings, from the Saracen's Head Inn in Snow Hill, just off what is now Holborn Viaduct, where Mr. Squeers recruited new victims for Dotheboys Hall, to Mrs. Todgers' commercial boarding house near the Monument, where the Pecksniffs stayed.

Very little of the City that figures in English literature survives except in place names. The brick and stone City that replaced the wooden one destroyed in 1666 slowly disappeared in the course of the Victorian era, when the resident population, which hitherto had made it a self-contained community of shops and dwellings, moved to other parts of the metropolitan area opened up by the introduction of railways and omnibuses. The City was left to fulfill its new destiny as the financial center of the nation and the Empire. Conspicuous among the buildings the emigrants left behind them, scattered among the new banks, insurance companies, warehouses, and commodity exchanges, were the precious old churches and livery halls which were fated to be blasted in 1940–41.

What with the altered function of the City and the ravages of the Blitz, comparatively little remains of the quaintness preserved in old prints. The predominant impression the visitor now has of the City is one of mass and solidity, the effect provided by the gray and buff façades of the late Victorian and Edwardian banks and offices. In their own way, the vistas offered by the region centering on the Bank of England and the Royal Exchange are as staunchly and identifiably English as any other. The crooked streets allow the stately building fronts to be viewed from several angles, with differing effects, and the omnipresent gay window-ledge plantings of petunias, marigolds, snapdragons, geraniums, and hydrangeas relieve the severity of the Portland stone. These structures, breathing dignity from every crevice, have now been joined by an equal number of new office buildings, simpler, higher, lighter both in hue and in fenestration, and considerably less interesting.

But the transformation is not complete. Enough of the City of Donne, Milton, Richardson, and Keats remains to invite the explorer to plunge into its mysterious narrow passages, shadowed perhaps by aluminum-faced office slabs, in quest of hidden old shops and taverns and tiny, silent churchyards. And the ancient street topography, at least, will persist even when the rebuilding is finished. Although a few old thoroughfares have been vacated to permit the erection of large buildings across their sites, in general the layout of the City is still what it was in Pepys's and Dickens' time, a tangle of brief streets, alleys, courts, passages, and cul-de-sacs bearing their venerable names: Poultry, Seething Lane, Broken Wharf, Ireland Yard, Pudding Lane, Giltspur Street, Old Jewry, Cloth Fair, Beer Lane, Austin Friars, Eastcheap, Lamb's Passage, Knightrider Street, Vintners Place, St. Mary Axe, Cowcross Street, Seacoal Lane, Harp Lane.

The City covers an area of just over a square mile. Greater London, as defined in the act creating a new metropolitan government in 1965, is 620 times as large. Beyond central London lie wide expanses of formerly independent parishes and boroughs that have now coalesced into a single metropolis. It is a territory that embraces old-fashioned slums and new ghettos; islands of green felicity such as Hampstead and Dulwich, stubbornly defending their village air against the encroachment of the city; Victorian and Edwardian suburbs of tree-shaded ways (Laburnum Grove, Connaught Crescent, Khartoum Road, Kingsley Gardens) and modest semi-detached or detached houses ("villas" in British usage: the term's grander connotations are more or less peculiar to American speech) ; and out still farther, the pleasant open countryside on the fringe of the Home Counties.

I like to explore it all; all of it is London. But what interests me most, apart from the specific regions I have been talking about, is the London of the masses, the one that is directly descended from the London Dickens, Gissing, and Wells portrayed. It is essentially the same as that seen in the novels and plays of the proletarian writers of the thirties and the angry young men of the fifties, and it is bound to contain the material for some of the literature of the future, whatever form that literature may take and in whatever spirit it may be written. Seen from the sidewalk and the bus top, it is a London of once-dignified Victorian houses, now often peeled and crumbled into still-inhabited wrecks, sometimes bravely repaired and painted in what is probably a foredoomed attempt to resist the pervasive blight of cities. It is a London, too, of factory districts with their mingling of dismal old tenements, clusters of prefabricated shacks introduced during the war and not yet declared redundant, and public housing developments that have become shabby before they ceased being new.

Mile after mile of back-street life, if "life" is the right word: Television antennas surmount the smoking chimney pots; long lines of dejected dwellings are punctuated by a greasy repair garage, a dirty lunchroom, a pub, a corner hole-in-the-wall that sells papers, tobacco, candy, and notions (a mercantile operation just one thin rung above sidewalk peddling) . The only relief, if again that is the right word, is provided by an occasional school, public library, or hospital whose typical exterior—chocolate brown, irrelevantly ornamented, irretrievably ugly in the worst mode of nineteenth-century institutional design—steeps it in gloom.

Connecting these poverty neighborhoods are hundreds of miles

of commercial thoroughfares, many formed by the linking together of what once were the high streets of separate villages.
Now the cottages and trees and gardens are gone, their sites
buried beneath the asphalt over which the buses and lorries
pound. During the day the sidewalks are crowded with women
pushing prams, carrying the string shopping bags that accompany all British women on their rounds, or leading dogs—
or sometimes doing all three. Interspersed between the chain
stores—Express Dairy, Mac Fisheries, Sainsbury groceries, Woolworth's—are appliance stores stressing the ease and convenience
of installment buying (known familiarly as the "never-never
plan": you never get paid up), butcher shops with sawdust-
sprinkled floors, snack bars, fruit barrows at the curb competing
with greengrocers' shops across the pavement, second-hand book
and magazine establishments featuring piles of battered paperbacks and manuals on astrology and sex, former cinemas which
the competition of television has turned into bingo palaces.

To complete the scene there are fish-and-chip dispensaries,
tobacconists and chemists and pop-record shops, real-estate
agents displaying posters advertising desirable nearby properties for sale, and the offices of "turf accountants," the genteelism of the sign seeking to dignify the profession, which is
that of the (legal) bookie. Outside cheap clothing shops, hampering the sidewalk traffic, hang swaying thickets of coats and
dresses, and outside the butcher's next door, totally unprotected
from the air so laden with dirt and fume and germ, depend
plucked fowl with their heads and feet still on, as a guarantee of
authenticity. Although many ground-floor premises have been, in
the expressive British idiom, "tarted up"—that is, beautified
with chromium and synthetic tile and fluorescent lighting—one
looks higher and discovers that the building is, in fact, of Victorian origin; the weathered, old-fashioned lettering on the fascia
commemorates a long-vanished business that throve when horse
trams plied the street in front.

Everyday London seen in this mode has a tendency to blur

into one universal sense of monotony, ugliness, social decay. A dependable antidote to an overexposure of sidewalk sociology is a quick return to the most elegant streets of Mayfair or Belgravia; or to the Temple, that unbelievably serene precinct of lawyers in the very center of London, snug between Fleet Street and the Embankment, which lost a number of its oldest and most atmospheric buildings to the Nazis but, now reconstructed with its lawns and gardens restored, retains the peace it knew when Fielding, Goldsmith, and Lamb lived there.

Or one can always retreat to a London park. Although the city is well supplied with open spaces in almost every direction—Dulwich Park, for example, and Hampstead Heath, and Regent's Park with its cricket grounds and acres of rose gardens —it is most famous for its central "lungs," the unbroken sequence of parks through which one can walk in a direct line from Whitehall, in the very heart of Westminster by the Thames, all the way to Kensington. No other city in the world has so much green space laid out to such happy effect. There are clumps and long avenues of old trees; bordering the walks are meticulously tended flower beds which are aflame with color from early spring to autumn, and in Kensington Gardens a lovely sunken formal garden as well. Along the streams and ponds, brown ducks and geese and other fowl nest, swim, feed, or merely contemplate the businessmen and shop assistants on their way to or from work, and the people sitting on benches reading the newspaper or a new Penguin book. And in any season but the coldest and rainiest, those broad stretches of grass under trees that were old when Victoria died proffer hospitality, though scarcely much privacy, to young amorists intent upon their immemorial pleasure. Necessarily, the lovemaking is more circumspect in the rowboats that are piloted up and down the placid Serpentine, and no thought ever is given to the fact that it was here that Shelley's first wife drowned herself.

The parks are so spacious that only at their very borders, and at the points where Hyde Park is traversed by motor roads, is one reminded that he is in the midst of a great city. The hotels that face the northern and southern edges of Hyde Park and Kensington Gardens are satisfactorily distant, nor do the scream and roar of buses, vans, and motorbikes and their attendant fumes penetrate far into the greenery. Instead, the wide dirt track in the Knightsbridge sector of Hyde Park, known for centuries as Rotten Row, still invites the nervous clump of hooves as favored people from Belgravia, garbed in correct equestrian costume, exercise the horses they have drawn from nearby stables. Jet planes overhead, and below them Rotten Row witnessing the same sights it knew in the reign of the first Hanoverians: a perfect epitome, once more, of London's constant mingling of old and new.

The chain of central London parks has many aspects and many pleasures, but none, I think (once one has banished the inconvenient memory that Boswell used these lovely grounds for some of his most deplorable assignations), match the soft magic of St. James's Park, the easternmost of the four, on a warm night in spring or summer. It is tranquil as the country. Over the willows of the island in Charles II's bird sanctuary, a few stars are discernible (this in the very midst of London!). The towers of the Horse Guards are bathed in floodlighting. Lovers clasp on benches along the paths, and shadowy figures stroll past: policemen on their quiet rounds, or a pair of M.P.'s, perhaps, out for a bit of exercise and a chat before bed at their Westminster flats. Across the pond in the sanctuary, multitudes of birds that "sleep all the night with open eye" twitter and rustle when disturbed by something that goes splash in the dark . . .

This is London at its most enchanting.

*Ham House, Surrey*

# 3

# *Liquid 'Istory*

"THE THAMES," maintained Sir Roger de Coverley, "is the noblest river in Europe." This unequivocal judgment, as Addison goes on to remark, was but one "among many other honest prejudices which naturally cleave to the heart of a true Englishman." The actual nobility of the River Thames (properly so called) may well be debated; it bears little resemblance to the Hudson or the Rhine. But nobody can question its inseparability from the London scene, historically, geographically, and above all in the affections of both citizens and strangers. London without the Thames making its broad sinuous bend through the heart of two millennia of English history—what would London be without it?

Conventionally, in our tongue rivers are assigned the feminine gender. Not so the Thames, or at least not in the latter portion of his trip to the sea. As a matter of fact, the river's sex, like that of Virginia Woolf's Orlando, changes in the course of its journey. In her upper reaches she has been traditionally known to poets and Oxonians as the Isis. There, goddess-like, she is slender, no wider than an American creek; and on her quiet surface as she glides through Christ Church meadows innumerable generations of Oxford undergraduates have rowed or merely lazed, dreaming dreams of statesmanship, poetry, and (formerly) theology. But by the time she has entered central London she has renounced her femininity, and the river's new sex is unmistakably indicated by the huge masonry smokestacks of the Battersea power station that bulk opposite Pimlico. From then on, down to the looming, smogging oil refineries in the estuary, the River Thames is the fluent symbol of a masculine Britain, a man's world of commerce and commodities, of smoke and cranes and lighters.

John Burns, the Socialist politician and devout Londoner, is said to have declared to visitors from America, "Every drop of the Thames is liquid 'istory." And so it is. For as the stream winds through London it is attended by memories: of the long-vanished medieval London Bridge with its huddled, precarious shops and dwellings lining both sides of the roadway, a Britannic Ponte Vecchio (there is a scale model of it in the London Museum) ; of the "frost fairs" held on its frozen surface in exceptionally cold winters down to the start of the nineteenth century, seasons when the catchpenny pitches and amusements of Bartholomew Fair were transferred from dry land to the gelid element (the London Museum has a diorama of this also) ; of the skiffs and wherries that ferried truant Londoners across to Southwark for an afternoon's entertainment at the thatch-topped Globe playhouse, and Mr. Pepys on his business errands between Whitehall and the City, and Dr. Johnson and Boswell to and from their social engagements. The proprietors of these water taxis, which provided transport through the heart of London— the Thames indeed was the original urban throughway—were the progenitors, not so much of modern London cab drivers, who tend toward reticence, as of bus conductors, voluble, independent-minded, and argumentative when pressed. Once in a while they were part-time poets (the seventeenth-century John Taylor, for instance) and they were masters of abusive language to match the most resourceful fishwives on shore at Billingsgate.

It was to such a waterman that Dr. Johnson hurled one of his masterpieces of intellectual wit enlisted in the cause of insult: "Sir, under pretence of keeping a bawdy-house, your wife is a receiver of stolen goods."

Liquid 'istory, yes; and liquid literature too. For not only did the brisk breeze on the Thames invigorate Dr. Johnson's stout powers of invective; from Spenser's time onward the river touched the lyric sensibilities of poets. "Sweet Thames! run softly till I end my song. . . ." But by the middle of the nineteenth century, the Thames was anything but sweet. It had become an open sewer into which all the noisomeness of the sprawling metropolis was poured, and in hot weather it stank so abominably that Parliament, the windows of whose meeting place fronted directly on the fluvial cesspool, repeatedly had to adjourn.

Except as viewed from the air in sunshine, the Thames no longer is silver, as poets once described it. Although it no longer receives raw sewage, like rivers in all industrial countries it is polluted from other sources, and its gray-green tides are only to be seen and ridden upon, not bathed in. But it does not smell, and its casual cargo of flotsam and jetsam is no uglier than that of most heavily traveled streams. Canvassing it for stray material of possible worth, including human bodies for which rewards are offered, is no longer the potentially profitable occupation it was in the time of Gaffer Hexam in *Our Mutual Friend*.

To sample the Thames in its diversified locales and moods as it flows through metropolitan London requires amphibious travels, partly aboard the motor launches that ply upstream and down from the piers at Westminster Bridge and Charing Cross and partly afoot, along country towpath and city embankment. Emerging from the wheatfields and meadows of rural England in the vicinity of Windsor and Eton, it becomes a London stream at Hampton Court Palace. It was between here and the then village of Chelsea, one remembers from the film *A Man for All Seasons*, that Sir Thomas More commuted; how lovely the river must have been then! But even now, when the Thames is flanked by Lon-

don suburbs, it still has idyllic green reaches as it meanders from
Hampton Court in successive directions that finally average out
to be northerly. On a summer Sunday afternoon the river is alive
with small craft—powerboats, cabin cruisers, sailboats, sculls,
even humble rowboats—and more ride at moorings, some being
worked on by their owners. Set among trees on the banks are
intermittent rows of weekend cottages. Whatever alarms and
forebodings may be riding the invisible waves of radio and television, in this happily insulated swath which the river cuts
through the abrasive outside world there are only strollers along
the bankside paths, picnickers in the fields beyond, and local
residents sitting at ease in the little village parks and by the
landing stages. And to add the final desirable touch, there are
the swans, much-coddled aristocrats of the sweet river, whose
ancestors no doubt bowed gravely to Sir Thomas More as he was
rowed upstream to interview his sovereign.

Out here, in the region of Teddington, Ham, Richmond, and
Kew, there is plenty of scope for the dry-land explorer. Late one
May morning, I disembarked from a train at Richmond, an attractive town whose streets are lined with shops catering to a
prosperous clientele and the lilac-embowered villas in which they
live. I made my way along the river to the Three Pigeons, a well-
situated pub with a garden overlooking the water, where I was
provided with the ale and the sandwiches requisite to further
wandering. Deserting the road, I took a leisurely, appreciative
walk along the towpath toward Petersham and Ham. An hour
before, I had been passing through an unlovely industrial part of
the city, heavy with smoke from diesel engines and burning oily
debris. Now, though still miles within the limits of Greater
London, I was in the country, walking through buttercup-
bespeckled pastures where cows grazed, and where, on benches
along the path, little groups of old women knitted and chatted.
Except for the lines of motor cruisers moored along the bank
awaiting the next weekend, and the frequent jets shrilling as
they descended toward London Airport, the twentieth century

was far away.

It remained so when I entered the grounds of Ham House, a seventeenth-century mansion fronting on a formal garden bordered in this season with masses of rhododendrons ranging from purple to flaming crimson. In contrast to its contemporary neighbors in western London, Chiswick House and Osterley House, Ham lacks the stateliness, the conspicuous display of wealth that marks the most notable monuments of the Age of Classicism translated into domestic architecture; it is smaller, less austere, providing the effect of elegance without any accompanying stiffness. Again unlike those more imposing mansions (both of which should be visited), Ham House has not had to be restored. Its decoration and furnishings—rich red damask hangings, wall and ceiling paintings by Dutch artists, a number of Lely portraits, elaborately carved chairs and tables—have been preserved as they are described in an inventory of 1679. One is able to see it, therefore, exactly as it appeared to the diarist John Evelyn, who left an admiring description of the house and its contents.

By a delightful and unexpected sequel, chance enabled me to remain in the Restoration period a little while longer. Regaining the river, I came to a landing at the tip of Eel Pie Island, a favorite picnic spot in the eighteenth century for London families like Fanny Burney's. At that moment there arrived, with its cargo of two or three passengers, a genuine water taxi—a skiff that provides regular ferry service at this point in the river's course. For ninepence I was conveyed to the Twickenham side by a muscular, freckled young waterman who, as he rowed, commented with amusement on the earnest efforts of a schoolboy crew who crossed his bows as their coach, megaphone strapped to mouth, kept pace with them on a bicycle along the towpath. Ninepence is a small price to pay for the privilege of fancying oneself a Pepys on a transriparian errand—or, moving into another literary context for the sake of an exact topographical correspondence, to be Arthur Gowan crossing to the Meagles' home by this very ferry, as Dickens describes him doing in the seventeenth chapter of *Little Dorrit*. It was the cheapest sentimental journey I ever made, as well as one of the most satisfying.

Now that I was at Twickenham, my next objective was clear enough. I walked through a walled lane onto which waterside villas backed and across the Twickenham esplanade with its benches, refreshment stands, and warnings on the steps and in low-lying parking areas that they can be affected by high water. (One does not ordinarily think of the amiable Thames as capable of even a minor flood, but the spring tides can be high.) At length I came upon the well-traveled road called Cross Deep, and, a few hundred feet along on the left, St. Catherine's Convent, a girls' school built on the riverbank site of Alexander Pope's villa which was torn down in 1809. The problem: What had happened to the poet's celebrated grotto? For twenty years Pope collected from his friends all manner of rocks, fossils, and shells with which he decorated the tunnel leading under the road from his house to his garden. It was an occupation appropriate to an Augustan man of taste, and the result was a showplace which people came to visit for many years after Pope's death. Its fame was assisted by Dr. Johnson's dry comment: "A grotto is not often the wish or pleasure of an Englishman, who has more frequent need to solicit than exclude the sun; but Pope's excavation was requisite as an entrance to his garden, and, as some men try to be proud of their defects, he extracted an ornament from an inconvenience, and vanity produced a grotto where necessity enforced a passage."

On a previous survey of the neighborhood, in 1958, I had failed to establish the fate of Pope's subterranean plaything; the nearest I came to an answer was a public house, newly built of red brick in a vaguely Georgian manner, which paid tribute to the *genius loci* in its name: Pope's Grotto. This time, however, I was emboldened to inquire of an elderly crossing guard across the road from the school. Yes, he said at once: it was right over there. And he pointed to a descending flight of concrete steps alongside the building behind him, which was an annex of the school, built on the site of Pope's garden. The nuns and girls use the tunnel every day to cross from one building to the other. Deeming it somehow inappropriate under the circumstances to ask to explore the grotto, I contented myself with photographing its entrance. But I can now vouch for the fact that the grotto has been preserved, at least in part, even though Pope's house has itself vanished.*

From the town of Twickenham, where it is crossed by a simple stone bridge over which Horace Walpole often rode, the Thames re-enters spacious parkland as it divides the Old Deer Park and Kew Gardens (on the right-hand, or Surrey, side) from the grounds of Syon House, another well-preserved seat of the Age of Elegance. Then, by a sequence of leisurely twists, the river drifts toward central London. Now and again, as at Strand-on-the-Green and Hammersmith, there are charming little rows of eighteenth-century houses fronting a strip of waterside mall. But from Barnes and Chiswick onward, there is much commercial activity—small docks, breweries, timber yards, and petroleum depots.

Directly opposite the four-stacked Battersea power station is Churchill Gardens, an extensive City of Westminster housing estate, built in the 1950's, whose individual eight-story buildings bear such names as Coleridge, Keats, Shelley, Chaucer, Hallam, Elgar, Chippendale, Jane Austen, De Quincey, Marryat, Martineau, Wedgwood, Blackstone, Nash, Gifford, and Erskine. One wonders what influence, if any, the presence of such talented spirits has upon the minds and ambitions of the children who clamber over the brightly painted retired road roller set in the middle of one of their playgrounds. Just downstream from Churchill Gardens is the fashionable Dolphin Square apartment

---

* A distinguished student of eighteenth-century English literature, less timorous than I, reports that he has been inside the school and viewed all that remains of the grotto. He gained access by first visiting Horace Walpole's nearby Strawberry Hill, now a training school for an order of Irish priests; the rector there, learning of his interest in Pope, got on the hot line to his opposite number, the sister superior at St. Catherine's, and arranged for the visit.

complex, which, in contrast, commemorates British sea dogs and naval heroes, Frobisher, Drake, Raleigh, Beatty, and the rest. Beyond it, in turn, is an older public housing development, built about streets bearing such names as Erasmus, Herrick, and St. Oswulf. Here the component structures recall the history of English art: Millais, Mulready, Ruskin, Reynolds, Morland, Rossetti, Turner, Gainsborough, Stubbs, Wilkie, Lawrence, Landseer, Leighton. (Oddly, I failed to notice any house named for Constable or Hogarth.)

It comes close to the peculiar essence of the English temperament, I think, this stout praise of famous men of letters, jurists, sea adventurers, and painters—a broad spectrum of the nation's genius—in a region not only dominated by a power-generating station but oppressed by the incessant roar and smell of big lorries in the bordering Grosvenor Road. Here we are prepared for the broader symbolism inherent in the next several miles, as the Thames sweeps majestically through the heart of London. At the beginning, opposite the Tate Gallery with its unsurpassed collection of English art, is Lambeth Palace with its grim huddled towers and walls, the seat of the Church of England; at the end, downstream, lies the Port of London. Between these two points, history and modernity, the monuments of the English spirit and those of English maritime commerce, mingle in a series of contrasts and complements.

Symbolism wholly apart, from Westminster past Somerset House and the Temple to the City this curving reach of the Thames is visually one of the finest panoramas to be found in any city on earth. I never tire of contemplating it from any of the several bridges between Vauxhall and Southwark, at any time of day or night and in any weather. First, a sight on the west bank identifiable even by severely disoriented American tourists who think, as I have actually heard them say, that Lambeth Palace is the Tower of London: the long Victorian Gothic range of the Houses of Parliament, extending from a public garden at the end toward the Tate to the foot of Westminster Bridge. Then, an imaginative piece of urban planning which deserves the praise customarily directed to Paris' treatment of the Seine: the Victoria Embankment, one of London's pleasantest locales. Never more than a minute's walk from Whitehall, Trafalgar Square, the Strand, and Fleet Street, the explorer may idle along the esplanade at the river's edge from Westminster Bridge all the way to Blackfriars. On the landward side, the Embankment consists of a continuous strip of park and garden, a miniature version of St. James's Park on the other side of Whitehall. Here at noon on summer days crowds of workers from the nearby offices sun themselves, read, eat lunch, and listen to a military band. Behind the trees rise large stone blocks of government ministries, grave and impregnably solid as only London office buildings erected in the brief Edwardian summer can be; and farther along, the no-nonsense white 1933-functional Shell-Mex House, London's first gesture toward a skyscraper.

As the river completes its north-to-east bend at Blackfriars Bridge, commerce takes over again. On both shores are almost unbroken lines of wharves, not platforms along the stream as one might expect but flat-walled warehouses, six or eight stories high, to which big gangling cranes and hoists protruding above the doors transfer the cargoes of small freighters and lighters moored beneath. Unpainted, undecorated, and weathered, these London wharves are the very definition of gray utilitarianism. It is not a landscape to please the beauty-minded. Yet even here literary memories prevail, for these are the reaches that figure in so many of Dickens' river scenes, from *Oliver Twist* to *Our Mutual Friend;* and even though the word is no longer on many lips, there is pleasure in the awareness that the occasional flights of steps by which one descends from the foot of a lane to a (now disused) landing stage are the "stairs" that Pepys and Boswell often refer to and that are marked on old maps: Wapping Old Stairs, Pelican Stairs, King James's Stairs, New Crane Stairs . . . The simple word is redolent with London history.

The Port of London, one of the world's largest, has the romantic, exotic flavor common to all ports. The addition of parabolic radar scanners before ships' masts and the disappearance of coal smoke from their funnels have detracted little from the aspect of London River (the Thames's familiar local name) as books prepared one to find it. Alongside the sleek white fruit boats and elongated tankers riding low in the water the river voyager still sees a fair number of rusty, bilge-spouting tramp freighters such as Masefield celebrated. This is the port, too, which figures in the travel sketches of H. M. Tomlinson, a Thames-side shipping clerk turned journalist—one of his books, *Gallions Reach,* is named for a stretch of the river below Greenwich—and which serves as background for the once popular short stories of W. W. Jacobs, who was born in Wapping, the son of a wharf manager.

Between the Pool of London and Greenwich Reach the Thames is best inspected from one of the sightseeing boats based at Westminster and Charing Cross. It is well populated with shipping and ancillary craft—tugboats plowing upstream with a following of low-slung, snub-nosed barges, colliers heading for the electricity plants in the central city and beyond, launches of the Port of London Authority and the river police, timber ships from the Baltic proceeding slowly up the river or anchored in midstream. At length, as the almost continuous twin line of warehouses thins out, its place is taken by other graceless and immense monuments of modern commerce and industry: flour mills, chemical plants, sugar refineries, more petroleum dumps and power stations, their stacks giving off white, black, or yellow smoke, with appropriate river craft and cargo boats tied alongside their piers. And along the way are equally familiar accessories to any busy waterway: gulls and other seafowl flapping and swooping and chattering in the wake of the traffic and perching on pilings and floating debris as they consider their next move, and once in a while a rotting barge lying alongside an abandoned pier or beached on a mud flat.

Dockland proper, however, the five systems of man-made basins lying inland from the river, is pretty well concealed. Its presence is indicated only by forests of cranes and funnels seen at some distance beyond the bank. But on certain days in summer the Port of London Authority conducts special boat tours, leaving from Tower Pier, which go beyond Greenwich and then ascend through a lock to the Royal Albert and King George V Docks at East Ham, where ranks of moored freighters from East Africa and New Zealand and Scandinavia are seen discharging their cargoes and receiving in return the bulky, boxed tokens of foreign exchange. The trip is well worth the trouble of making the advance reservations it requires, especially because it is the only way one can gain a glimpse of the working docks. On the landward side they are heavily fenced and guarded against persons not on official business.

Such persons, if like me they have an appetite for the ambience of a busy river even in its most starkly commercial moods, have plenty of walking routes to choose from. Beginning at the Mile End Underground station, I once walked through the unlovely streets of Poplar, which still bears many evidences of wartime damage, to the congested East India Road, lined with the usual appurtenances of a port—seamen's homes, employment offices, missions, pawnbrokers' shops, and cheap clothing emporiums. (Are these last still called "slop sellers," as they are in old nautical fiction?) Then, steering, as I often like to do, not by compass and chart but by mere instinct, I followed a circuitous route upstream, skirting the West India Docks on the Isle of Dogs. The pedestrian's closest contact with maritime life in this region is at the swing and draw bridges that span the channels connecting the docks with the river. Now and again a gate bottles up road traffic as a tug passes through, towing a dozen barges loaded with crated Ford of England products on their way to Port Elizabeth and Auckland, or even a big freighter in outsize majesty towering over the accumulated buses and cycles. Finally I arrived at Island Gardens, a small park on the tip of the Isle of Dogs, and after resting on a bench I proceeded *under* the Thames. A passenger lift housed in a little rotunda took me down to a long,

echoing tunnel by which I walked—I could have ridden if I had
brought a bicycle, as regular users do—to the far bank, where
another lift delivered me to the streets of Greenwich. There the
explorer has a choice: he can head either for the National Maritime Museum, a fine comprehensive collection of the relics, documents, and art of Britain's naval history housed in buildings
Wren designed for the former Greenwich Hospital, or for a pub.
Having inspected the museum on a previous occasion, I therefore
bent my steps to the Yacht Inn, which has a terrace directly
overlooking the water. There I relaxed over lunch as I watched
the river traffic and listened to the gentle slapping of the waves
against the pilings. Apart from its fine location, I cherish the
Yacht as the only pub so far (in my limited experience) where I
have found ham-and-apricot sandwiches at the buffet.

Nearer central London on the Surrey side the stout-soled
walker has available a route that takes him through a waterside
region penetrated by but one London visitor out of every hundred thousand. The only navigational principle involved is to
stay as close to the river as possible, even though it is seldom
visible: bear left wherever a choice must be made. Beginning at
Waterloo Bridge, just downstream from the Royal Festival Hall
and the slowly rising cultural complex neighboring it, the way
leads through narrow chasms formed by the wharves that line the
river opposite Blackfriars and the City. Bracketed between Waterloo Bridge and Southwark Bridge is Bankside, the people's
playground of Elizabethan London. Here, in a region beyond the
jurisdiction of the Puritan-minded City authorities, the available
amusements ranged from animal baiting and brothels to Shake-
spearian plays; vestiges of the site's former use survive in such
names as Bear Garden and Rose Street (named for a theater
built here in 1587). Set into a wall of the Courage Barclay
brewery is a tablet marking the approximate location of the
Globe Playhouse, which housed, among other original-cast productions, those of *Hamlet, Othello,* and *King Lear.* This is not
the only literary association the spot possesses, because the

present brewing firm incorporates the one owned by Dr. Johnson's good friend Henry Thrale, for whom a little nearby square is named. How little some things change in England! Over two centuries ago, Johnson, congratulating Thrale on his present "floating on the spring-tide of prosperity," referred to Thrale's "ambition of *out-brewing Whitbread.*" The competition persists to this day: witness the ubiquitous rivalry of the Courage Barclay and Whitbread advertisements in newspapers, and on billboards and Underground posters.

The name of a tiny waterside street, the Clink, recalls that this area south of the Thames once was noteworthy for its prisons. Only a few minutes' walk from Bankside stood the Marshalsea debtors' prison, where Ben Jonson, George Wither, and Dickens' impecunious father were confined and where much of the action of *Little Dorrit* takes place. A tiny court on the site is named for Dickens' heroine. Nearby was King's Bench, another debtors' prison, where Thomas Dekker, Tobias Smollett, and Mr. Micawber served time, and where the mad poet Christopher Smart died. In the neighboring Horsemonger Lane Gaol Leigh Hunt resided for two years as a consequence of having described the Prince Regent, in his paper *The Examiner,* as (among other things) "a violator of his word, a libertine, over head and ears in disgrace, a despiser of domestic ties, the companion of demireps, a man who has just closed half a century without one single claim on the gratitude of his country, or the respect of posterity!" Never was a convicted libeler's imprisonment made happier. Hunt papered his walls with a trellis of roses and his ceiling with clouds and sky, installed bookcases and a piano, and held open house for his friends; Charles Lamb, according to Hunt, "declared there was no other such room, except in a fairy tale." Outside this luxurious cell was a small plot of ground in which Hunt raised flowers and, lounging under an awning, read his favorite poets. But there is no point in looking for the building in which this jocund incident in literary history occurred. It, along with the other less easeful prisons in Southwark, was torn down long since, and only its memory—and a little street named for Leigh Hunt—survives in this shabby region of commercial and near-slum London.

From the approach to London Bridge, where a massive railway viaduct comes within a few feet of knocking a corner off the tower of Southwark Cathedral, the explorer's route leads him past Potter's Field—like the Clink, the original bearer of what has become a generic name—into Bermondsey, a maze of erratic and often discontinuous streets and byways fragrant with spices and grain and bearing such names as Jamaica Road, Bombay Wharf, Cherry Garden Pier, Cathay Street, and Paradise Street. It is not a comely region, but occasionally the prevailing city-scape of warehouses and lorry parking lots is relieved by such vestiges of the past as the church of St. Mary Rotherhithe, tranquil in its shaded yard, and across the street a charming eighteenth-century schoolhouse with weathered wooden figures of a boy and girl set into niches in the brick façade.

In this dreary and war-battered neighborhood the English enthusiasm for injecting a hopeful tinge of culture into the life of the masses is again manifest. In Wolseley Street is the Dickens housing estate for the families of dock workers. The units are named Tapley, Brownlow, Dombey (there is also a Dombey Street in Bloomsbury), Bardell, Pickwick, Carton, Copperfield, Havisham, Spenlow, Rudge, Micawber, Darnay, Weller, and Oliver. There is also a Fleming House, a fairly obscure choice of name, for how many readers can remember offhand that the orphan Rose Maylie, in *Oliver Twist*, was really Rose Fleming? The nomenclature adopted here in the Dickens estate provokes speculation. Brownlow, Pickwick, and Spenlow can be accounted for by the hearty benevolence that marks those characters; but why, then, no Cheeryble House? And why memorialize, in so domestic a milieu, the rapacious Widow Bardell, who sued Mr. Pickwick for breach of promise, and the vindictive jilted bride, Miss Havisham? The absence of Fagin, Carker, Quilp, Rogue Riderhood, Steerforth, and Scrooge from the premises is understandable. But the name Micawber is not a happy choice for a housing block, where one of the prime virtues must always be the ability to keep up with the rent.

In any case, a trudge through this stretch of river-oriented London may well conclude with a subaqueous excursion to an authentic period piece. One crosses the Thames by the pedestrian walk of the Wapping-Rotherhithe vehicular tunnel and then, having emerged in the King Edward VII Memorial Park on the north bank, finds one's way to the Wapping tube station—the station that (it is easy to imagine) London Transport forgot. It lies at one end of a tunnel which was a famous engineering feat in its day. Built in 1825–43 by Sir Marc Isambard Brunel and his son Isambard Kingdom Brunel, the tunnel was intended to carry road traffic under the Thames but was never used for that purpose. Instead, toward the end of the century it was acquired by the Underground, which then built Wapping station. The station itself is an unaltered relic of sixty and more years ago. The narrow platforms, precipitous stairs, rough stairwells and walls, and primitive electric lighting are just as they were when the area the station obscurely serves was a crowded, suffering, crime-ridden waterfront slum and the clientele of its smoke-belching trains was roughly dressed dockers and seamen and their beshawled Cockney women.

Thus to the modern investigator by boat and road, the Thames is a twisting watery magnet that brings him back again and again to partake of its constantly changing moods and scenes, a kaleidoscope of London's past and present. To me, the most irresistible portion of that magnet remains the dramatic sweep downstream from Westminster Bridge. At night the festoons of lights on both banks and the floodlit buildings provide something of the effect of the illuminated Seine, less spectacular perhaps, more soberly English, but pleasing just the same. The buses, their top decks forming oblongs of luminescence, glide across the bridge; Big Ben chimes the quarter-hours, and atop its tower with its great illuminated dials a light signifies that Parliament is sitting; on the dark river, points of red, white, and green slowly move with a tugboat or launch, itself unseen; far downstream is the lighted dome of St. Paul's. The taxis keep swishing by with the slick sound of rubber against asphalt. It is an uncoordinated, indeed wholly unplanned, coalescence of *son et lumière;* it is London at night; it is what Vaughan Williams' London Symphony contains.

And yet, when I look from the middle of Westminster Bridge toward the Embankment and downriver in another circumstance —in the lovely golden light of late afternoon, after a day of low scudding clouds and sudden spatters of rain has miraculously ended in cleared skies, and the outlines of trees and buildings are sharp as they never are when London moisture is in the air: an atmosphere, in short, meant for a Canaletto rather than a Turner—then it is not Vaughan Williams but Wordsworth that I hear. There are certain literal difficulties, because neither the bridge on which I stand nor the modern scene I admire is the one Wordsworth knew, and the time of day also is wrong. But how beautifully, nonetheless, the spirit of the Thames panorama was caught and preserved in 1802:

> *Earth has not anything to show more fair:*
> *Dull would he be of soul who could pass by*
> *A sight so touching in its majesty:*
> *This City now doth, like a garment, wear*
> *The beauty of the morning; silent, bare,*
> *Ships, towers, domes, theatres, and temples lie*
> *Open unto the fields, and to the sky;*
> *All bright and glittering in the smokeless air.*
> *Never did sun more beautifully steep*
> *In his first splendour, valley, rock, or hill;*
> *Ne'er saw I, never felt, a calm so deep!*
> *The river glideth at his own sweet will:*
> *Dear God! the very houses seem asleep;*
> *And all that mighty heart is lying still!*

*London Transport's South Kensington Station*

$●,$●,$●

---

*4*

---

# The Style of London Transport

IN SOUTH KENSINGTON there is a station on the Underground
named Gloucester Road. Most riders, looking up from their papers as their train brakes to a stop, identify it by the multilingual
signs erected to guide disembarking passengers to the adjacent
West London Air Terminal. It is a busy junction, where the
Circle line, arriving from Kensington High Street and points
north, meets the District line which has come in from the western
suburbs. On a lower level are the tracks of the Piccadilly line.

These topographical details must be specified in order to make
clear the Gloucester Road station's literary associations. For here,
in 1895, the body of Cadogan West, the unfortunate Woolwich
Arsenal clerk in the Sherlock Holmes story of the Bruce-
Partington Plans, was deposited on the roof of a Circle line train
and conveyed to the Aldgate station in the City, at which point it
fell beside the tracks. An on-site inspection allows the investigator to verify the scene as Conan Doyle reports it in the story.
Before entering the station from the north, on a brief stretch of
trackage which is out of tunnel, eastbound Circle trains often
must stop for red signals. Above them are the back walls of a row
of Victorian houses, and it was from the window of one of these

that West's body was laid on such a waiting train. It must be admitted that the distance from window to track strains one's credulity: a long throw and an accurate or extremely lucky one would be required to hit the train roof. It is most unlikely, moreover, given the number of station stops and rail junctions between Gloucester Road and Aldgate, that the body would have remained on the roof of a moving train all that distance.

I do not know whether T. S. Eliot, who was sufficiently a student of the Holmes saga to work echoes of "The Musgrave Ritual" into *Murder in the Cathedral,* ever pondered this matter as he awaited his train at Gloucester Road. But there is no question that he knew the station well, for, as he told his brother, it is the one alluded to in "Burnt Norton":

> *Descend lower, descend only*
> *Into the world of perpetual solitude,*
> *World not world, but that which is not world.*
> *Internal darkness, deprivation*
> *And destitution of all property,*
> *Desiccation of the world of sense,*
> *Evacuation of the world of fancy,*
> *Inoperancy of the world of spirit;*
> *This is the one way, and the other*
> *Is the same, not in movement*
> *But abstention from movement; while the world moves*
> *In appetency, on its metalled ways*
> *Of time past and time future.*

In these lines, F. O. Matthiessen pointed out, "a descent into the London underground . . . becomes also a descent into the dark night of the soul." To take the Piccadilly line train on its "metalled ways" to his office in Bloomsbury, Eliot could descend from the street or the level of the District and Circle line platforms in either of two ways, by lift or by spiral staircase ("the same, not in movement/ But abstention from movement"). In his typical manner, Eliot used a fragment of the Londoner's daily experience to frame a solemn philosophical observation.

The Underground figures elsewhere in *Four Quartets*. It is probably unique among the transit systems of the world, in that it is, in "East Coker," the subject of a Homeric simile:

> . . . *as, when an underground train, in the tube, stops too long*
> *between stations*
> *And the conversation rises and slowly fades into silence*
> *And you see behind every face the mental emptiness deepen*
> *Leaving only the growing terror of nothing to think about . . .*

It was once argued in a learned journal that the refrain in the same poem, "In my beginning is my end," refers to the Circle line, which has no terminus, its trains plying in both directions, clockwise and counterclockwise, around the ellipse connecting a number of main-line railway stations. But Dickens had already used the idea in Chapter 34 of *Dombey and Son*, which was written thirty-six years before the Circle line was completed: "In this round world of many circles within circles, do we make a weary journey from the high grade to the low, to find at last that they lie close together, that the two extremes touch, and that our journey's end is but our starting place?" And the notion was, of course, a literary commonplace even then. But there is a unique pleasure in riding on a route whose design induces echoes of both Eliot and Dickens—to say nothing of Dante.

It is highly appropriate that Gloucester Road should be the most literary of the world's subway stations and that the Underground should have repeatedly inspired one of our age's great poets; for their owner, the London Transport Board, is the most literate of the world's urban transportation authorities, a patron of the arts and a quoter of poetry as well as daily mover of millions by train and bus.* From its earliest days as a loose con-

---

* To say nothing of being the landlord of two famous twentieth-century authors. In Chiltern Court Mansions, a London Transport property built over the Baker Street Underground station, H. G. Wells lived from 1930 to 1937, and Arnold Bennett died in a flat in the same building, after an occupancy of only a few months. To stretch the point a little, William Cobbett in a sense also was a tenant of London Transport, though in long retrospect. In 1820, as operator of a seed farm, he lived in a cottage on the land now occupied by the Kensington High Street station.

federation of separately owned Underground lines and then as the London Passenger Transport Board, it conceived of itself also as a purveyor of humane culture and entertainment to its passengers. It has always felt that minutes spent waiting for bus or Underground train should be well spent. Hence, for instance, its much-admired poster campaign.

In 1963, as part of its elaborate centenary celebration of the opening of the first Underground line, London Transport took over the Royal Institute Galleries in Piccadilly for an exhibition of the art it had commissioned since 1908. On display were some 124 posters commissioned from such artists as Sir Frank Brangwyn, E. McKnight Kauffer, Rex Whistler, Sir Jacob Epstein, Graham Sutherland, Len Deighton, Dame Laura Knight, Hans Unger, and Clare Leighton. (The façade of London Transport's headquarters at 55 Broadway, Westminster—stilted over the St. James's Park station—bears once-controversial sculptures likewise commissioned from Epstein, Eric Gill, and Henry Moore.) These posters, in many moods and styles from Georgian pastoral to abstractionism and surrealism, from montage to flat color, had been displayed, as their current progeny continue to be, at hundreds of London bus stops and Underground platforms. Advertising exhibitions and other public events, or calling attention to various points of interest and recreation to be reached by London Transport, they provided a vivid retrospective view of the evolution of fine poster art, and incidentally of the flavor of London life, since Edwardian days. In 1908 a gay evocation of a summer fair urged passengers to "Book to Hampstead or Golders Green!" In 1914 a Tony Sarg poster illustrating the latest models of aircraft recommended attendance at the flying exhibitions held at Hendon. A Kauffer design in 1924 advised that "Winter sales are best reached by Underground!" An Austin Cooper poster in 1928, boldly headed LEPIDOPTERA, suggested going by Underground to the South Kensington Natural History Museum, where moths and butterflies could be inspected in bright abundance. And so the colorful procession went, with themes as diversified as brass rubbing, the circus, Kew Gardens, the Woolwich Free Ferry, the Round Pond at Kensington Gardens, a Picasso exhibition, Harrow Weald, and the Elgin Marbles.

Accompanying the art was text to match—often not merely a caption but a captivating snatch of poetry or prose. Posters celebrating the English seasons, as many of them did, quoted appropriate lines from Longfellow, Hood, Robert Louis Stevenson, Richard Jefferies, Swinburne, and Milton ("Lycidas" on one occasion, the "Tractate of Education" on another). Sometimes the letterpress was composed for the occasion. An Eric Kennington poster (1944) of an improbably handsome uniformed woman officiating on a platform of the wartime Underground bore tributary verses from A. P. Herbert:

> *Thank you, Mrs. Porter,*
>   *For a good job stoutly done;*
> *Your voice is clear, and the Hun can hear*
>   *When you cry "South Kensington!"*

> *The world must hurry homeward,*
>   *The soldier on his way,*
> *And the wheels whizz round on the Underground*
>   *At the voice of the girls in grey.*

> *And though the skies are noisy,*
>   *How calm the voices are—*
> *"Upminster train! That man again!*
>   *Pass further down the car!"*

From time to time, anonymous poetasters in London Transport Publicity's nest of singing birds contributed to the municipal cheer:

*A professional poet from Sarratt*
*Wooed his muse in a frost-bitten garratt.*
*When his scansion * broke down*

---

* *He should have put another shilling in the metre.*

*She would dash up to Town*
*To revive her enthusiasm among the bright lights and warm*
*gaiety of the West End.*

A montage made up chiefly of old photographs of railroad rolling
stock was explicated by the lines

*A psychology pstudent of Pstaines*
*Psaid his ego was pshattered by trains*
*Pso he took it to psee*
*The pceremony*
*Of Changing the Guard which takes place every morning at the*
*Horse Guards and on most mornings at Buckingham Palace or*
*St. James's.*

This may perhaps be called the London Transport house
limerick stanza. It starts off bravely enough, with four brief,
properly stressed lines, but at the end the structure breaks down
completely under the stress of having to convey a packet of practical information which cannot be compressed into a suitable
fifth line:

*A gardener (it might have been yueue)*
*Kindly gave up his place in the queue*
*To explain to a stranger*
*The obvious danger*
*Of thinking that Kwewe should only be visited in lilac time. The*
*gardens are always superb and admission is only 3d. Kwewe*
*Gardens station is 5 minutes walk. Many buses stop near the*
*gates.*

Every so often, this year as in each of the preceding sixty, a new
London Transport poster blossoms forth everywhere in Greater
London to gladden the passenger's eye and touch his sensibility
or evoke his smile. Because this constant use of tasteful and often
sophisticated popular art to sell public transportation has earned
many admirers, London Transport, always eager to be of service,

has reproduced many of its posters (full size) for sale. They can be bought, quite cheaply, at its publicity department in the Marylebone Road. Five of them brighten my university office today.

The authority's well-developed esthetic concern extends to every aspect of design. As much thought and talent, it has said, are devoted to the shape and aspect of a litter box or a bus-stop post as to the pattern of upholstery on a new batch of trains or the architecture of a new station. London Transport's most important contribution in this field, however, was the development of a distinctive style of lettering to be adopted in all its signs and notices and in much of its printed material: the sans-serif alphabet, commissioned in 1915 from Edward Johnston, the most distinguished English type designer of his period, and used ever since. This clean and legible style, graceful and functional to equal degrees, inspired the many seminal innovations in lettering and typography which occurred in the 1920's under the leadership of Johnston's friend and most famous pupil, Eric Gill, who designed a similar font, Gill Sans-Serif, for the Monotype Corporation. Its influence has spread far beyond London Transport until it has become, along with its variations, almost the standard style for direction signs and notices throughout Britain, and has lately been spreading through the Continent.

In addition to its posters, London Transport encourages the use of its buses and trains (in off-peak hours and on weekends) by issuing a wide variety of leaflets and guidebooks on interesting places to visit and how to get there. These are among the most informative and dependable of all the *vade mecums* available to the London visitor, as they are among the most attractive. The text is always written with a clarity and economy, and not infrequently with a quiet dry humor, that every professional writer may well envy. This expertly colloquial type of "public prose," so blessedly innocent of the cluttered, jagged jargon which ordinarily disfigures the genre, is perhaps seen to best advantage in the notices of advice, instruction, and admonition

posted throughout the authority's premises. Here is an example
of the way London Transport's official prose combines instant
intelligibility with informality:

### DON'T DESPAIR

About 330,000 articles left on the buses and Underground arrive
at London Transport's Lost Property Office in Baker Street every
year.

London Transport would like every one of these to get back into
the hands of its owner.

So if you have lost anything go along to the Lost Property Office
at 200 Baker Street, N. W. 1 (near Baker Street Station). It is
open from 10 00 to 18 00 on Mondays to Fridays (19 00 on Thurs-
days for London's late night shoppers), but closed on Saturdays,
Sundays, and Bank Holidays.

*Or you can write, if you prefer.*
Please note, the missing article may not reach Baker Street until
a day or two after it was lost. Give it a chance to get there.

If it is left on a London Transport green country bus outside London or a Green Line coach, it is held for two days at the local
bus garage before being sent to Baker Street, so that you can
call there if you wish.

Could any prose be clearer or tonally better fitted for its purpose
than this? It makes losing an umbrella on London Transport
almost enjoyable.

This is the friendly public image—a repulsive term that I hope
never enters London Transport's mind—which the authority has
always sought to cultivate. Its shrewd and enlightened public
relations policy, its successful projection of a jaunty idea of its
corporate self, surely must rank among the most sustained and
successful of all such enterprises. In a field dominated by vulgarity, London Transport's publicity policy has always been marked
by remarkable intelligence and taste.

As a glance at any of the authority's freely available comprehensive pocket maps of its system will show, the bus and tube networks are complicated. (Tube or Underground: in practice the terms are used interchangeably, though there actually is a distinction. The tube, properly speaking, is that portion of the transit system which has been bored at some depth through London's subsoil, while the Underground has been built by the cut-and-cover method of excavation just below street level.) But navigation is made as easy as humanly possible. On the Underground, maps are everywhere, enlargements of the familiar card-size schematization which every Londoner carries in his pocket if not in his head, the way Calais was written on Mary Tudor's heart. The same map is inserted into most London guidebooks. Each of the eight lines—the newest, just opened, is the Victoria line to the northern suburbs—has its distinctive color, blue for the Piccadilly, red for the Central, green for the District, and so forth; and all references to each route, on maps and signs, display the appropriate color. Thus London Transport caters to the varying capacities of its users—for the educated, quotations from Bacon on its posters; for the illiterate, colors to interpret words.

The Underground, so intelligibly charted, is one of the most effective means by which modern London endears herself to the visitor. It is not an anglicization of New York's shame, for the platforms are clean, the trains are quiet and smooth-running, and the seats are upholstered. Candor requires one to add that smoking is allowed in many cars, the result being an unholy fug as well as a litter of squashed butts on the floor. Queues at the "booking office" can often be avoided by using one of the adjacent battery of coin-in-slot machines, which sell tickets for many of the most popular stations in the entire system.

Although, street traffic being what it is, the Underground is unquestionably the most expeditious way of moving about London, the sensible reader will point out that it is the very worst way of *seeing* London, since most of its mileage supposedly—

witness its name—lies in round black tunnels. But this neglects the fact that in their outer reaches the lines emerge, blinking, into the daylight, and for the remainder of their trackage supply the rider with glimpses of the back-garden London he otherwise would miss.

I am not one to regard a ride in the Underground as a mere, barely tolerable means to an end, the end being the surrender of one's ticket to the collector at the exit and the resumption of one's business. On the contrary, to me it can be a pleasurable experience in itself. I cannot count myself a member of the numerous band of American and British urban-transit enthusiasts, for I have none of the near-professional expertise that they boast. But, as an amateur of amateurs, I recognize and understand the drives that lead the former to operate open-air trolley museums on weekends and the latter to flock to the several excellent English railroad museums. When I am in London, I always pay a refresher visit to the Museum of British Transport, a superlative collection of colorful and improbably immaculate cars and engines, trams, buses, operating accessories, and memorabilia skillfully displayed in a former bus garage a few steps from Clapham Common. When I spent childhood vacations in New York City in the early 1920's, I found unclouded happiness in riding the subway and elevated lines eight hours a day at the cost of a single nickel. In the process, I memorized all the stations on the BMT and IRT systems in correct order, the way other boys memorized batting averages. And so it is clearly a reversion to youthful addiction that has led me, many years later, to cover every mile of the London Underground in like manner. I find comfort in the awareness that my singular preference is not unshared. Several years ago I read of an American officer attached to London naval headquarters who had written a whole book about the Underground and the distinctive atmospheres of the various lines. (I don't think it was ever published.) Best of all, I have the company of a most respectable English poet, John Betjeman, who has recalled how in his own childhood he accomplished saturation coverage of the Underground as it existed in the 1920's:

> *Great was our joy, Ronald Hughes Wright's and mine,*
> *To travel by the Underground all day*
> *Between the rush hours, so that very soon*
> *There was no station, north to Finsbury Park,*
> *To Barking eastwards, Clapham Common south,*
> *No temporary platform in the west*
> *Among the Actons and the Ealings, where*
> *We had not once alighted. Metroland*
> *Beckoned us out to lanes in beechy Bucks—*
> *Goldschmidt and Howland (in a wooden hut*
> *Beside the station) : 'Most attractive sites*
> *Ripe for development'; Charrington's for coal;*
> *And not far off the neo-Tudor shops.*
> *We knew the different railways by their smells.*
> *The City and South reeked like a changing-room;*
> *Its orange engines and old rolling-stock,*
> *Its narrow platforms, undulating tracks,*
> *Seemed even then historic. Next in age,*
> *The Central London, with its cut-glass shades*
> *On draughty stations, had an ozone smell—*
> *Not seaweed-scented ozone from the sea*
> *But something chemical from Birmingham.*

Whatever the attractions of the Underground, Gladstone's observation that London is best seen from the top of a bus still holds. The red double-deckers that are as familiar a symbol of the city as the Houses of Parliament cover all of central London with fifteen hundred miles of route. Some of the "services" are so long as to require two or more hours to travel from one end to the other. A few days spent riding a selected number of routes in various directions can give one a more comprehensive view of urban London than is otherwise obtainable. The 37 bus, for

instance, begins at busy Peckham in the southeast, passes through
the placid village of Dulwich, and then works in a generally
westerly direction through the built-up regions south of the
Thames—Brixton, Clapham, Wandsworth—coming out, finally,
in the riverside suburbs of Richmond and Isleworth. On the
other side of the city, Number 107 weaves a circuitous path from
Ponders End and Enfield through a great swath of near-north
suburbia, panting up hills, second-gearing down them, passing
the Home of Rest for Horses (founded 1885) on Furzehill Road,
leaving the main thoroughfares to thread through housing estates,
stopping to absorb queues of workers from the National Cash
Register plant and the MGM studios, touching at all the Bar-
nets, at Elstree, at Borehamwood, at Canon's Park—and pulling
up, eventually, at the Edgware terminus of the Underground,
where one can board a swift train back to town.

There are many such lengthy routes, some extending like the
spokes of a wheel from the center of London, others proceeding,
like the ones described, along the city's farther margins. There
the red buses meet and are supplanted by double-deckers painted
green, which cover the outer suburbs. A third London Transport
system, the Green Line coaches, is composed of a number of
express routes which strike directly across Greater London from
various directions, beginning at a town on one edge of the commuter belt, passing through the central city, and ending at a
town on the opposite side: from Tunbridge Wells on the southeast, for example, to Windsor on the west, or from Guildford on
the southwest to Hertford on the north. They are the best way to
see a considerable portion of the Home Counties if one doesn't
have a car.

The queue at the bus stop is England's permanent melting
pot. It gathers under London Transport's benevolent signpost
the bespattered hod carrier on the way home, the restless schoolboy in his little cap and blazer, the middle-class housewife with
her shopping bag, the City broker with his bowler, umbrella, and
attaché case. The conductor—the word covers both sexes—is the

master of ceremonies on board, and, when the bus is full, something of a petty tyrant in addition as he adamantly forbids access
to his domain. Regulations limit the number of standees on the
lower deck, and no standing is ever permitted upstairs. Running
the managerial end of a London bus is an occupation only for
the agile and the tireless, for the conductor is forever scuttering
up and down the tight curving stairs that lead to the top deck.
Communication with the driver in his little isolation booth over
the right front wheel, maintained by the traditional bell cord
when the conductor is belowdecks, takes a cruder form when he
or slack-trousered she is aloft. The signal to proceed, after a
glance at the mirror at the head of the staircase has shown
that all is clear on the rear platform, is a couple of sharp
stamps of the foot on the upper deck. The London equivalent of
the New York subway guard's adjuration to "washa daw" is the
appeal, as the bus sways alarmingly around the arc of Hyde Park
Corner, to "hole tie!" I for one always do, trying at the same time
to remember that London buses are built with so low a center of
gravity that they almost never tip over.

The ticket-selling routine aboard a bus is part of the London
experience. The conductor arrives topside, jingling his heavy
apron of change and uttering the inarticulate monosyllable that
sounds something like "kew" and is, in fact, the bus-top version
of the "thank you," however pronounced, which in England is as
universal in casual human intercourse and serves as many purposes as the Scandinavian "tak." In bus parlance the introductory
"kew" means "fares, please." The passenger either states his destination, in which case the conductor calculates the fare, or, if he
already knows what the fare is, asks for a ticket of the appropriate
value. Coins are then given up for a receipt which takes the form
of a supermarket-register tape ground out from a machine suspended above the conductor's diaphragm. The transaction is concluded by another "kew" from the conductor, now really meaning
"thank you," and, like as not, by an echoing "kew" from the
passenger, which serves as the American "you're welcome," a

phrase unknown in England. The purchase of a bus ticket can be quite a ritual.

The cheerful, pungent-tongued Cockney conductors of former generations have been replaced to a considerable extent by Negroes and Pakistanis, members of the recent immigrant wave which has supplied both transport and Post Office with low-paid labor and the country with an increasingly ugly racial situation. I always doubt whether these exotics know London, or even their single route, well enough to reckon fares exactly. In fact, I marvel that anyone can master the rate card which is based on the distance between any two points along the route. More often than we imagine, the fare quoted is probably a rough approximation or even a wild surmise.

A speaker of English would not expect to encounter a language problem on London buses, but sometimes he does. Not long ago I overheard an amusing—and significant—contretemps. A young passenger, an African Negro who spoke impeccable English, asked the conductor, a white man of unascertainable nationality, for information. The conductor's reply was perfectly unintelligible, not through any malice but through simple failure to speak English. His dialect may have been a peculiarly obscure variety of Cockney, though I doubt it, because Cockney speech is fast vanishing. Even after repetition his words were still incomprehensible, not only to the Negro but to me. Thus today, in Britain, the linguistic shoe is on the other foot: the foreigner speaks the indigenous language of the country, and the natives, or at least an occasional member of the London Transport staff, do nothing of the sort. Perhaps London Transport should start language courses for its conductors. Or perhaps it has already done so.

But one would not wish to demand more of a public agency that already has its hands full, what with its posters, maps, booklets, travel enquiry bureaus, and documentary movies—a whole battery of public relations services that have brought good taste in pictures and prose and sprightliness of spirit to the London scene for these many years. I wonder if ordinary Londoners regard with the same affection the visitor does that most familiar of all trademarks on the metropolitan scene, London Transport's red circle bisected by a black crossbar (for buses) or a blue one (for the Underground). As one plods wearily through a portion of London whose allurements have palled after a long day of strenuous exploration, the sign which betokens a bus stop or a tube station is as welcome as an oasis in a desert. It is not mere transportation that London Transport sells: it is transportation with a certain style.

*The ruins of Paternoster Row (1958). The site is now covered by a shopping precinct.*

# 5

# The Scars of London

LONDON EXERTS its spell most strongly over those who have the most active sense of the past. But it is only an occasional visitor, perhaps, who is much burdened with a sense of London's most recent past, the years of nightly thunder and fire and horror when the Germans sought to wipe out the capital of the Anglo-Saxon world. Those who are young and have no personal recollection of what happened here a quarter of a century ago may overlook or casually dismiss the testimony remaining of the city's prolonged ordeal. Unless they wander into certain sections of London, for the most part off the ordinary tourist's track, where the devastation remains so extensive as to be apparent even to the dullest eye, or unless they eventually respond to the cumulative evidence provided by many small observations, the magnitude and grievousness of that ordeal may escape them. They may need to be reminded of events that are engraved into the English memory beyond the possibility of oblivion, even though they are seldom talked of now. The scars London still bears, so long after the event, inescapably add a note of threnody to any account of the city that presents itself to the modern explorer.

It is an experience attended by a persistent feeling of melancholy irony to read books about London published, say, in the middle 1930's and to realize the degree to which events, feared even then by a prescient minority but not really credited by the common run of men, would transform many of those pages, read with hindsight, into a roll-call of prospective annihilation. "Here," for example wrote E. V. Lucas in *London Afresh* (1936), "is the Guards' Chapel, for which you should find a Sunday morning—if only to hear hymns sung with verve and vigour." On a certain Sunday morning in 1944, when the chapel in Birdcage Walk was crowded with guardsmen singing hymns, it may be assumed with verve and vigour, a German flying bomb landed squarely in their midst, obliterating the chapel and most of the worshipers. . . . History has savagely rewritten those tributes to a proud and supposedly impregnable city, requiring their authors' placid present tense—the "present" being the epoch of Hitler's rise to power—to be replaced by the bitter tense of the irretrievable past. In those years of peril, a repeated literary prophecy came close to total fulfilment. In 1774 Horace Walpole had had a vision of a traveler from Peru beholding the ruins of St. Paul's; later Shelley had imagined a time when "St. Paul's and Westminster Abbey shall stand, shapeless and nameless ruins in the midst of an unpeopled marsh"; and Macaulay in 1840 foresaw the day "when some traveller from New Zealand shall, in the midst of a vast solitude, take his stand on a broken arch of London Bridge to sketch the ruins of St. Paul's." On many a watchful night in 1940–44, Londoners were confronted with the imminent reality of this fanciful cataclysm.

So critical, prolonged, and destructive a passage in London history, one which reached into every home and every life, cries out for a worthy chronicler. But so far it has not found one. If we except some of Churchill's oratory and possibly a few other pieces, London's—and the nation's—near-mortal ordeal resulted in no prose or poetry that is likely to be read, as literature, a hundred years from now. Unless somewhere a precious diary lies hidden in manuscript, it seems that the Blitz went unrecorded

by any eyewitness with the rare gift of a Pepys. Perhaps the best
hope lies in the chance that a new Defoe will appear. Defoe
himself, one recalls, synthesized his unfadingly graphic "Journal
of the Plague Year" (the year was 1665, when he was five) from
printed narratives by actual witnesses. Someone, perhaps un-
born in 1941, may yet apply the same documentary technique to
the subject of mid-twentieth-century London under siege, and
produce a permanent masterpiece.

No one who acquired his proprietary love of London from
books, however, needs to read other books to be stirred and
grieved by the story, for as his explorations proceed he soon is
aware that an all too substantial portion of the London best
known to readers of English literature perished then. Although
no section of the metropolis escaped bombardment, the loss was
greatest in the City, the locale of Pepys and Defoe and Dr. Johnson, and to a great extent that of Dickens as well. There, on the
Sunday night after Christmas, 1940, the Nazi bombers, in the
forerunner of what were to prove many so-called "Baedeker
raids," lit a holocaust whose consequences, though relatively
light in terms of death and suffering, were severest of all when
measured by violation of the sense of the past and the wholesale
destruction of symbols of the English spirit. It was a short raid as
raids at the height of the Blitz went, only two hours early in the
evening, but it was unusually heavy, and, thanks to a malign
combination of circumstances, far more catastrophic than usual.
There being at the time no compulsion to guard them, most City
premises—banks, mercantile offices, shops, warehouses, livery
companies, churches—were locked up tight and deserted; so that
when they took fire, one by one (there were some fifteen hundred
separately ignited blazes), it was many minutes, sometimes hours,
before the firemen could take their positions inside or on adjacent roofs, and by that time the buildings were doomed. In addition, an emergency water line laid from the Thames to the
Regent's Canal was severed by a bomb; the extraordinary number of pumps at work reduced the pressure in the regular mains;

at the crucial hour there was an abnormally low tide in the Thames, so that other hose lines ended on mud flats, a number of feet disastrously removed from precious water; fireboats were prevented from coming to the land brigades' assistance by an unexploded parachute mine downstream; and a stiff westerly wind blew at fifty miles an hour. And so, as tangles of waterless hoses snaked limply across the streets and thousands of firemen and wardens watched helplessly, the individual fires merged into two vast crackling, crashing infernos, the larger of which leveled the whole area bounded by Moorgate, Aldersgate Street, Cannon Street, and Old Street. On the edge was St. Paul's, whose miraculous survival—it is fair to call it "miraculous" even though the devotion and heroism of the cathedral's firewatching staff can never be overpraised—strengthened Londoners' determination thereafter as perhaps no other single event, or non-event, did. If Paul's had gone, either on that dreadful night or later, who knows what would have happened to the morale of the countless weary people who looked every dawn, after the All Clear had sounded, to be sure the dome was still there?

Although it was on this single night that the City suffered its most grievous blow, further damage was sustained during many other raids, notably the incomparably extensive and protracted one on the night of May 10–11, 1941, when the glow of London's fires could be seen reflected in the sky as far away as Oxford. (It is to this single night that Richard Collier's *The City That Wouldn't Die,* the most vivid book I have yet read on London in wartime, is devoted.) Fortunately, this raid was the last on such a scale; one or two more might well have won Hitler his victory over the people of London.

By the end of the Blitz, of the 460 acres of built-up land in the City, 164 had been devastated. To the literary visitor, possibly the most poignant sites in the ruined City were those immediately north and east of St. Paul's. Here, ever since Shakespeare's time, had been the center of English publishing and bookselling.

Many thousands of books from the sixteenth and seventeenth centuries bear on their title pages the notice that their printers and sellers had their shops in the curving street called St. Paul's Churchyard, which bordered the cathedral grounds, or in the nearby Ave Maria Lane. After the Great Fire of 1666, the center of the book trade shifted to Paternoster Row, which was no farther away than one could cast a reasonably heavy folio, and here it remained until 1940. On the night the City burned, the greater part of the extant records of London publishing, most of them still unexamined, were lost forever. We shall never know how much valuable correspondence with authors and other material important to the study of English literary history was destroyed in those few flaming hours. But we do know that five million printed books, the entire stocks of a number of important firms, were consumed then.

The worst toll was that of the Wren churches, themselves the products of the rebuilding that occurred after the fire of 1666 when most of the City was leveled. Along with St. Paul's dome, the graceful spires and towers of the forty-seven City churches—including a number which were not by Wren, several of these being older buildings which had been spared in 1666—provided London with a skyline, seen from the Thames, which as we have noted remained essentially unaltered from the late seventeenth century to 1940. To Englishmen at home or in colonies on the other side of the globe, that skyline was as proud a symbol of British permanence as Big Ben (which did survive). After the bombing, there were fewer spires and towers; and of those that still stood, a number lacked their accompanying churches.

Until quite recently, ruined churches were so much in evidence in the City as to stir sadness wherever one walked. Sometimes hemmed in by commercial buildings old or new, sometimes standing in conspicuous starkness where the surrounding acres contained nothing but leveled-off foundations enclosing weed-grown rubble, the shells of stone or brick stood in eloquent

muteness. The roofs were gone, and in the windows, once colorful with glass, were only twisted outlines of old leading, or else
sheer vacancy. The debris that was left after the explosions and
fires—the timbers of the collapsed roofs, the once-exquisite
carved wood of reredos and pulpit, the gallery and pews and
organ—had been removed, and what remained in the bare interior, open to every season of the English climate, were the
memorial tablets on the walls and the well-worn inscriptions on
the stone slabs laid into the floor. Now their pious messages spoke
to no one; their service was over. But somewhere near the gate, or
at the steps before the church that now led nowhere, there was
posted a message of another kind, an urgent appeal, weathered
and forlorn, for funds to restore that one of Wren's masterpieces
to its former glory.

> *St. Augustine, Watling Street . . . Christ Church, Newgate
> Street . . . St. Dunstan-in-the-East . . . St. Mary Alderman-
> bury . . . St. Alban . . . St. Swithin . . . St. Mildred,
> Bread Street . . .*

Close against these bare, ruined choirs were—as they still are
today—little churchyards, burial places for many generations of
men and women and children when the City was still a populous
place of residence instead of a center of commerce and finance
that is deserted after business hours by all except policemen,
charwomen, and night watchmen. Often the tombstones remain,
though frequently undecipherable because London rain and
London smog have eroded their surfaces. But here the churchyards are more the possession of the living than of the dead, and
typically they are what they were before the German fury: little
patches of flower garden, with neat graveled paths and benches
where old people come to take the sun or gossip or doze, and
clerks and stenographers eat their lunches and feed the crumbs to
the hardy pigeons and sparrows.

*St. Andrew, Holborn . . . St. Mary Abchurch . . . St. Nicholas, Cole Abbey . . . St. Mary Aldermary . . . St. James, Garlickhithe . . . St. Michael, Paternoster Royal . . . St. Magnus the Martyr . . . St. Stephen Walbrook . . . St. Giles', Cripplegate . . .*

All but eleven of the City churches damaged or destroyed in the Blitz have been rebuilt. Thanks to the loving antiquarianism that has led the English to preserve minute descriptions, drawings, and photographs of their most prized buildings, the restoring architects sometimes were able to create churches that were virtual replicas of the vanished originals. Sometimes, however, their fidelity was to the spirit rather than to the strict letter. In either case, as a rule the reconstructed churches are as lovely in their various ways as the ones they replaced. And so the strollers and bus riders who watch the surging Strand traffic divide at the "island" church of St. Clement Danes need not be aware that this graceful building, like the nearby printers' and journalists' church of St. Bride with its odd wedding-cake spire poking up from an obscure court, was nothing more than a gutted shell at the end of the war.

*St. Vedast . . . St. Mary-le-Bowe . . . St. Lawrence Jewry . . . St. Andrew-by-the-Wardrobe . . . the Temple Church . . . All Hallows, London Wall . . . St. Botolph, Bishopsgate . . . St. Olave, Hart Street . . . Austin Friars . . . All Hallows, Barking . . .*

And yet, painstaking though the restoration has been, these churches, like all the other London landmarks that have risen from their own rubble, are not the same as they were. No replica, however faithful, can wholly replace the genuine article. The visible authenticity may be complete, but emotional authenticity —which is more important—is lacking. One cannot help being conscious that here the link with the past is but illusion; the design may be old, but the materials are new. This is not the actual pulpit from which Restoration preachers delivered their sermons, these are not the carved pews that beheld weddings and funerals in Defoe's time or Dr. Johnson's; all that remain genuinely representative of the past, a true physical link with the London life of the past two and a half centuries, are the walls and the tower—and sometimes even these had to be built anew. Thus there is only the barest satisfaction in reflecting that this is the exact way things appeared to people who came here to worship or look around them in 1700 or 1800, for these are not the same things.

The sad roster, however, contains more than churches. Equally devastated were another class of buildings deeply embedded in London history, the homes of the many livery companies: lineal descendants of the medieval tradesmen's and artisans' guilds, organizations proud of the venerable traditions, ideals, prerogatives, and practices of their respective occupations, powerful too in municipal politics; the suppliers to the City of its aldermen and, at their head, of the Lord Mayor himself.

Each of these companies had its own hall, some dating from the decades just after the Great Fire. As befitted the official homes of occupations that prospered as London grew in size and waxed richer and richer, the company halls were elaborately decorated, especially the chambers dedicated to banqueting in the high style appropriate to well-to-do middle-class citizens. These halls were as much a symbol of English pride and wealth as the private mansions of the nobility in Bloomsbury and, later, the West End.

They too suffered; the Vintners' Hall, in fact, was one of the very few to escape serious harm and the Stationers' Hall was lucky to escape with only a burned-off roof and blast damage. The roll—eighteen (out of a total of thirty-six) utterly destroyed or damaged beyond repair—is as mournful as that of the churches:

*Fishmongers' Hall . . . Mercers' Hall . . . Saddlers' Hall
. . . Grocers' Hall . . . Haberdashers' Hall . . . Carpen-
ters' Hall . . . Leathersellers' Hall . . .*

Their ruins, too, have slowly disappeared. As the livery companies rebuilt, they restored to their new headquarters the great
old shining services of plate that accommodated their banquets,
and on the freshly plastered and painted walls were hung once
again the portraits of the company's dignitaries down through
the centuries, and in cases of honor were placed the memorabilia
—the documents, the *realia* peculiar to each trade, the relics of
long-past events—which survived the Blitz. But a great deal did
not, and our connection with London's economic and social history is to that degree the more tenuous.

*Wax Chandlers' Hall . . . Cordwainers' Hall . . . Gird-
lers' Hall . . . Barbers' and Surgeons' Hall . . . Coopers'
Hall . . . Butchers' Hall . . . Merchant Taylors' Hall . . .
Clothworkers' Hall . . .*

A new City gradually absorbs the wide spaces of desolation;
the walls of ravaged warehouses, having stood for a generation as
ugly monuments to London's trial by fire, now disappear, and
sprawling office cubes take their place. I have seen the transformation progressing in the ten years I have known London. In
1958, when I first viewed the ruins in the manner of Macaulay's
New Zealander, more than a dozen years had passed since V-E
Day, but the rebuilding of the wasteland had barely begun, at
least as measured by the scope of the destruction to be made
good. Since that time, despite Britain's chronic economic distress,
more and more of the bombed area has been filled in by new
construction. But gaps remain. Within a walk of a minute or two
from the great red-brick modified Georgian or steel-and-glass
buildings that now hem in St. Paul's and the shopping precinct
that covers the site of Paternoster Row are still derelict ware-

houses and empty sites used as parking lots. Here and there remain arched masonry foundations, their debris overgrown with Oxford ragwort, Canadian fleabane, bracken, and willow-herb.

The City as it could be seen immediately after the war is best represented—or was when I last saw it—in Upper Thames Street, from near Blackfriars to London Bridge. This pocket along the river is as yet largely unreclaimed. Just east of the Cannon Street Station, itself an unlovely casualty of the Blitz although it has been patched up and kept in service, is a large ruinous space that was the site of the church of All Hallows the Less, destroyed in the fire of 1666. The plaque that commemorates the fact can still be seen, rent in two, in the ruins of whatever building succeeded the church and *its* successor—Wren's church of All Hallows the Great, torn down at the end of the nineteenth century—and suffered the same fate 274 years later.

Long after the City is entirely rebuilt, the East End will continue to bear its scars. Of all the regions within metropolitan London, those adjoining the river and the docks—Poplar, West Ham, Bermondsey, Deptford, Stepney, Wapping, Whitechapel— had the greatest toll of human lives and human misery. By the end of the war a quarter of all the buildings in the East End were destroyed or rendered uninhabitable. The results still appall, so many years later. Along the main streets in Whitechapel and Limehouse one sees row after row of shops, blasted, decaying, and derelict, or at best carrying on business at ground level while the upper stories exhibit nothing but wall and empty windows. And everywhere one walks in the labyrinths of mean back streets, there is the same evidence: gutted schoolhouses and factories, long successions of small wall-to-wall dwellings boarded up and marked dangerous and unfit for occupancy. On some cleared sites rise large blocks of low-cost public housing, but on many other such plots remain clusters of wallboard-sided "temporary" huts, cramped, unsanitary, dismal refuges for families for whom English society has as yet been able to provide nothing more inhabitable. For the people in the East End, the Second

World War is not over. They still live on one of its battlefields.

But so do all Londoners, even if in the best-known areas most of the evidence has now vanished. Some of the devastated buildings, such as Queen's Hall, for many years a center of British musical life, have not been replaced. But most have been re-erected or repaired, leaving no trace of the wholly or partly desolate condition in which the end of the war found them: the House of Commons, Westminster School, Charterhouse, Guildhall, Staple Inn, the British Museum (which lost about 150,000 volumes), University College, the Natural History Museum in South Kensington (whose botanical collections were decimated), Lambeth Palace, Dulwich Gallery, the Old Vic, the Royal Court Theatre, Chelsea Old Church with its Thomas More associations. Most of the central London hospitals, including St. Thomas' and Guy's, were badly damaged, and no single railroad station escaped being put out of commission for a time. The several inns of court, Gray's Inn, Lincoln's Inn, and the Middle and Inner Temples, with their quadrangles of venerable buildings—in the great hall of the Middle Temple Shakespeare's own company performed *Twelfth Night* in 1602, and Lamb was born and grew up in the Inner Temple—suffered severely. And this is not to take account of the thousands of shops and other business properties which were bombed out.

Apart from the frequent parking lots on bombed sites and the remaining gaps in rows of houses in the residential streets and squares, the West End's scars are pretty well erased. The parks, which throughout the war were the sites of anti-aircraft batteries, now bear no trace of military occupation. But the farther out one goes, the more abundant are the vestiges of the war. The losses in the City and the West End naturally were the most publicized because the buildings involved were the most famous and their destruction the cause for the deepest regret; but it cannot be forgotten that for four years Lewisham and Islington, Fulham and Wimbledon and Paddington and Kentish Town and a hundred other sections of Greater London were also under attack.

Time after time, walking through a neighborhood whose present intactness evokes no suggestion of a city once under siege, the stroller comes unexpectedly upon a gaunt ruin, as in the residential area near Regent's Square, Bloomsbury, where the silent shell of the Greek Revival church of St. Peter stands in its space of green. Churches, indeed, are the most conspicuous casualties remaining in all parts of London. Gradually the bombed cinemas and almshouses, the garages and libraries and small factories and schools have been torn down and replaced. But, doubtless for economic reasons, the pathetic roofless walls and boarded-up windows of devastated churches, belonging to various faiths and various epochs, seem destined to be permanent landmarks.

In the expanses of everyday London beyond the central city, the quality of the feeling with which one looks upon the remaining evidences of the Blitz is different than it is in the City and the West End. In the latter, apart from the thousands of families in Westminster, Mayfair, Knightsbridge, Chelsea, and elsewhere whose houses and flats were destroyed, the effect was felt principally by business firms or the community as a whole; the loss was relatively impersonal. Because it could be distributed, it was blunted. In the square miles of middle- and working-class dwellings and shops outside central London, however, each well-directed missile spelled a violent, perhaps irremediable disruption of personal lives, if not their outright loss. The wounds delivered from the sky, irrespective of their extent, were more personal because they were suffered by the neighborhood in which one lived and by the people one knew best. The men and women, now middle-aged and elderly, who lived here during the war know the intimate significance of every scar, or site of a now-vanished scar, they pass every day. They scarcely forget the explicit private circumstances of each (euphemistically so called) "incident." And it is these—to him—anonymous local tragedies that the walker recognizes in the overtones of the devastated places he finds in Wandsworth or Croydon. The evidence of war is a gap in the middle of the row of houses, with heavy timbers wedged across the vacancy to support the walls of the adjacent survivors, walls that still bear the outlines of the floors and the stairways of the vanished house, and sometimes weathered fragments of bedroom wallpaper or a hob grate that no one will ever reach up twenty feet to light. It is an empty lot, separated from the sidewalk by a low brick parapet topped with barbed wire and now grown over with the tramp vegetation that thrives on misery. It is, especially in the poorer districts, an expanse of façade, consisting of brick walls and boarded-up rectangles that once were the windows and doors of dwellings; there is nothing behind them but piles of the debris that once was floors and ceilings and roofs. Or—the clues here are a bit less obtrusive—it is a sound, inhabited dwelling or shop with no trace of wartime experience except for a telltale band of relatively new bricks and mortar across the top: a building, obviously, which like Dr. Johnson's house in Gough Square lost its roof or even an upper story or two, but the fire wardens were on the job and the fire brigade was not long in coming, so the damage was not irreparable.

Such sites must depend upon local memory for whatever significance they may convey to future generations, because unlike Paris, whose walls bear many reminders of the deaths of men of the resistance in street fighting, London has not chosen to memorialize the scenes of her people's suffering and heroism. At the busy Bank corner in the City there is nothing to remind the stroller that here was once a huge crater where an exploding bomb caused the whole roadway to cave into the tube station when the platforms were crowded with people and two trains were standing there. In New Cross Road in southeast London stands a typical Woolworth's with nothing to signify that it replaces a former store which a buzz bomb tore apart at noon one Saturday in November, 1944, killing between seventy and eighty shoppers in the store itself as well as a hundred more waiting in queues up and down the street. Instead, the windows are filled with the accessories of a peaceful world, picnic equipment, grass and flower seed, beach chairs and beach balls; and inside, the candy counter invites one to "pick 'n' mix"—choose your own assortment, a quarter-pound for tenpence. Directly across the road, in case one has a taste for irony, is the Deptford Civil Defence Headquarters. In Coventry Street, a few yards off Piccadilly Circus, is the spot where sightseers gathered one evening in March, 1941, as mangled casualties in evening dress and uniform were passed one by one from the wreckage of the Café de Paris, where a bomb had plunged onto the crowded dance floor just in front of the band. The Café de Paris is back in business at the same site, advertising "afternoon tea dancing" and "evening dancing" as if the sound of revelry had never been interrupted.

These are the kinds of places, prominent and obscure, which present-day Londoners who went through the Blitz cannot overlook, much as they would wish to. To the peripatetic stranger, as to them, they are an ineradicable part of the past: of, indeed, one of the noblest chapters in British history. The remaining walls of burned churches, the decapitated rows of shabby Whitechapel shops, are as evocative as the better-known formal monuments to older events. Contemplating them, one is easily able to reconstruct the atmosphere of a London bombarded from the air, month after month, year after year: the warning sirens, the shudder of arriving bombs, the bells of fire engines and ambulances, the scurrying of the helmeted fire wardens, the rumble of falling walls and the crackle of flames. And, next morning, new sights of destruction (the corner pub, the chemist's shop, the parish church, the neighborhood cinema "caught a packet last night") ; the smell here of burning and there of damp plaster, the choking clouds of dust from walls being toppled by demolition crews, the craters in the streets, the mountains of debris spilling into sidewalk and roadway, the pools of broken glass from premises shaken by bomb blast but otherwise relatively unscathed, the resultant filling of the vacant windows with drafty makeshift curtains; the gushing of water from broken conduits and sewers, the severing of gas and electric service, the disruption of transportation schedules, the re-routing of trains, buses, and trams around impassable spots . . . "London can take it!" was the defiant slogan of those years. London did. But no one who walks her streets with attentive eyes can long remain ignorant of the cost. It is an epic story which still awaits its poet.

*Quadrangle of Corpus Christi College, Cambridge: Christopher Marlowe and John Fletcher occupied the ground-floor rooms shown in the center of the picture.*

$\mathbf{9 \! a 9 \! a 9 \! a}$

---

*6*

---

# Hawthorne:
# The "Appetite for English Soil"

WHILE I WAS writing these chapters I read, for the first time in their entirety, Nathaniel Hawthorne's *English Notebooks,* the most intimate record in existence of a perceptive American's encounter with the country to which he felt a strong atavistic attraction. Few people know the complete book, because it has been published only in a small edition by the late Randall Stewart (Modern Language Association, 1941). Hawthorne often drew upon these journals, which run to over 300,000 words, when he was writing *Our Old Home* (1863), a considered but nonetheless vivacious distillation of his thoughts about various British places and topics, and after his death his widow published fussily bowdlerized excerpts in *Passages from the English Note-books* (1870). This selection is most inadequate, and not only because Mrs. Hawthorne deleted all her husband's pungencies. The whole series of notebooks should be reissued in more accessible form, because only they convey the full flavor of Hawthorne's English experience and his detailed novelist's-eye view of English scenes.

Often, as I turned the six hundred pages of Professor Stewart's edition, I echoed the imprecation Lowell once uttered in a letter to Longfellow: "Confound those who plagiarize from us before we were born!" The particular objects of Hawthorne's interest, his impressions, predilections, and dislikes are not merely private idiosyncrasies but the constant mirror of one's own. For instance, like at least one modern cathedral-stroller, he repeatedly deplores the placing of choir screen or organ in the middle of a cathedral's nave, thus effectively curtailing the long vista which might otherwise be had. (So, incidentally, does Emerson in *English Traits*.) One is tempted to find in Hawthorne the very archetype of the literate American, of whatever era, who is enthusiastically bent upon exploring and understanding England. The way he looks at things is determined by a subtle but not unusual coalescence of concerns: esthetics, literary reminiscence, history, topography, amateur sociology, social psychology—and sheer unlimited curiosity.

It is extraordinary how fresh and applicable Hawthorne's observations remain today. Hundreds of his paragraphs could be transferred unaltered to a book on modern England, and, as the present reader will soon discover, a few of them have been. The startling extent to which it is possible to see contemporary Britain through Hawthorne's eyes is a witness to the changelessness of so much that the American visitor most values in England. Included among the scenes he describes and the excursions he narrates in the years 1853–57, when he was United States consul at Liverpool but had plenty of time to go about, are many of the very ones that remain central to our own experience.

He was an indefatigable and unapologetic sightseer; in him there was no nonsense about being superior to the interests of the tourist, at least the intelligent literary type. His Anglophilia, or what he called, in another connection, the "diseased American appetite for English soil," was of long standing, and when he took up President Pierce's appointment to the Liverpool consulate, he was enabled to indulge it to the full. He soon discovered that his was yet another case of *déjà vu:*

> . . . *history, poetry, and fiction, books of travel, and the talk of tourists [he wrote in* Our Old Home], *had given me pretty accurate preconceptions of the common objects of English scenery, and these, being long ago vivified by a youthful fancy, had insensibly taken their places among the images of things already seen. Yet the illusion was often so powerful, that I almost doubted whether such airy remembrances might not be a sort of innate idea, the print of a recollection in some ancestral idea, transmitted, with fainter and fainter impress through several descents, to my own. I felt, indeed, like the stalwart progenitor in person, returning to the hereditary haunts after more than two hundred years, and finding the church, the hall, the farm-house, the cottage, hardly changed during his long absence,—the same shady by-paths and hedge-lanes, the same veiled sky, and green lustre in the lawns and fields,—while his own affinities for these things, a little obscured by disuse, were reviving at every step.*

Hawthorne understood, probably better than any other writer on the American's repossession of England, the psychology behind both his motive and the actual quality of his experience. In a single sentence he explained why the American's sense of the past in England is so acute: "To an American there is a kind of sanctity even in an English turnip-field, when he thinks how long that small square of ground has been known and recognized as a possession, transmitted from father to son, trodden often by memorable feet, and utterly redeemed from savagery by old acquaintanceship with civilized eyes." Exactly. Hawthorne knew instinctively what the research of modern historians has established: that nearly all the villages on the modern map were already in existence when the Domesday Book was compiled in 1086, and that some of the compact pattern of fields, lanes, and hedgerows which divides the countryside today was familiar to the peasants who worked the land as long ago as the Middle Ages. More of it was known to the Tudor husbandmen, and practically all to the countrymen who, like Wordsworth and John Clare, came in the aftermath of the great eighteenth-century enclosure movement. Nothing in one's experience of England is more powerful than the sense of great age and continuity which the environment everywhere conveys.

The comparative instinct was as lively in Hawthorne as in any other traveler. Unlike some, however, he exercised it not for the sake of balancing the virtues and deficiencies of two different societies but usually to discover additional felicities in English life. He appreciated the occasional English institution which has no counterpart in America, the public footpath, for instance, which makes it possible for walkers everywhere in Britain to leave the road and strike unhindered across country:

> . . . a fresher delight [than is found on the highroads] is to be found in the foot-paths, which go wandering away from stile to stile, along hedges, and across broad fields, and through wooded parks, leading you to little hamlets of thatched cottages, ancient, solitary farm-houses, picturesque old mills, streamlets, pools, and all those quiet, secret, unexpected yet strangely familiar features of English scenery that Tennyson shows us in his idyls and eclogues. These by-paths admit the wayfarer into the very heart of rural life, and yet do not burden him with a sense of intrusiveness. He has a right to go whithersoever they lead him; for, with all their shaded privacy, they are as much the property of the public as the dusty high-road itself, and even by an older tenure. . . . An American farmer would plough across any such path, and obliterate it with his hills of potatoes and Indian corn; but here it is protected by law, and still more by the

*sacredness that inevitably springs up, in this soil, along the
well-defined footprints of centuries.*

To his mention of stiles, incidentally, Hawthorne might have
added kissing gates, another indigenous detail. They are gates
between pastures, hung in a U- or V-shaped enclosure so as to
allow human passage but prevent bovine exodus.

Today, when so many great houses and estates of England
have been turned into tourist attractions to help their lordly
owners make ends meet, it is startling to discover that this is no
new phenomenon induced by the stiff taxation laid upon the
very rich. The present Duke of Bedford with his picture gallery,
deer herd, zoo, and amusement park at Woburn Abbey and Lord
Montagu with his old-automobile museum and jazz festival at
Beaulieu had noble precedent in Hawthorne's time. At Blenheim Palace, the Duke of Marlborough " (with a thrift of which
even the hero of Blenheim himself did not set the example) sells
tickets admitting six persons at ten shillings; if only one person
enters the gate, he must pay for six; and if there are seven in
the company, two tickets are required to admit them. The attendants, who meet you everywhere in the park and palace, expect
fees on their own private account,—their noble master pocketing
the ten shillings." Hawthorne speculated on the happiness so
wealthy a man might possess; at the very moment he, Hawthorne, was admiring the vast Blenheim gardens, His Grace
might have been in the same gardens, "and, if in a condition for
arithmetic, was thinking of nothing nobler than how many ten-
shilling tickets had that day been sold."*

Hawthorne was the perfect London perambulator. His habit is
noted in his journal entry for September 7, 1855: "Yesterday fore-
noon, I went out alone, and plunged headlong into London, and

---

* When he wrote this in *Our Old Home,* Hawthorne dropped a footnote to
say that the Duke's successor had made "much more liberal arrangements."
One hesitates, incidentally, to think what Hawthorne would have said of the
present Marquess of Bath's gay London posters advertising his Longleat as
"England's most with-it stately home."

wandered about all day, without any particular object in view, but only to lose myself for the sake of finding myself unexpectedly among things that I have always read and dreamed about. The plan was perfectly successful." In the notebooks he alludes time and again to the pleasure of getting hopelessly lost, or at least disoriented, in his long inquisitive wanderings. I can testify from long practice that there is no better way of acquiring a knowledge of London far more intimate than that of the casual tourist. And the result of such aimless walking today, in some of the very regions Hawthorne mentions in this connection, is precisely what he found it to be when he recorded with satisfaction, "I trudge through Fleet Street and Ludgate Street and along Cheapside with an enjoyment as great as I ever felt in a woodpath at home; and I have come to know these streets as well, I believe, as I ever knew Washington Street in Boston, or even Essex Street in my stupid old native town."

On the other hand, he confessed that, however tireless he was on the street, he soon grew weary in art galleries and museums because of his own lack of expertise and the multitudinousness of the exhibits, which resulted in a hopeless blurring of impression. To his private pages he confided heresy: he found visiting the galleries of the British Museum "always a most wearisome and depressing task." Some of the antique sculptures "were doubtless grand and beautiful in their day, though it is by no means plain to me that their merit has not been vastly over-estimated." But his spirits and strength revived as soon as he and his son Julian escaped into Holborn and thence to Cheapside; the boy, he wrote, "seems to have my own passion for thronged streets and the intensest bustle of human life."

Hawthorne is a sympathetic companion not only for the traveler but for the writer who ventures to follow in his path at the remove of over a century. As a striving artist, he correctly recognized the ultimate futility of trying to embody in words the essence of the traveler's impressions. "What nonsense," he exclaimed, "to try to write about a cathedral! . . . It is utterly useless; there is no possibility of giving the general effect, or any shadow of it; and it is miserable to put down a few items of tombstones, and a bit of glass from a painted window, as if the gloom and glory of the edifice were thus to be reproduced. . . . Cathedrals often make me miserable from my inadequacy to take them wholly in; and, above all, I despise myself when I sit down to describe them."

Similarly with the English landscape; but note what he does with the subject as he is about to complain that he can do nothing with it:

> *The first part of the journey [from Gloucester to Basingstoke] was through as beautiful a tract of country as I have seen in England; hilly, but not wild; a tender and graceful picturesqueness—fine trees, and clumps of trees, and sometimes wild woods, scattered over the landscape, and filling the nooks of the hills with luxuriant foliage. Old villages scattered frequently along our track, looking very peaceful, with the peace of past ages lingering about them; and a rich, rural verdure of antique cultivation, everywhere. Old country-seats—specimens of the old English hall, or manor-house—appeared on the hill-sides, with park-scenery about them; and the gray churches rose in the midst of all the little towns. The beauty of English scenery makes me desperate, it is so impossible to describe it, or in any way to record its impression, and such a pity to leave it undescribed . . . English scenery, to be appreciated, and to be reproduced with pen or pencil, requires to be dwelt upon long, and to be wrought out with the nicest touches. A coarse and hasty brush is not the instrument for such work.*

So too did Oxford defeat him—he thought:

> *I am in despair about the architecture and old edifices of these Oxford colleges; it is so impossible to express them in*

*words. They are themselves—as the architect left them, and
as Time has modified and improved them—the expression of
an idea, which does not admit of being otherwise expressed,
or translated into anything else. Those old battlemented
walls, around the quadrangles—the Gothic ornaments and
quaint devices—the many gables—the towers, the windows,
with stone mullions, so very antique, yet some of them
adorned with fresh flowers in pots, a very sweet contrast—
the ivy, mantling the gray stone—and the infinite repose,
both in sunshine and shadow—it is as if half a dozen bygone centuries had set up their rest here, and as if nothing of
the present time ever passed through the deeply recessed
arch-way that shuts in the college from the street.*

While thus lamenting his incapacity to do even minimal justice
to cathedral, landscape, or Oxford, Hawthorne nevertheless wrote
scores upon scores of carefully circumstantial pen-pictures which
everyone who follows him to the places he describes must admire
for their fidelity and eschewing of literary flourish. Hawthorne
saw with an artist's eye so clear that, as we read the notebooks, no
alien sensibility seems to interpose itself between the scene and
the vicarious observer. It is not accidental that the present pages
contain no descriptions of cathedrals except in one or two particular respects, of the English countryside, or of Oxford. Hawthorne has been there before us.

*Kipling's home, Bateman's, Burwash, Sussex*

# 7

## Stone in the Abbey

WHATEVER *frissons* it once evoked in older generations of visitors, Madame Tussaud's today is among Britain's most staid entertainments. In its dignified rooms, one may look upon the minutely faithful effigies of current royalty, ecclesiastical dignitaries, American presidents, and eminences of the sporting and entertainment worlds; and in elaborately detailed permanent tableaux the death of Nelson, the arrest of Guy Fawkes, and the execution of Mary Queen of Scots are re-enacted. We may admire, as we should, the fine craftsmanship reflected in these naturalistic congealings of actuality, but we miss the classic emotions of pity and fear. This is equally true of the Chamber of Horrors, the basement annex to Madame Tussaud's from which its deliciously grisly old reputation chiefly stemmed. Even though the viewing areas down there are kept suitably murky, the sights themselves—waxen figures of distinguished criminals along with miscellaneous engines of torture and death and memorabilia of crime, such as the police poster reproducing one of Jack the Ripper's impudent messages and asking the public to come forward and identify the handwriting—fail to evoke the proper response. To those in quest of the macabre and the monstrous,

Madame Tussaud's is, frankly, a disappointment.

London's true Chamber of Horrors, though never advertised as such, is Westminster Abbey. True, only the blind could be insensible of the Abbey's overriding magnificence. "The heart aches, as one gazes at it," wrote Hawthorne, "for lack of power and breadth enough to take its beauty and grandeur in." But the trouble with the Abbey is that one is too easily distracted from the church by the monuments it contains. Its aisles, ambulatories, and transepts are crowded with marmoreal monstrosities, funerary pomposity on a scale as colossal as its style is eclectic, the riotous results of centuries of mortuary competition. By virtue of their gigantism, extravagance, ornateness, and sheer bad taste, its hundreds of monuments make it unique among the world's most famous buildings, sacred or secular. Here death and its solemnities give rise to irrepressible laughter—the only possible honest reaction, as Hawthorne, who was a little troubled by its inappropriateness, several times admitted. "Ridiculous" is the word he chose to describe the Abbey's memorials. He was right, though "preposterous," the term Horace Walpole applied to the monument to Shakespeare erected in 1740, may also serve.

During the Second World War, the British expressed fears that their island would sink under the sheer weight of assembled Allied armament and troops. They need not have worried. Any piece of land that can support so heavy a burden of marble as is collected within the compass of the Abbey could bear the whole population of China without giving an inch. In the side aisles the monuments are packed in with utter irrelevance to suitability or effect. There are, indeed, two tiers of them, one against the walls, the second, containing no less elaborate specimens, placed on the window ledges. You lift up your eyes from the ground level specimens, hoping to encounter the Lord, and discover instead more of the same: layer after laboriously soaring layer of memorial ostentation.

In the shadowy northwest corner of the nave, to the left as you enter from the west door, there is a helter-skelter assemblage of heroic statues which it is permissible to believe, without putting them to the test, could do with a good dusting. The effect is of suddenly being thrust into a Brobdingnagian sculptor's studio at a time when all his unsold products were shoved into a corner, along with an overstock of folding chairs, while the premises were being decorated. In the north transept the enormous statues of a number of Britain's great political leaders—the Earl of Chatham and his son and namesake William Pitt, Charles James Fox, Canning, Castlereagh, Peel, Palmerston, Gladstone, Disraeli —constitute a kind of perpetual summit conference of eighteenth- and nineteenth-century English statesmen. Captured in the act of orating or studying a book, they are lined up as if to watch a parade, which in fact they do, for past them flows a ceaseless stream of sightseers from every country on the globe, having alighted from their tour coaches, cameras a-dangle, for half an hour's hectic communion with the British past.

In its eastern portion, where irreverence has no scope, the Abbey holds the bones and dust of ancient royalty, gorgeously enshrined and commemorated; in the western half, it is the nation's pantheon, where on tombs and tablets are inscribed the names of its celebrated statesmen, warriors, builders and defenders of Empire, philanthropists, and scientists. But mixed among them are a numerous company of mediocrities and nonentities: minor military and naval officers, titled nullities, and their relics and progeny. Who now, without the assistance of the epitaphs, is able to identify Mary Beaufoy, Martha Price, George Graham, William Dalrymple, Adam Lindsay Gordon, Dr. Joshua Ward, Clement Saunders, or Susannah Davidson? The Abbey commemorates many men and women who could hardly have been called persons of importance even in their own days. Some claimed burial here solely on the strength of having died young; one—"old Parr"—by having lived to the alleged age of one hundred and fifty-two years; and more than a few by mere possession of a nine-hundred-year-old family name. Thus, in the case of these otherwise forgotten figures, the pious intent of their memorializers is achieved, though not quite in the way they had in mind; for it is not the decedents' admirable qualities *per se* that have earned them posthumous fame but only the accident that those virtues are set forth in the nation's most-visited shrine. "You find," said Hawthorne, "that the fame of the buried person does not make the marble live, but the marble keeps merely a cold and sad memory of a man who would else be forgotten."

Compassionate man that he was, he tried to appreciate the "nobodies' " point of view, "forgotten people, with great piles of sculpture, often as high as the eaves of an ordinary house, built up over their miserable bones; so that the visitor keeps saying to himself—'What right has this fellow among the Immortals?' . . . But it is too bad to judge these poor dead folks—so hungry for fame while they lived—in this hard way. So let each century set up the monuments of those whom it admires and loves; and there is no harm, but, on the whole, much pleasure in having such a record before the world's eyes. . . . It is the historical and biographical record of each successive age, written by itself, and all the truer for its mistakes."

Both the sentimentalist and the historian argue well. Furthermore, this indiscriminate mingling of the deservedly eminent and the obscure has a kind of justice to recommend it. Here, as the poet Gray might have observed, the high and the humble are embraced in the democracy of death. But even in a democracy there are scales of value, and in the Abbey no correspondence whatever exists between the size and complication of a monument and the degree of (permanent) fame it represents. Some of the Abbey's most grandiose productions in marble are dedicated to the memory of vanished reputations, or even to reputations which never, so to speak, got off the ground. The tallest monument in the whole Abbey, thirty-six towering feet, was raised to the first Baron Hunsdon, Queen Elizabeth I's lord chamberlain. It set a lamentable precedent. In succeeding centuries the magnitude of memorial had less and less correlation with true fame, the latter-day artificers seeking to make their venerative point

simply by outbuilding—one might almost say outquarrying—
their predecessors.

This persistent reaching for epic proportions was limited only
by space and logistic difficulties. Installation of the cumbrous
General Wolfe monument made it necessary to destroy the screen
of the Chapel of St. John the Evangelist and dislodge the monument of an ancient abbot; and the colossal proportions of
Nollekens' monument to the "three captains," William Bayne,
William Blair, and Robert Manners, who were killed fighting the
French in the West Indies in 1782, required the very font of the
church to be transferred to the western end of the nave. When
the equally weighty memorial to James Watt, of steam-engine
fame, was dragged to its position in the Chapel of St. Paul (the
much-denounced statue itself, by Chantrey, has now been exiled
to the Museum of British Transport at Clapham, where it is
more at home among the locomotives), the pavement gave way,
and only the foresighted provision of planking at the site saved
the toiling workmen from tumbling, along with tons of stone,
into the crypt below. When representation reaches such a scale,
one's sense of proportion is seriously disturbed. On Sir Isaac
Newton's monument, the allegorical figure of Astronomy is portrayed contemplating a celestial globe, which is about four feet
in diameter. But in view of the scale prevailing in the surrounding works of art, it is natural to mistake the globe for Newton's
apple.

Putting aside the irritable question of whether most of these
defunct celebrities or non-celebrities deserved their elaborate
monuments, or vice versa, and with equal tact evading embar-
rassing problems of esthetic justification, it is possible to find as
much delight in the Abbey's exhibits as in Madame Tussaud's.
Marble, no less than wax, is capable of depicting vigorous action,
and in the Abbey is a wide assortment of violently dramatic
scenes executed in haut relief or full three-dimensional sculpture.
The Abbey's dramatic iconography tends toward desperate naval
engagements and military assaults. On Wolfe's monument the

British troops are perpetually landing at Quebec and storming the Plains of Abraham; on Admiral Tyrrell's, his ship, H. M. S. *Buckingham,* handily defeats three French men-of-war, and on that of Lieutenant-General Hargrave one beholds what appears to be the collapse of the walls of Jericho but probably isn't. The first such action to be so represented was the Battle of Nieuport (1600), on the tomb of Sir George Holles, who is also the first hero to be depicted standing erect. The tombstone activity extends also to peacetime violence. On the tomb of Thomas Thynne, a favorite of Charles II, is a portrayal of his murder by three ruffians who attacked his coach as it passed through the Haymarket. It is the easily recognizable prototype of a thousand movie sequences involving desperadoes, rearing horses, and people trapped in a coach.

The allegorical and symbolic components of the tombs are as replete with movement, or at least dramatic posture, as the realistic scenes. Calcutta, personified, kneels at the feet of Rear-Admiral Watson, who avenged the Black Hole; History busily records William Pitt's oratory, as Anarchy, alias the French Revolution, cowers in bondage at his feet; Liberty holds the dying Charles James Fox in her arms as a Negro thanks him for helping sponsor the abolition of slavery. The monument of the second Duke of Argyll (whom Scott portrays in *The Heart of Midlothian*) is laden with allusion: History, inscribing his titles, stops at "Gr—" as a sign that the dukedom of Greenwich died with him; Eloquence with outstretched hand represents the power of his oratory, and to make sure the point is unmistakably clear, at her feet are volumes of Demosthenes and Caesar's *Commentaries;* and the summary of his character and principles is completed by a sculptured Temple of Liberty and a cherub holding up the Magna Charta. The singular thing about the concretions of grief and adoration who attend so many of the Abbey's figures is the variety and intensity of their postures and demeanors. Whatever their allegorical role may be, they are *busy* at it; their forms are studies in the dynamism of funerary passion.

Sometimes, though, the precise nature of their feelings is hard to determine. There are a number of figures, including several Britannias, who are nominally supposed to be devoting themselves to wholehearted mourning, but who seem instead to be in the throes of indignation. Or is it permissible to believe they are embarrassed by having to participate in this many-scened mortuary charade?

In one of the Abbey's most dramatic arrangements, a skeleton Death, emerging from underneath the tomb, is about to hurl what appears to be a spear at Lady Elizabeth Nightingale (d. 1731) and her husband, who are deployed atop the vault. The latter, his arm lightly encircling his lady, looks properly alarmed, but she exhibits hardly more than fatigue, certainly not horror. Death's missile is, in fact, a thunderbolt: the lady died of a miscarriage brought on by her being frightened by lightning. Perhaps in the ghostly shadows of a moonlit Abbey the monument does have the effect once attributed to it, of scaring a robber so violently that he fled, leaving behind both the tools of his trade and his wits. Walpole called the Nightingale tableau "more theatric than sepulchral," but the same objection could be made equally well to a score of other Abbey monuments. For this reason it is a little strange to find Lamb, who knew the Abbey well, singling out the statue of David Garrick for particular condemnation on the same score. "I was struck," he wrote, "with the affected attitude of . . . the celebrated Mr. Garrick. . . . I own I was not a little scandalized at the introduction of theatrical airs and gestures into a place set apart to remind us of the saddest realities." But "theatrical airs and gestures" dominate monuments that long antedate Garrick's.

The inscriptions on the tombs are at least as ornate and flamboyant as the figures, and often more pompous; and in overstatement and superfluous accessory they easily match the architectural design of the most baroque monuments upon which they are carved. But in the midst of their verbosity can be found precise explanations of their subjects' lien on everlasting fame and directions to the beholder as to the feelings he might most suitably summon up. In these extensive annotations, which often amount to miniature appreciative essays, the iconographical suggestion of the figures is reduced to explicit statement. Ambiguity is not one of the literary qualities prized by epitaph writers.

Without necessarily imputing hypocrisy to their composers, it is possible to say that these inscriptions often strain both credulity and patience. As Alexander Pope remarked, alluding, some say, to Robert Freind, the headmaster of Westminster School, who wrote a number of the Abbey inscriptions:

> *Friend, for your epitaphs I'm grieved*
> *Where still so much is said,*
> *One half will never be believed,*
> *The other never read.*

But Pope was willing enough to supply his own brand of mortuary verse, and the results were not always fortunate. In his essay on Pope in *Lives of the Poets,* Dr. Johnson subjects several of his Abbey epitaphs to stringent critical analysis. For the monument to Sir Godfrey Kneller (who, sensible man, declared, "By God, I will not be buried in Westminster . . . they do bury fools there"—and he wasn't) Pope wrote:

> *Kneller, by heaven, and not a master taught,*
> *Whose art was nature, and whose pictures thought;*
> *Now for two ages, having snatched from fate*
> *Whate'er was beauteous, or whate'er was great,*
> *Lies crown'd with Princes' honours, Poet's lays,*
> *Due to his merit, and brave thirst of praise.*
> *　Living, great Nature fear'd he might outvie*
> *Her works; and dying, fears herself may die.*

Dr. Johnson's criticism was explicit and concise: "Of this epitaph the first couplet is good, the second not bad, the third is deformed with a broken metaphor, the word *crowned* not being applicable to the *honours* or the *lays,* and the fourth is not only borrowed from the epitaph on Raphael, but of very harsh construction." But Pope had anticipated him with a much harsher self-judgment: the lines on Kneller, he said, were the worst thing he ever wrote in his life.

The best lines Pope wrote for an Abbey monument were never inscribed on it: the epitaph on Newton, ending with the couplet "Nature and Nature's Laws lay hid in Night:/ God said, *Let Newton be!* and all was Light." No other famous poet achieved the same felicity in his Abbey exertions, although a number, including three laureates, were obliged to try—Dryden (to Sir Palmes Fairborne, governor of Tangiers), Wordsworth (to Southey), and Tennyson (to the explorer Sir John Franklin and the diplomat Stratford Canning).

Even before Pope reproached Freind and Dr. Johnson reproached Pope, Abbey inscriptions, as much as any other form of literary expression, stirred judicious criticism. In the *Spectator* (1711) Addison wrote of the "extravagant epitaphs" which were already so numerous "that if it were possible for the dead person to be acquainted with them, he would blush at the praises which his friends have bestowed upon him. There are others so excessively modest, that they deliver the character of the person departed in Greek or Hebrew, and by that means are not understood once in a twelvemonth." Addison may have been thinking of the monument to the two wives of Sir Samuel Morland, improver of the fire engine and inventor of the speaking trumpet, who were eulogized in Hebrew, Greek, and Ethiopic as well as English. Two generations later, Dr. Johnson delivered a verdict on the bill of particulars—not by Pope—adorning Sir Isaac Newton's elaborate tomb: "Had only the name of Sir Isaac Newton been subjoined to the design upon his monument, instead of a long detail of his discoveries, which no philosopher can want, and which none but a philosopher can understand, those, by whose direction it was raised, had done more honour both to him and to themselves." It is too bad that Johnson never applied his genius for succinct summary to Abbey purposes. He did not lack opportunities to do so, because Louis François Roubiliac, who sculpted a number of the Abbey's most imposing monuments, including those to Mrs. Nightingale and Handel, repeatedly asked Johnson to compose epitaphs worthy of his—Roubiliac's— works. He did not get them.

Allowing for the mannerisms inseparable from the panegyric or pathetic occasion, the epitaphs in the Abbey offer a reliable anthology of the changing English literary styles from Tudor times to our own. Their floridity of language and conventionality of sentiment are apt unfairly to obscure their frequent individuality; their flavor is not only of the age in which they were composed but of the persons who composed them. Fanny Burney's tribute to her musician father, for instance, came unmistakably, exclamation points and all, from the same animated pen that wrote her inimitable diary and her domestic novels:

> . . . *the pride of his family, the delight of society, the unrivalled chief, and scientifick historian of his tuneful art! beloved, revered, regretted, breathed, in Chelsea College, his last sigh! leaving to posterity a fame unblemished, raised on the noble basis of intellectual attainments. High principles and pure benevolence, goodness with gaiety, talents with taste, were of his gifted mind the blended attributes; while the genial hilarity of his airy spirits animated, or softened, his every earthly toil; and a conscience without reproach prepared, in the whole tenour of his mortal life, through the mediation of our lord Jesus Christ, his soul for heaven. Amen.*

Throughout the range of epitaphs runs, of course, the strong evidence of their Roman inspiration. This is true also of the figures themselves, and it is responsible for the incongruities that startle the Abbey wanderer at every turn. In heroic monuments dating from after the first quarter of the seventeenth century (here again Sir George Holles was in the vanguard of change) Roman garb was virtually obligatory, contemporary costume being regarded as undignified in such a context. Thus the troops skirmishing before Fort Ticonderoga on Lieutenant-Colonel Townshend's tomb are—however improbably—dressed as gallant Romans, and so is Sir Robert Peel as he addresses the House of Commons in early Victorian days. But the most memorable toga-wearer, indeed to many connoisseurs of the Abbey's excesses its supreme achievement, is Sir Cloudesley (or as the *Dictionary of National Biography* spells it, Clowdisley) Shovell, a seventeenth-century adumbrator of Sir Joseph Porter, who rose from humble life to become Commander of the Fleet. Unlike Sir Joseph, Sir Cloudesley seems to have been a genuine hero—he achieved his final eminence by repeated feats of daring—but his sculptor, the great Grinling Gibbons, inadvertently reduced him to the level of farce. "Instead of the brave rough English admiral, which was the distinguished character of that plain, gallant man," wrote Addison not long after Gibbons finished his work, "he is repre-sented on his tomb by the figure of a beau, dressed in a long periwig, and reposing himself upon velvet cushions, under a canopy of state." This is accurate as far as it goes, but what Addison and later commentators on Sir Cloudesley's effigy desist from mentioning is the fact as he lies on his side, uncomfortably we should think, his drapery has fallen away, revealing a consid-erable naked belly.

The belly is, in a double sense, obtrusive; and it hovers some-where in the twilight zone where realism and fancy meet, for what is an admiral's bare midsection, taken by itself, but a realis-tic detail, yet when conjoined with toga and full-bottomed wig a flight of free invention? In the Abbey, verisimilitude and extrav-agance are forever confronting each other. On the one hand, there is the smallpox-pitted face of Admiral Sir Peter Warren; on the other, Rear-Admiral Richard Tyrrell rises out of the sea, where he was buried, and "looks for all the world," commented

Joseph Nollekens, who did not hesitate to disparage another sculptor's work, "as if he were hanging from a gallows with a rope round his neck." The sight inspired Arthur Penryhn Stanley, Dean of Westminster, who knew the Abbey's monuments better than any other man, to one of his rare moments of wit. "The idea of the monument," he wrote, "seems to be to represent the Resurrection under difficulties."

That, it seems to me, is the right spirit in which to wander through the mad *mélange des genres* that is Westminster Abbey west of the crossing. Yet alongside the monstrosities, often overshadowed by their arrogance and pomposity, are memorials which are rendered affecting by their simplicity or palpable sincerity of style, their aptness to character and circumstance. The effigy of the Duchess of Newcastle, whom her husband eulogized in his inscription as "a wise, wittie, and learned lady, which her many bookes do well testifie" and of whom Pepys, for his part, recorded privately that "her whole story is a romance and all she does romantic," is equipped with an open book, a pen case, and an ink horn, ready for any sudden inspiration that might visit her in the grave. Addison was "very much pleased" by the sentence in the inscription: "Her name was Margaret Lucas, youngest sister of Lord Lucas of Colchester—a noble family, for all the brothers were valiant, and all the sisters virtuous."

The further one goes back in time, the more genuine—that is, the more devout—the sentiment behind the tomb seems to be. This may be an illusion, but it is a persuasive one. The reclining effigy of the Elizabethan lawyer Sir Thomas Hesketh, clad in a black and red gown and lying under a painted and gilt canopy, and the lovely tomb of Sir John and Lady Puckering, whose alabaster effigies are attended by seven prayerful children in ruffs and gowns, are typical of the many pre-Restoration memorials which survive from the days when the Abbey was as yet free of the megalomaniac abortions with which three further centuries of misguided "taste" were to encumber it.

I have said nothing of the Poets' Corner, for that is too familiar ground and the additional element of literary sentiment inevitably complicates one's reaction to the crowded floor and walls. Yet we may appropriately end there, for the sake of the very latest inscription in the Abbey. It is on the plain slab laid alongside Tennyson's, which is flanked on the other side by Browning's. This newest marker commemorates T. S. Eliot and bears the words: "The communication of the dead is tongued with fire beyond the language of the living." But with what an antic babel does the Abbey resound!

*The Parsonage (Brontë Museum), Haworth, Yorkshire*

## 8

# In the Public Domain

FORTUNATELY for the transatlantic admirer of their books, the English are proud of their literary heritage and have exerted themselves to preserve or restore places associated with great English authors. That they continue to do so even today when some house with literary associations is in peril of decay or destruction —Laurence Sterne's Shandy Hall in Yorkshire is the leading case at the moment I am writing—is a tribute to the enduring power of honest sentimentality in a resolutely non-sentimental age.

Buried deep in the English psyche is the traumatic memory of what happened at Stratford-on-Avon when, well over a century ago, national bardolatry turned that inoffensive Warwickshire market town into one of the first literary tourist lures on record. The main attraction was (as it remains) the so-called "birthplace" of Shakespeare, a typical Warwickshire Tudor cottage which the dramatist's father certainly owned although there is no proof that William was born there. No authentic relics of the Shakespeare family's occupancy survive, and only the basic fabric of the house is as it then was; for in the course of the years the cottage was allowed to fall into dilapidation, "the filthy remnant of a butcher's shamble, with its ghastly hook," as it was described by a magazine writer in 1847, its frontage low and crazy and the rooms "squalid and forlorn." In that year it was bought and endowed with a curatorship and subsequently rehabilitated into the museum-like edifice known to modern tourists. Meanwhile Anne Hathaway's cottage, several miles distant, was similarly "restored," and, with the addition of large stocks of brummagem souvenirs (the first having been artifacts made from a seemingly inexhaustible supply of wood from a mulberry tree Shakespeare was reputed to have planted), Stratford was ready for the business which has never ceased coming. Some of the episodes attending the exploitation of a national piety for the sake of local industry were pathetic, some comic; and in the aggregate they represented the strong streak of vulgar commercialism in the English character which the English character in its loftier moments never ceases to deplore. As a result, Stratford is something of a permanent embarrassment to the English, the very symbol of culture equipped with a turnstile.

Actually, I think the case against Stratford is overstated. Perhaps it has lost much of its earlier force in recent years because of the distinguished Shakespeare productions in the brick Memorial Theatre that was built on the banks of the Avon in the 1930's, replacing a Victorian mistake whose burning elicited nationwide cheers led by George Bernard Shaw. But apart from that: the commercialism which troubled people in the nineteenth century is not oppressively in evidence in the town. On its sidewalks Stratford residents in the legitimate discharge of their business outnumber American sightseers. There is, naturally, a constant plethora of tourist coaches in the parking lots, but such a phenomenon is hardly peculiar to Stratford. True, there are gift shops with every conceivable kind of Shakespeare knickknack, and the local W. H. Smith bookstore displays not only editions of the Complete Works and the Lambs' *Tales from Shakespeare* but a wide selection of the latest scholarly studies. There are a Judith Shakespeare Tea Shop and a Shakespeare Garage and (to make the ordeal of attending a Literary Shrine relatively bearable for George F. Babbitt's progeny) an American soda fountain, an American cocktail bar, and the Stars and Stripes and the Union Jack flying side by side overhead. But the Avon as it flows under the ancient Clopton Bridge is still a charming English stream, with swans and rowboats and willows; there are green meadows on the bank opposite the playhouse; and in front of the theater itself are broad acres of lawn and, behind, a brilliant flower garden.

The hard truth is that as vulgarizers the British are, and always have been, incompetent. If they invent cheap gewgaws for people to take home as mementoes of their improving visit to the Bard's shrine, they immediately salve their conscience by planting more flower gardens. They simply do not have the gift other nations possess for cashing in on cultural windfalls. Passing over the numerous American triumphs in this kind of enterprise, consider what continental nations do. The sure-fire prescription for a successful tourist promotion (I have in mind the town of Odense, Denmark, where Hans Christian Andersen was born) is to take a couple of the town's back alleys, freshen up the tumbledown houses, and advertise the result as "fairy tale streets" or whatever phrase best fits the particular local deity being exploited. The tourists will come and find the tumbledown houses converted into shops hideous with yellow Kodak and red Coca Cola signs, the "picturesque" sidewalks lined with stands and racks laden with junk devised for the spendthrift holidayer. This is the way shrewd promotion can parlay a slum into a fortune. The English, however, have not learned the trick to perfection at Stratford or anywhere else I know, although, surprisingly, they have come closest to it in a Yorkshire village called Haworth.

Haworth was, of course, the home of the Brontë sisters and the locale of *Wuthering Heights*. Few works of English fiction are so permeated with a sense of place: the bleakness, inhospitality, and isolation of the Yorkshire moors remain in readers' memories long after details of character and plot have faded. Haworth is today, as it was in the Brontës' time, a sufficiently picturesque village in its grim, tight-lipped way, with a steep, narrow street and all buildings constructed of the prevalent dark brown sandstone. Conceivably it might have become a tourist attraction without the aid of formerly resident celebrities, the way prettier places like Broadway in the Cotswolds did. But Haworth prospers today because of its Brontë industry. It no longer possesses the isolation that once entered so strongly into its character; the village is pretty well swallowed up on the western fringes of the Bradford-Leeds industrial conurbation. More specifically, it is a satellite of the manufacturing town of Keighley (pronounced, with the aberrant logic that is one of the glories of the English tongue, "Keethly") . But the famous Parsonage remains at the top of a cobblestoned lane that climbs from the main street, and, though considerably altered since the Brontës lived there, it is worth seeing for its collection of their personal belongings and household effects such as the Rev. Patrick Brontë's nightcap, samplers worked by the sisters, and family china and clothing; and from the front windows one looks across the tenebrous graveyard to the church, which, however, replaces the one of which Patrick was rector. Of special interest to Americans is the wing recently added to the Parsonage which houses the superlative collection of Brontë manuscripts and drawings made by a Philadelphian, Henry Houston Bonnell, and bequeathed by him to the Brontë Society—a rare case of an English literary treasure being returned from America to the place of its origin.

To reach this authentic literary shrine, after passing the Black Bull Tavern where the doomed Brontë brother, Branwell, drank himself to ruin (no marker on the building conveys this information) , one must run the gauntlet of tourist-trade establishments, the Brontë Cafe, the Brontë Guest House, and the Brontë Bookshop. This last enterprise, with its display of souvenirs, postcards, and maps of the "Brontë country," boasts over its door a sign which to me represents local ingenuity's attempt to extort the last drop of sentimental association from the materials it has to work with. "This," the sign reads, "was the post office in the time

of the Brontës and here their famous manuscripts were posted."
Well (thinks the incorrigible nit-picker), not *all* of them, at any
rate, for Charlotte sent the manuscript of *Jane Eyre* to London
by what we today would call railway express—as we know from a
letter to her publisher in which she apologizes for not prepaying
the carriage charge, "as money for that purpose is not received at
the small station-house where it is left."

And, putting aside the sign's palpable inaccuracy, to designate
a post office as an adjunct literary shrine is setting a dangerous
precedent, for how many other English buildings are entitled to
the same recognition? One thinks of the Charing Cross Post Office
in London which figures in the romantic story of the author of
"The Hound of Heaven," the poet Francis Thompson. In 1887
Thompson, a ragged down-and-outer of the sort still to be seen
along the Embankment and in the London parks, sent a soiled
sheaf of manuscript to Wilfrid Meynell, editor of the periodical
*Merry England,* with an accompanying note saying, "Kindly
address your rejection to the Charing Cross Post Office." Meynell,
who was not the most methodical of editors, pigeonholed the
submitted copy without bothering to examine it, and only six
months later did he get around to doing so. Impressed, he then
wrote at once to the author in care of the Charing Cross Post
Office, but received no reply. Either the letter miscarried or, more
likely, Thompson by this time had tired of applying for mail that
never came. After seven more months Meynell tried the device of
publishing one of Thompson's poems, and this succeeded in
flushing the poet out. Meynell finally caught up with him, no
shirt under his coat, no socks on his feet, his shoes broken, at a
chemist's shop in Drury Lane which replaced the post office as an
accommodation address. Thus began a troubled friendship in the
course of which Thompson's irregular habits and self-serving
character made Meynell and his wife Alice—persons of infinite
patience and mercy—eligible for canonization among the mar-
tyrs of English literature.

And so the Charing Cross Post Office, if the lead of remote

Haworth were to be followed, should have a marker to the effect
that "on this site Francis Thompson failed to receive Wilfrid
Meynell's letter, August, 1887." But if, as I say, Haworth sets a
dangerous precedent in this respect, in another there is fortuitous
fitness in distinguishing this particular post office, because one of
the addresses to which Brontë mail was sent from here is also
marked. This is 32 Cornhill, London, the headquarters in Victorian times of the publishing firm of Smith, Elder, and Company. One panel in the modern carved doors at this location
recalls a famous episode that occurred here, but uses considerable
license in doing so.

In July, 1848, J. Cantley Newby, the unscrupulous publisher
of "Ellis Bell's" (Emily Brontë's) *Wuthering Heights* and
"Acton Bell's" (Anne Brontë's) *Agnes Grey* and *Wildfell Hall*,
sought to cash in on the critical and popular success of "Currer
Bell's" (Charlotte Brontë's) *Jane Eyre*—published by Smith,
Elder—by implying in his publicity that all these novels were by
a single author. Disturbed by this chicanery, Charlotte and
Anne, who like Emily were known to their publishers only under
their masculine pen names, suddenly resolved to go to London
and set the record straight. After tea, as Charlotte recounted in a
letter, they "walked through a snow-storm to the station" (yes: in
July) and took the night train for Leeds and London.

The next morning they walked from their inn unannounced
to the Smith, Elder office, where they asked a young man at the
counter if they could see Mr. Smith. "He hesitated, looked a
little surprised. We sat down and waited awhile, looking at some
of the books on the counter. . . . At last we were shown up to
Mr. Smith." Smith later recalled that when the clerk entered his
office on that Saturday morning "I was very busy and sent out to
ask their names. The clerk returned to say the ladies declined to
give their names but wished to see me on a private matter. After
a moment's hesitation I told him to show them in." They turned
out to be "two rather quaintly dressed little ladies"—rural Yorkshire's fashions were not London's—"pale faced and anxious

looking. . . . One of them came forward and presented me with a letter—addressed to 'Currer Bell, Esq.' I noticed that the letter had been opened, and said with some sharpness: 'Where did you get this from?' 'From the post-office,' was the reply, 'It was addressed to me. We have both come that you might have ocular proof that there are at least two of us.' " According to Charlotte, at this Smith looked so baffled she could scarcely keep from laughing. Then "A recognition took place—I gave my real name: Miss Brontë. We were in a small room—ceiled with a great skylight—and there explanations were rapidly gone into: Mr. Newby being anathematized, I fear, with undue vehemence. Mr. Smith hurried out and returned quickly with one whom he introduced as Mr. Williams"—the reader who, as the consequence of a long Sunday absorbed in the manuscript of *Jane Eyre,* had strongly urged its publication. "Another recognition and a long, nervous shaking of hands. Then followed talk—talk—talk. . . ."

The wood sculpture at 32 Cornhill, however, portrays not George Smith but William Makepeace Thackeray welcoming the Brontë sisters. The depicted scene is faithful to Thackeray's appearance—he is shown with spectacles and a misshapen nose, broken in a fight when he was a boy at the Charterhouse—but not to the event. In 1848 Thackeray had not yet become a Smith, Elder author, and although later he attended the office regularly when he became the first editor of the firm's *Cornhill Magazine,* one doubts that he ever added to his duties that of official greeter. Charlotte met him first at Smith's home in Kensington, eighteen months after her first visit to the publisher's office, and later was a guest at Thackeray's own house in Young Street.

But no matter. Few of the crowd who hurry by, in this heart of the London financial district—only three doors from the site of Thomas Gray's birthplace, by the way—know the carved scene is even there, let alone that it dilutes fact with fancy. In Haworth, however, the Brontë legend does anything but blush unseen. The lowering Sunday I investigated it, the whole industry, from pot-holed pay-as-you-enter parking lot to the house itself up the lane, was doing a capacity business. At the opening hour the Parsonage door was pressed by a crowd that would have done credit to Barnum's Museum. Men, women, and children, some seventy thousand a year, says the official guidebook: surely not more than one in twenty has ever read a line of any of the Brontës? Or do I underestimate the fierce local pride the county feels for these gifted sisters, a pride that requires their books to be read over and over, more than a hundred years after their deaths? Or is the popularity of Haworth due merely to the lack of anything else to do on a Yorkshire Sunday?

Thanks partly to the National Trust, a public foundation which owns and maintains hundreds of literary and historical buildings and sites, but even more to various individual associations of enthusiasts who somehow scraped up the requisite purchase money, a considerable number of homes once occupied by great writers are in the public domain, so to speak. Hawthorne, who visited as many as were accessible over a century ago, nevertheless decried the practice:

> I do abhor this mode of making pilgrimage to the shrines of departed great men; there is certainly something wrong in it, for it seldom or never produces (in me, at least) the right feeling. It is a queer truth, too, that a house is forever spoiled and ruined, as a house, by having been the abode of a great man. His spirit haunts it, as it were, with a malevolent effect, and takes hearth and hall away from the nominal possessors, giving all the world (because he had such intimate relations with all) the right to enter there.

Hawthorne was writing specifically of Scott's baronial mansion, Abbotsford, which was then, as it is today, in private hands, though open to the public; possibly his sense of intrusiveness would have been less bothersome had the houses he visited not been still occupied as private dwellings. Whether or not such houses produce "the right feeling" depends on the individual case. The success with which they recall to the visitor the personality, tastes, and habits of their former illustrious occupant is largely a matter of accident. Too often the dispersal of furniture and personal effects at some time following his death or departure to another house, and alterations carried out by subsequent owners, have made the building little more than an irrelevant shelter for stray memorabilia.

Occasionally, however, fate favored the project. Probably the most satisfactory literary home in London proper is Carlyle's house in Cheyne Row, Chelsea, where he lived from 1834, when he came from Scotland to find his fortune as a writer, to 1881, when he died as a craggy, venerated national sage. After his death there was a fourteen-year interval during which the house was at times untenanted and neglected and at others rented to such occupants as an eccentric woman with a flagrant surplus of cats and dogs and the purveyor of a nostrum called "Balm of Columbia." But despite this period of neglect, when the house was bought for the nation in 1895 with the proceeds of a public campaign, it was quickly returned to the condition in which the Carlyles knew it. The restoration, down to the placement of the original furniture and bric-a-brac and the patterns on the wallpaper, was made possible by the remarkable amount of information that survived, not only in the Carlyles' letters but in the memory of people still living in 1895 who had known it when the Carlyles lived there, in a number of leases and specifications drawn up in connection with their tenancy, and even in a series of photographs made of the rooms in the 1850's. No other English literary house is so well documented.

This is fortunate, because the house plays a far more important role in the biography of its occupants than do most houses which figure in literary history. It might be said to have a biography of its own, because it is, apart from Thomas and Jane themselves, the chief character in Thea Holme's engaging domestic chronicle, *The Carlyles at Home* (1965). Here the irascible Carlyle and his long-suffering but far from meek Jeannie entertained their friends, coped with erring maidservants, added small luxuries as their income increased, querulously shared their illnesses, had shrill arguments, and still could not do without each other. One can still see the kitchen where on winter nights Carlyle and Tennyson smoked their pipes in silent communion, and behind it the tiny walled-in garden where they did so on summer evenings, and where Jeannie's beloved dog Nero was buried. Atop the house is the "soundproof" study Carlyle had built when the combination of street noises, his neighbors' crowing roosters, and their young daughters practicing on the pianoforte promised to drive him out of his mind. As a sad footnote it must be added that the room turned out not to be soundproof after all. Up there, Carlyle even heard new noises, distant railway bells and whistles and the like, of which he formerly had been blissfully unaware.

Scottish peasant though he was by birth, Carlyle was a Londoner most of his life, and with his rugged face and flowing cape he was a familiar passenger on the horse omnibuses running to Piccadilly from the Chelsea that, like so many regions which are now totally absorbed by London, still had a village quality. Of another Londoner-by-adoption, Charles Dickens, who knew every inch of the Victorian metropolis more intimately than anybody else in his time and wrote about it with unmatched vividness, only one London residence survives. This is 48 Doughty Street, Holborn. Young Dickens lived here in 1837–39, the very time he rocketed into fame with *Pickwick Papers* and went on to consolidate his position with *Oliver Twist* and *Nicholas Nickelby*. After he left it for larger quarters, the house went through various hands and in 1903, when a marker was placed on it, it was a boarding house. None of Dickens' furniture remains except a chair or two and his worktable, but some of his books and personal belongings and a few manuscripts are here. The walls are covered with a motley collection of pictures of Dickens and of various other places associated with him, and with many illustrations of characters and scenes from the novels. But here, of course, the biographical interest gives way to the sentimental, and indeed the whole emphasis at Doughty Street is epitomized by the presence in the basement of a fanciful recreation of the Dingley Dell kitchen in *Pickwick Papers*. Dickens House reflects the tastes of its owner, the Dickens Fellowship, which bought it in 1923. The Fellowship is an old-established sodality of enthusiasts who used each year to set aside a Dickens novel for intensive study and devised for their corporate delight fiendishly difficult "examination papers" covering minute details in the canon. Dickens the storyteller and character-creator was their man, not the complex human being and serious artist whom modern scholarship and criticism have revealed. Thus Dickens House is predicated on an old-fashioned and now largely discarded version of its hero.

Dickens' last home, incidentally, can still be seen on the right side of the highway from Gravesend to Rochester, some twenty-five miles from London. It is at the top of Gad's Hill, famous as the locale of the farcical highway robbery in the first part of Shakespeare's *Henry IV*, and on the opposite side of the road is a mediocre pub named for the anti-hero of that event, Sir John Falstaff. This red brick house, in whose dining room Dickens had his fatal stroke in June, 1870, is now a girls' school, partly hidden from the road and, I believe, not identified as Dickens'. The gate merely bears a small brass plate reading "Gad's Hill Place."

A third great man of letters who was also a professional Londoner ("Sir, when a man is tired of London he is tired of life") was Dr. Johnson, who lived from 1749 to 1759 in Gough Square, a cul-de-sac achieved through a narrow alleyway off Fleet Street. Of the fifteen places where Johnson told Boswell he had lived in London, this is the only one to survive. Surrounded for some years by wartime ruins, it is now again hemmed in by buildings associated with the printing trade, such as the headquarters of inkmakers in whose display windows may be seen startling iridescent pictures of nude girls—a feature of the latter-day neighborhood (the pictures, not the girls) on which we would welcome

Johnson's comments. After Johnson left the house, it was occupied by Hugh Kelly, the "poetical stay-maker," and then, following the pattern, it went through various other hands. Carlyle visited it in 1832 and left the following account:

> *The actual occupant, an elderly, well-washed, decent-looking man, invited us to enter; and courteously undertook to be* cicerone; *though in his memory lay nothing but the foolishest jumble and hallucination. It is a stout, old-fashioned, oak-balustraded house:* "I have spent many a pound and penny on it since then," *said the worthy Landlord:* "here, you see, this Bedroom was the Doctor's study; that was the garden" *(a plot of delved ground somewhat larger than a bed-quilt)*, "where he walked for exercise; these three garret Bedrooms" *(where his three Copyists sat and wrote)* "were the place he kept his—Pupils in!" *Tempus edax rerum! Yet* ferax *also: for our friend now added, with a wistful look, which strove to seem merely historical:* "I let it all in Lodgings, to respectable gentlemen; by the quarter or the month; it's all one to me." *—*"To me also," *whispered the Ghost of Samuel, as we went pensively our ways.*

The building remained a rooming house for many more years, after which it was taken over by a printing firm. When it was finally bought for the nation in 1910, its purchaser, the newspaper magnate Cecil Harmsworth, called it "perhaps the most dilapidated and forlorn tenement in London." In these circumstances, it would be futile to hope for much Ghost of Samuel to remain. The main interest of the house is simply the layout Johnson knew, two decent-sized rooms flanking the staircase on each of the floors, and in the attic (burned during the Blitz but now restored) the space occupied by what would in today's academic circles be called Johnson's Dictionary Factory, where the harmless twenty-three-shilling-a-week drudges Carlyle mentions helped compile his most famous book. The house contains a modest assemblage of Johnsoniana, engravings of the Doctor and members of his circle and a few books, but virtually no authentic furniture or memorabilia.*

The other house of Johnsonian memory, his childhood home, is in the marketplace at Lichfield, Staffordshire. I doubt if any but the most dedicated Johnson enthusiast would find it worth a special detour. Apart from a fairly respectable reference library on Johnson and his circle, and the inevitable random miscellany of prints, portraits, and silhouettes on the walls, it is a meager display. It contains little furniture, and such alleged personal effects of Johnson as it contains—teapot, mug, punch bowl, shoe buckles, walking stick, snuffbox, and the rest—are, to put it charitably, of uncertain authenticity.

Happily the dejected air that pervades the Lichfield house is not often encountered in English literary homes. The Keats devotees who have restored and now manage Wentworth Place, the Keats Museum in Hampstead, have little more to exhibit than is found in either of the Johnson homes, yet they have succeeded in evoking the spirit of the young poet who once lived there. A cream stucco house located in a quiet tree-lined street only a block or two from Hampstead station, Wentworth Place was built by Keats's friends Charles Armitage Brown and Charles Dilke. After his brother Tom died late in 1818, Keats moved into Brown's half of the two-family house, and here he lived off and on until he left for Italy in September, 1820. Meanwhile, in May, 1819, Fanny Brawne, the girl with whom he was in love, had moved with her mother into the other side of the house, and the two cared for him as his tubercular illness progressed. It was a time of poetic inspiration—much of Keats's "miraculous year,"

---

* Since the event is too recent to have found its way as yet into most guidebooks, it might be added that the summer house Johnson often enjoyed while staying with the Thrales at suburban Streatham, a sort of log cabin with a conical thatched roof, has been restored after a century and a half of neglectful exile at Knockholt, Kent, and erected in the grounds of Kenwood House, Hampstead.

during which he wrote "Hyperion," "The Eve of St. Agnes," "Lamia," and the great odes, was spent here—as well as of passionate hope and despair. And somehow, despite the paucity of association pieces, in Keats House one senses his continuing presence. Before the living room window is a "sopha bed" of the kind from which the feverish youth looked out on what was then a portion of Hampstead Heath, though now built upon; on the walls are copies of some of Severn's pictures of members of the poet's circle, and in display cases are the holographs of some of his incomparable letters. By a happy thought, the annotative cards alongside the various items, written in beautiful italic script, quote passages from the letters referring to Keats's life in these rooms. This means of restoring the spirit of a long-gone occupant is better, because more subtle, than the display of Brown's furniture would have been had it survived.

These four London houses, Carlyle's, Dickens', Johnson's, and Keats's, are the ones most often visited by conscientious literary tourists. A fifth is less well known, partly because it is remote from the beaten path (in the northern suburb of Walthamstow, a long bus ride from central London through the slums of Hackney and Clapton) and partly because the fame of the literary figure whose home it once was is not as wide. This is Water House in Lloyd Park, Forest Road, now renamed the William Morris Art Gallery. Morris' mother lived in it in 1848–56, after the death of his wealthy father and while the future poet, craftsman, and socialist was at school and university. In these rooms Morris' career as an astonishingly versatile (and in some respects highly influential) craftsman is illustrated by a wide sampling of Morris-designed and Morris-executed tapestries, rugs, furniture, tiles, chintzes, and wallpapers, the colors of the latter two categories remaining surprisingly fresh after all these years. Added to them are samples of the work of other members of the Pre-Raphaelite group, Rossetti, Burne-Jones, and Hunt, as well as some of Morris' original designs for the textiles and wallpapers and a few Kelmscott Press books. There is little relating to

Morris as a person, but I found a satisfying aptness in the extraordinarily dirty hands of the attendant who presided at the door the day I was there. They reminded me of the wonder Rossetti expressed at the surpassing ability "Topsy," as they called Morris because of his thick unruly hair, had for attracting dirt to his person.

Morris' other homes are still standing and occupied, though none are open to the public. The dark, gabled Red House he had his architect friend Philip Webb design for him and his bride, Jane Burden, can be found in Bexley Heath, an eastern suburb of London. Red House Lane, off Upton Road, which in turn is off Bexley High Street, is a dull neighborhood of rather antiquated villas, and Red House itself, a pioneer attempt to free Victorian domestic architecture from the bonds of formula and stereotype, is hardly distinguishable from its neighbors except in the extent of its grounds. (When it was built, it stood in open country.) Perhaps it can be said to have paid the penalty of its own success: once its style caught on, it was imitated all over England. Later, Morris moved his family to Kelmscott Manor, on the stripling Thames some miles above Oxford. It can be reached by car from the Oxford-Lechlade road: one turns into a rural road at the Trout public house and follows it past an ancient-looking hamlet built wholly of the native gray-brown stone. The road narrows still more into a lane, and just beyond, on the right, is the low manor house of late Elizabethan origin. It is half hidden behind a hedge fence, visitors are not welcomed, and a picture angle can be found only by climbing the barbed wire fence on the other side of the lane and maneuvering in a nettle-filled field.

Morris' last residence, also called Kelmscott, is easier to find and photograph. It is in the Upper Mall, Hammersmith, one of a row of eighteenth-century houses directly overlooking the Thames and Hammersmith Bridge. The river at this point is an unlovely industrial stream, but as if in deference to Morris' dream of a factoryless England where handicraftsmen would work in pleasant tree-shaded shops, the tract of the bank directly opposite the Upper Mall has been preserved as an interval of greenery. Morris conducted one of his own industries here, at two different addresses in the immediate vicinity. But this was the least offensive of all manufactures—the making of beautiful books by hand. The Kelmscott Press made no smoke, consumed no oil, and contributed nothing whatsoever to the pollution either of air or of water.

This little strip of waterside Hammersmith, hemmed in on the landward side by the heavily traveled Cromwell Road extension, is unusually rich in literary associations. Kelmscott House itself, before Morris acquired it, was the home for ten years of the poet and novelist George MacDonald. A few yards away, nestling between a lane and the river bank, is an old inn, the Doves, where the eighteenth-century poet James Thomson is said, on rather fragile authority, to have composed the "Winter" section of his *The Seasons.* Just downstream from this, at 19 Lower Mall, is the headquarters of the Furnivall Sculling Club, and beyond it, adjoining Hammersmith Pier, a public garden bearing Frederick J. Furnivall's name. This many-interested Victorian philologist, textual editor, and organizer of literary and scholarly societies was an amiable (when unaroused), dogmatic, moderately eccentric character who deserves the full-length biography which no one as yet has written. He had a somewhat overdeveloped relish for controversy: probably his most famous passage at arms was a six-year-long exchange of printed billingsgate with Swinburne over the relative validity of the purely esthetic and the rigidly historical approaches in Shakespeare criticism. Neither party wound up with much dignity left. One of Furnivall's passionate but non-controversial lifelong avocations was rowing. Not only did he coach young ladies' crews on this very reach of the Thames, but he was himself a fixture on the river. His white beard, streaming behind him as he sculled, is reported to have made him seem the very incarnation of Father Thames. It is fitting, therefore, that his name should be preserved along the river's bank. In due course, one hopes, similar recognition will be given to Furnivall's successor as—to compound a necessary word —the tuteliterary divinity of Hammersmith Reach, Sir Alan Herbert.

Furnivall was a friend of William Morris, and both of them knew George Bernard Shaw. In the 1880's Furnivall commissioned Shaw, then a poor but willing young journalist, to make an index for a limited edition of Thomas Lodge's works issued by one of Furnivall's printing societies, the Hunterian Club. Index-making was not one of Shaw's preferred *métiers,* and even the prospect of a five-guinea fee did not offset his distaste for the job. He procrastinated until the club was frantic and eventually, to Furnivall's relief as well as his own, passed the job on to someone else.

Shaw often attended meetings of the Hammersmith Socialists in Morris' coach house, which became available for this purpose after Morris moved his hand weaving equipment, previously housed here, to another location. Shaw was also a frequent house guest of the Morrises, and his recollections of their personalities are among the most intimate and vivid we have of the energetic craftsman-poet-propagandist and his shadowy, silent wife.

For a number of years later in his life Shaw, along with Barrie and Galsworthy, had town quarters in the Adelphi, a group of houses between the Strand and the Victoria Embankment which were considered gems of Adam architecture and whose demolition in 1935–38 to make room for office buildings was a catastrophe still execrated in histories of the London scene. But Shaw's country residence, simply called "Shaw's Corner," is still preserved and is open to the public. It is at Ayot St. Lawrence, Hertfordshire, an out-of-the-way spot which, though hardly beyond the limits of Greater London, is reached only by one-lane roads. If the time-pressed explorer can afford only one experience of this sort, the tracking down of an obscurely situated literary home, guided only by map and an occasional signpost, I recommend the trip to Shaw's Corner as an exemplar of all such quests.

It is also among the most rewarding. The house is just as Shaw left it when he died in 1950, no other tenant having intervened. Surrounded by modest lawns and gardens and more distantly by open fields, there is nothing pretentious about it. Shaw and his wife lived comfortably and informally, not opulently. In the well-lighted study are all the implements of the busy nonagenarian: a Remington Noiseless Portable, packs of unused air letter forms, several cameras, and filing cases with drawers marked "Ayot," "Self," "Keys and Contraptions," "Motoring," "Russia," "Bibliography," "Collected Ed.," "Rehearsal Copies"—G.B.S. in a nutshell. The bookshelves are in the genial condition of working disorder all bookshelves probably acquire if a typewriter is in the vicinity. Among the up-to-date reference works Shaw owned the year he died, we notice, were *Who's Who* and Kelly's *Handbook to the Titled, Landed and Official Classes.*

The other parts of the house have the same authentic, well-used appearance. The books lying about on the living-room tables are the usually inconsequential best-sellers of the forties, the sort of commodity that would have been sold for a few shillings to a second-hand dealer had their late owner not been a man named Shaw. Even the magazines are, to say the least, unliterary (such as the May, 1949, issue of *Business: the Journal of Management in Industry*). Somehow they befit the man who exercised on the stationary bicycle found in another room. And everywhere are the casual mementoes of the Shaws' wide acquaintanceship among the celebrated men and women of their long day. An American's eye is especially caught by the gold dress watch given Shaw by William Randolph Hearst and Marian Davies.

An interesting contrast with the literary personality implied in the atmosphere of Shaw's Corner is available if one travels the same distance from London in the opposite direction, to a spot near the Sussex town of Burwash. Here is Bateman's, a large stone house built in the middle of the seventeenth century by the ironmaster whose name it still bears. It stands today as an emblem of what success could mean to a highly popular writer in the early twentieth century, for Rudyard Kipling lived here on the fruits of his pen. During his long occupancy Kipling preserved the original character of Bateman's—the first owner obviously had been successful in his own line of work—but at the same time he made it the scene of gracious living as his own era understood it. It is the perfect Home Counties residence of a gentleman-farmer by avocation and a writer by calling, surrounded by lovely formal gardens, kitchen gardens, and stables (now converted into workshops and storage places). Like Shaw's Corner, it is kept as its owner left it. And it is as perfectly representative of Kipling as the Ayot St. Lawrence house is of Shaw. In the latter, one is reminded ineffaceably of the jaunty iconoclast, the self-created fictive character; at the somewhat more staid Bateman's, Kipling still presides, the very type of solid English middle-class accomplishment, the arch-Conservative and singer of Empire.

Two houses in the Greater London region preserve in authentic detail the way of life enjoyed by prosperous novelists in the Victorian era. They are heavy with the stateliness that gave way to the comparative relaxation of the Edwardian and later epochs; they reflect a far greater, or at any rate a more overt, consciousness of social class than do Shaw's Corner and Bateman's. One is Knebworth House, Bulwer-Lytton's mansion in Hertfordshire, north of London. Knebworth is a showplace depicting what life was like when one was both a man of title and a politician, as well as the author of popular novels. At base the house is early Tudor, but the present décor is relentlessly pre-Victorian Gothick, because in 1811 Bulwer's mother cement-veneered the brick exterior and added pseudo-medieval ornamentation both outside and inside. The result is a poor imitation of Walpole's Strawberry Hill. The stained-glass windows, meretricious arches, and other adornments fail to make Knebworth a thing of beauty, but we find no difficulty in believing this was the way it looked when Bulwer-Lytton lived here. His imposing study is lined, as nine-

teenth-century baronial studies usually were, with bookshelves
packed with standard works in leather bindings. They do not
appear to have been much read. But of most interest to the literary chronicler is the banqueting hall, presided over by a min-
strels' gallery and a collection of stags' heads, where Dickens'
theatrical troupe performed Ben Jonson's *Every Man in His
Humour* in 1850.

The other large estate near London with nineteenth-century
literary associations is Hughenden, two or three miles north of
the village of High Wycombe, Buckinghamshire, where Disraeli
lived during his years of celebrity. Hughenden reflects his dual
success, first as a novelist and then as a politician and prime minister. The two roles were not unconnected. Reputedly (for the oft-
repeated story, however credible, may be apocryphal) part of the
notoriously winning way he had with his queen was his habit of
reminding her that he, author of *Sybil* and *Coningsby*, and she,
author of *Leaves from a Journal of Our Life in the Highlands,*
were tied by the rare bond of literary sympathy: "We authors,
ma'am. . . ."

Some of the rooms in this large house, which is no gem of
architecture, are preserved as Disraeli knew them, their Victorian
décor and furnishings intact; others are used largely as galleries
for the display of portraits of his friends and colleagues. Only one
room contains personal memorabilia, including the manuscript
of *Coningsby*. The most eminent public figures in the high Victorian age, if one can judge from the houses that survive them,
lived in rather oppressive, heavy-hued splendor; those of the preceding generation, such as the Duke of Wellington, enjoyed more
glitter and color. But at Hughenden, as at Wellington's Apsley
House facing Hyde Park Corner, personality seems to me to be
lacking. These houses are display pieces valuable for recalling the
atmosphere of a departed age, but the master somehow is no
longer present.

Nor, for that matter, is he present in a tiny thatched cottage at
Chalfont St. Giles, a crossroads hamlet only a few miles from

Hughenden. A different age, a different kind of politics, a different kind of genius, surely: Milton had little enough in common with Disraeli. We do not find him in this, the only extant building associated with the poet, who fled here from plague-stricken London in 1665. The cottage is more interesting simply as an example of the cramped, low-ceilinged quarters in which seventeenth-century rural folk lived than as a place with exalted poetic associations. It boasts a fairly good collection of original Milton editions, including a first of *Paradise Lost* presented by United States Senator David Reed of Pennsylvania, but no personal relics, unless we are to count a lock of hair alleged to have been his but which the knowledgeable elderly lady who cares for the place cheerfully admits to be "bogus." The cottage, she says, has a hard time earning expenses: it is off the well-traveled highways, and the sightseeing coach companies cannot be persuaded to include it in their itineraries. Perhaps the main reason is that people do not read Milton nowadays with the avidity that supposedly marks their addiction to the Brontës.

Outside the London area, among the most interesting museums associated with English literature is one that virtually nobody visits and few have even heard of: the Cowper Museum at Olney, a Buckinghamshire town of stone, somnolence, and one very wide street. The man who was largely responsible for founding the museum, a garrulous multi-purposed enthusiast and antiquarian named Thomas Wright (biographer of Cowper, Pater, and FitzGerald), maintained in his autobiography that no other literary museum has so large a quantity and variety of exhibits. Wright was much given to self-congratulation, but in this instance he did not stretch the truth. The museum is housed in a late seventeenth-century red brick building fronting the town's triangular marketplace. It resembles a small warehouse rather than a residence, but it has always been used as two dwellings. Between 1767 and 1786, when he moved to a village two miles away, the unfortunate poet lived in one of them, the portion which is now the museum. The story of his quiet life in Olney is

among the most circumstantial domestic sagas in English literature, because in his retirement, enforced by his proneness to religious mania and the morbidly depressive state that often accompanied it, Cowper amused himself by writing to his friends long
letters that described, with a grace and humor which entitle
them to rank with the classic personal correspondences of Lamb,
Keats, Dickens, and FitzGerald, the small beer of daily life in this
little Buckinghamshire town.

In the Cowper house, the letters come alive. In the wall of the
front room one still sees the two-foot-square hole, connecting
with the kitchen, through which Cowper summoned his pet
hares for a familial evening by the fire; and in the garden, now
much overgrown, is the summer house where he wrote when the
weather was warm. Among the extensive miscellaneous exhibits,
which include Cowper's shoe buckles, household implements,
and other diurnal trivia, is the crude galvanic machine by which
it was hoped to alleviate the paralysis that struck down his devoted friend Mrs. Unwin. I like to recall what is evidently forgotten at Olney, that the neighbor from whom the electrotherapy
apparatus was borrowed was a Mr. Socket.

Everywhere are homely relics of an ill-starred man's life in
which friendships and literary exercises competed on unequal
terms with dreadful imaginings. The morbid tenor of Cowper's
inner life is implicitly memorialized in the room devoted to
items relating to John Newton, the reformed slave-ship captain
who turned Calvinist preacher—the spire of his church can be seen
from the room—and unluckily exacerbated Cowper's religious
gloom. The brighter side of his experience is recalled by the
room dedicated to Lady Hesketh, another of the generous women
who brought unstinted sympathy and assistance to Cowper. Of
the literary exercises themselves there are abundant relics. In still
another room are gathered the many editions of Cowper's popular ballad, "The Diverting History of John Gilpin," the story of
which Lady Austen related to him in a successful attempt to
divert his brooding mind. Another reminder of that lady's wise

efforts at therapy is a chaise longue, the subject of a poem
Cowper wrote literally to her order: "The Sofa." And hanging
on a wall is the subject of another much-anthologized poem, "On
the Receipt of My Mother's Picture out of Norfolk."

I could wish that these many relics of a tragic yet beguiling
man were better displayed and that money was available for the
thorough rehabilitation of the premises; repainted, freshened,
and put in order, they could be made into an enjoyable way station for those in search of English poets. At the same time, a note
of caution is in order which might well be applied to all such literary museums. When I visited Olney, the curator of the Cowper
house was a white-haired retired army officer, well versed in matters Cowperian, who sported a clipped mustache and a jaunty
trilby hat. In the course of the two-hour item-by-item tour upon
which he conducted me, he exhibited a glass ink jar he had recently dug up in the garden. Although there was not a scintilla
of evidence linking it with the poet except the accident that it
had turned up behind the house where he had lived two hundred years earlier, the Colonel had already labeled it "believed
to have belonged to Cowper." Thus do false attributions get
started, the *"believed"*—a weasel word in the first place: believed
by whom?—soon being quietly dropped. Not all curators are as
scrupulous as the lady at Milton's cottage. I have no idea what
proportion of the miscellaneous items packed into those three
stories at Olney are of unassailable provenance (Thomas Wright
himself was not excessively endowed with critical discrimination). No doubt a sizable number of them are dubiously ascribed.
But the Cowper Museum is not unique in this respect.

There are probably a hundred Janeites to every Cowperite,
but at her house at Chawton, in Hampshire, admirers of Jane
Austen receive what strikes me as a thin treat. The small rooms
contain little if any genuine Austen furniture; although the
walls are covered with framed letters and other documents, one
quickly discovers that most of them are mere photographic
copies; and while a number of personal relics are displayed, such

as a quilt Jane made with her mother, a silk shawl, and a dress, the authenticity of some is not beyond question. Of course, Janeitism being the consuming enthusiasm it is, I have no doubt that many addicts find adequate delight in whatever has any connection with the Austen family, who receive as much attention in the exhibits as Jane herself. Actually, the fact that she was a novelist is largely overlooked at Chawton; the stress here is all on the woman and the late eighteenth-century provincial society in which she lived, not on the real reason why her house attracts visitors in the last third of the twentieth century. But after all, this ironic neglect of her literary fame has precedent in the brass tablet dedicated to her on the north wall of Winchester Cathedral. It too says nothing about her having written novels. She was to be remembered solely as a daughter of a respected county family.

While one is in the neighborhood, though, a detour along a bumpy, muddy road to the isolated village of Selborne is well worth the time. The village itself is of interest, because it is typical of the numerous tiny places in Britain which the paved roads have not reached and which therefore are almost as representative of the sixteenth century as of the nineteenth. But apart from the thatched cottages and single narrow street, Selborne contains The Wakes, the home of Gilbert White, the naturalist-parson who died when Jane Austen was eighteen. The contents of the house itself have only a minor bearing on White, as they are a museum and library of natural history collected by an Essex man who bought the house in 1954 when a public collection to acquire it for the nation fell short. But the author of *The Natural History of Selborne* after all was an outdoorsman; and it is pleasant to walk across the ample lawn behind the house on the two-brick-wide path White laid out to enable him to cross, in dry-shod luxury, to the meadows and woods where he bird-watched to the eventual profit of English scientific prose.

Far to the north, on the eastern shore of Coniston Water in the Lake District, is Brantwood, the home of another nature-watcher

who made his own mark, albeit a quite different one, in the book
of prose style. In this large, comfortable house John Ruskin spent
many years at the end of his life—years clouded, as Cowper's had
been in far less easy circumstances, by the chiaroscuro of intermittent insanity. Although the bulk of Ruskin memorabilia was
dispersed by sale in the early 1930's, a fair amount remains at
Coniston, including some of his own watercolors. The windows
of Ruskin's study command a fine view of Coniston Old Man, the
peak across the lake. It was in this room, according to a possibly
apocryphal story which I want to believe, that at the end of the
day the maidservant would ceremoniously draw apart the curtains and announce to the brooding old man: "The sunset, Mr.
Ruskin!"

One finds Coniston after a drive through the still largely un-
spoiled scenery of the Lakes. The approach to Newstead Abbey,
Byron's home in his young manhood, is quite different. It begins
in the grimy environs of Nottingham and for completeness requires a brief intermediate stop at the parish church of Hucknall
Torkard. In the chancel of this church, which fronts on a
municipal parking lot flanked by public conveniences, is a tablet
marking the Byron family vault, in which the poet himself is
buried. His body arrived here at the end of a five-day procession
from London which was watched by crowds at every town and in
the final stage from Nottingham was a quarter-mile long.

From Hucknall Torkard the route leads through mixed Mid-
land country—farms, collieries, culm heaps, power lines, factories, and golf links existing uneasily side by side—and eventually delivers one at the entrance to the Newstead Abbey estate,
now a park owned and maintained by the City of Nottingham.
Hawthorne, noting in 1857 that "I suppose ten thousand people
(three-fourths of them Americans) have written descriptions of
Newstead Abbey," proceeded as usual to write a better one of his
own. In essentials it needs little modification today. The house is
attained by a long road thickly lined with rhododendrons. Facing on a lake of some size which is connected with a series of

waterfalls, it is the result of the familiar English process of building by accretion. To the central fabric, incorporating fragmentary walls of the medieval abbey, subsequent owners added large extensions over the centuries.

Enough of the old monastic building remains, including the cloister, the crypt, and the large abbot's guest room, to explain why the atmosphere of the place powerfully stimulated Byron's Gothick sensibilities when he lived here as a youth. Here, as every biographer recounts, he and his friends defied the decencies by garbing themselves in monks' robes and holding self-consciously wicked ceremonies in the course of which they drank wine from a human skull ("now reburied," adds the modern printed guide to the house). Much of the furniture the present-day visitor sees in Byron's bedroom was there in his time; it was kept against his promised return by the man to whom he sold Newstead Abbey. In this room and elsewhere are numerous personal relics, including his boxing gloves, dueling pistols, and the wooden lasts from which were made the shoes he wore on his crippled feet as a boy. In the large high-beamed salon is a collection of the first editions of his various volumes, some letters, and the manuscripts of a few minor poems. Outside, in the formal gardens behind the house, is the heavy gray tomb ("larger than most Christians get," commented Hawthorne tartly) of Byron's Newfoundland dog Boatswain, for which he wrote the inscription included in all collections of his poetry.

At Newstead Abbey, as at Selborne and the Morris Gallery with its concomitant exhibition of the work of the artist Sir Frank Brangwyn, one is offered numerous displays of objects in which one has little if any interest, for after Hawthorne's visit the house also became a museum of the Crimean War, in which the brother-in-law of the then owner was notably involved. The house thus is only in part a literary museum. Like most guides, the employee of the City of Nottingham who conducted the requisite tour when I was there—a melancholy specimen, whose every sentence, querulously pronounced through formidable

adenoids and sprinkled with whistled sibilants, had a dying fall
—played no favorites. The ancient monks, Sebastopol, and Lord
Byron were all one to him, and one got the impression he didn't
have great passion for any. But despite these extraneities, the
Byroniana at Newstead Abbey is sufficient to warrant a detour to
this otherwise unrewarding section of the Midlands. Or if it is
not, one may well remember that this is D. H. Lawrence country
too.

*The Queen's House, Cheyne Walk, Chelsea: home of Rossetti, Swin-
burne, and Meredith*

$ewpewpe$

---

## 9

---

# The Plaques on the Walls

A SECOND, more numerous order of buildings with literary associations is composed of those one can view only from the outside.
Whereas neighborhood signposts usually aid the discovery of
houses open to the public, these places are harder to find. They
are distinguished, if at all, by markers set into the façade of the
building or the gatepost outside. These plaques add one more
agreeable element of surprise to the inexhaustible occupation of
walking the London streets. There are between three and four
hundred of them, thirty-four erected by the Society of Arts before
1902 and the remainder—the blue-and-white ceramic discs familiar to every Londoner—being the contribution, depending on
locale, of the City Corporation or of the London County Council
(now the Greater London Council).

Alas, many plaques, instead of saying "In this house So-and-so
was born, 1796," have to record, "In a house on this site . . ."
London's record for demolishing buildings with historical associations is the equal of New York's: probably more deplorable,
indeed, because London has had much more to work with and
has been working with it longer. And much of what London
itself managed to preserve down to 1940 was subsequently erased

by bombing. I personally find little instruction in looking upon mere "sites"; the satisfaction in plaque-hunting lies in being able to see the very house, albeit somewhat altered in the course of the years, in which Goldsmith or Trollope lived. Apart from the wholesome exercise the trip would afford, there is no profit in walking to Lambeth, for example, to find the location of Hercules Buildings, in the garden of which a now discredited story avers William and Catherine Blake were once discovered playing Adam and Eve in native costume. Hercules Buildings have long since disappeared, along with whatever suggestion of Eden the region may once have had, and in their place is an ugly working-men's housing block called—Blake House.

The only reward in site-finding is the vague one of a slightly improved sense of topography and neighborhood. The neighborhood itself, however, may have changed so drastically over the years that its present condition bears no suggestion of its appearance when a celebrity *in esse* or merely *in posse* lived there. One London neighborhood remaining much as it was in the lifetime of the people memorialized on the plaques is Kensington Square, which has been a fashionable address ever since it was built in the late seventeenth century. At least five of the tall houses that face on the square bear markers. In one, Tallyrand lived during the early years of the French Revolution; in another lived the composer Sir Hubert Parry; next door is John Stuart Mill's residence in 1837–51; on the west side is Mrs. Patrick Campbell's home; and on the north, finally, is the home of Sir John Simon, the great Victorian pathologist and sanitary reformer. (The last-named, in particular, may seem far removed from the literary student's sphere until it is remembered that Sir John's niece and adopted daughter, Jane Faulkner, once was said to have been the girl whose derisive laughter when Swinburne proposed to her caused him to write his bitter poem "The Triumph of Time." Modern scholarship has exploded that story by proving that at the time of her alleged rebuff Jane was only ten years old.)

Nestling dwarfed against the rear of Barker's department store in Young Street, the narrow thoroughfare that connects Kensington Square with bustling Kensington High Street, is the red brick Queen Anne dwelling where Thackeray wrote *Vanity Fair, Pendennis, Henry Esmond,* and part of *The Newcomes.* This charming house with its pair of bow windows flanking the fanlighted central doorway was unoccupied and neglected for many years after the war. I was pleased later to find that it had been restored to its pristine condition and was occupied by a firm of architects. A minute's walk directly across the High Street brings one into Palace Green, the broad tree-lined avenue that leads northward past Kensington Palace to the Bayswater Road. The second house on the left, set well back from the street, is Thackeray's last residence. He designed it himself—it too is in the Queen Anne style, reflecting his temperamental and literary affiliation with the early eighteenth century—and in it he died suddenly in 1863. The house is now the Israeli embassy, an irony of some weight because Thackeray, like many men of his time, did not suppress his dislike of Jews.

West of Palace Green, in the quadrant beyond the steep Kensington Church Street with its antique shops, is Campden Hill, the abode for the last century of prosperous artists and now an attractive neighborhood of studios and residences. Plaques commemorating eminent artists, along with a few men of letters, abound on the Victorian villas that remain and on the modern flats that have succeeded the others. To have an idea of how a particularly successful Victorian artist lived, in Holland Park Road, a bit to the south, you can visit the sumptuous house where Lord Leighton, president of the Royal Academy, lived for thirty years (1866–96). It is never crowded: the register at the doorway records no more than an average of a dozen visitors a day, and I suspect the house is something of a burden and embarrassment to the Kensington Borough Council, which "gratefully accepted it" a generation ago. But it well exemplifies one aspect of mid- and late-Victorian taste with its elaborate Moorish entrance hall and salon (the latter with a fountain and square

pool inset in the floor) , a profusion of deep blue tiling, much of
it by the Chelsea potter William De Morgan, and a miscellaneous collection of pictures and sketches by Leighton and his
contemporaries. Some people may find more lively interest next
door, in the as yet modestly housed British Theatre Collection, a
representative display of costumes, manuscripts, playbills, photographs, props, and other memorabilia spanning the history of the
British theater from Garrick down through Ellen Terry and
Beerbohm Tree to Granville Barker and Gielgud.

In any event, the plaques in the Campden Hill neighborhood
bear witness that London honors its painters and sculptors
equally with its literary men. The most distinguished literary
person memorialized here is Macaulay, who lived in his last years
at Holly Lodge, Campden Hill Road, a house now used as a
hostel in connection with the adjoining Queen Elizabeth College
of London University. The location of Holly Lodge had special
meaning for Macaulay, because a short walking distance to the
west, enclosed in its own extensive park, was Holland House,
since the early eighteenth century the headquarters of the Whig
political coterie of which, in its final epoch, Macaulay had been a
prominent member. Addison had lived there after his marriage
to the widow of its former owner, the third Earl of Warwick; later
it had given to English politics the commanding figure of Charles
James Fox (Fox being the family name of the Hollands) ; and in
the last decades of the eighteenth century and the earlier ones of
the nineteenth, Holland House had been the meeting place of
the age's most celebrated politicians, intellectuals, wits, and artists. It was in fact the most brilliant salon of the time.

After the death in 1840 of Macaulay's host, the third baron, the
splendors of Holland House society faded, as Macaulay predicted
they would in the elegiac peroration to the essay on Lord Holland he wrote the following year:

> *In what language shall we speak of that house, once cele-*
> *brated for its rare attractions to the furthest ends of the*

*civilised world, and now silent and desolate as the grave?*
*. . . The wonderful city which, ancient and gigantic as it is,*
*still continues to grow as fast as a young town of logwood by*
*a water-privilege in Michigan, may soon displace those tur-*
*rets and gardens which are associated with so much that is*
*interesting and noble. . . . The time is coming when, per-*
*haps, a few old men, the last survivors of our generation,*
*will in vain seek, amidst new streets, and squares, and rail-*
*way stations, for the site of that dwelling which was in their*
*youth the favourite resort of wits and beauties, of painters*
*and poets, of scholars, philosophers, and statesmen.*

Macaulay's prophecy (he seems to have had a mild *idée fixe* about the lugubrious future of London) was fulfilled, but not in the way he anticipated. As London spread westward, it completely surrounded the wide acres of Holland Park but left them intact, as the last remaining private estate so close to the heart of the city. No streets, squares, or railway stations displaced the old groves and gardens. But in 1941 the stately Jacobean mansion was gutted by bombing. Nothing was done to preserve what remained, and the pitiful ruins were allowed to stand until the late 1950's, when the Earl of Ilchester, then the owner, sold the whole estate to the London County Council. It is now a lovely public park, in effect the westernmost (though separate) link in the chain of green spaces that begins miles to the east, at Whitehall. But, as Macaulay foresaw, one looks in vain for the mansion where night after night he had participated in—some said, distastefully dominated—the sparkling and learned conversation. Nothing remains of Holland House itself except a portion of the eastern wing, which has been incorporated into a youth hostel built on the site, and the lower story of the central part. The detached orangery is now a restaurant which in season caters to the Kensingtonians who come to enjoy the woods, the lawns, the formal gardens, the cricket matches, and the open-air symphony concerts given on summer evenings. The almost legendary headquarters of the Whig aristocracy now belongs to the people.

Little more than a mile or a mile and a half to the east, no trace survives of Holland House's rival, Gore House, where the Countess of Blessington, Byron's close friend in his last years, and her ambiguous ward, son-in-law, and lover, Count D'Orsay, maintained their own salon. If Gore House's society lacked the intellectual brilliance which distinguished the Holland House circle, it unquestionably matched it in sheer fashionableness. It is too bad that one or the other of these great houses has not been preserved; but after its mistress went bankrupt in 1849 and fled with Count D'Orsay to the Continent, Gore House's furnishings were auctioned off—a year or two earlier Dickens had written an oddly prophetic description of the proceedings in *Dombey and Son*—and after serving as a restaurant while the Crystal Palace exhibition of 1851 was held across the road, it was eventually torn down to make room for the Royal Albert Hall.

Southeast in Chelsea, the house of overriding literary interest, apart from Carlyle's, is that belonging to a dignified early Georgian row in Cheyne Walk, separated from the Thames embankment by only a strip of shady garden. At Number 16, called both the Queen's House and Tudor House, resided for a lively time in the 1860's the most colorful group of Victorian writers ever to live under one roof: Dante Gabriel Rossetti, Swinburne, and George Meredith, as well as Gabriel's comparatively staid brother, William Michael. The house and the garden behind it accommodated the menagerie collected by D. G. Rossetti. At one time or another the informal zoo is reported to have included a Pomeranian puppy, an Irish deerhound, owls, rabbits, dormice, hedgehogs, woodchucks, kangaroos, wallabies, lizards, parakeets, peacocks, a raccoon which hibernated in a drawer, an armadillo which burrowed into the kitchen next door and upon emerging is reported to have scared the housemaid out of her wits, a mole, a deer, white mice, a raven, chameleons, wombats, squirrels, salamanders, a zebra, and a laughing jackass which accidentally drowned in a tub of water. The premises also contained a

Brahman bull which Rossetti bought for twenty pounds because
its deep brown eyes reminded him of those of his frequent model,
William Morris' wife Jane. It is also said that Rossetti had ambitions to own an elephant but found the asking price beyond his
means at the time. No doubt it was, because he was also busy
cramming into the large house his compulsive purchases of bric-a-
brac and odd furniture, including a variety of convex mirrors
and a large collection of blue china. In such space as was left, the
occupants held high-spirited parties. Jane Carlyle once wrote to
complain of the noise, which was audible in Cheyne Row, a good
two blocks away.

Evidently Meredith could tolerate the animals, the blue china,
and the parties; but at length he moved out. His precise reason
for doing so is obscured by the numerous legends attending the
event. Was it because the others facetiously treated him to a pair
of new boots? Or because Rossetti, now a widower, was keeping a
woman in the house? Or because for breakfast Rossetti ate five
poached eggs piled atop bacon? Or because at dinner Rossetti,
emphasizing a point with a serving spoon, squirted gravy into the
face of a guest, the painter Whistler? Or (a possible variant of
the preceding) because Meredith called Rossetti a fool and
Rossetti forthwith threw a cup of tea in his face? The consensus
is that, whatever the precise circumstances, it was Rossetti who
was responsible for Meredith's sudden rageful departure. But
diminutive Swinburne, who was given to sliding down the banis-
ters, having tantrums, and tearing through the house without his
clothes, must have given equal offense. E. F. Benson, in his diverting "Victorian peep-show," *As We Were,* records that "Meredith on a highly critical occasion vowed that he would certainly
have kicked Swinburne downstairs had he not foreseen what a
clatter his horrid little bottom would have made as it bounced
from step to step."

Of all these wild proceedings a century ago, the chaste façade
of 16 Cheyne Walk gives the passerby no slightest hint. Yet, pausing in this vicinity it is impossible not to remember the scene de-

scribed by Edmund Gosse, in notes first published a few years ago in Cecil Lang's collected edition of Swinburne's letters. In 1871 or thereabouts, Gosse recorded, he was standing in the bow window of Bellevue House, a few doors away, which the poet and painter William Bell Scott had recently taken over. A hansom cab drove up.

> *Nothing happened at first, and then Walter Pater, delicately dressed, with lemon-yellow kid gloves, descended daintily, and was followed by Swinburne, who poised himself on the edge of the cab, and then dived forward on to the pavement, descending upon his two hands. His elegant top-hat sprang from him, and making a wide curve descended far away in the gutter. Presently Pater appeared in our upper room, talking with dreamy detachment on indifferent subjects, but of Swinburne I saw no more, and understood that he was taken into another part of the house to be cleaned and sobered.*

But once sobered up, Swinburne failed to remain sober; and by 1879 his friends deemed it a better than even chance that he would soon die an alcoholic death. To the rescue came his solicitor, a part-time man of letters named Theodore Watts (later Watts-Dunton), who spirited the ailing Swinburne to a duplex house with a remarkably ugly Victorian exterior at 2 The Pines, Putney Hill, where he lived in temperance, a much muted songbird, for the rest of his life. Now almost engulfed by modern buildings just off Putney's main thoroughfare, the house bears a plaque which, in the usual manner, merely states the fact of Swinburne's long residence here. It does not amplify by observing that the premises witnessed the tragicomic decline into bourgeois prosiness of a flamboyant but gifted poet whose personal habits had made him a Victorian Dylan Thomas. How useful it would be if the plaques would, where appropriate, bear footnotes referring the passerby to the places where he could read the full story behind the wall!*

An analogous case of benevolent but stultifying literary captivity is commemorated by a plaque on the other side of London. At the summit of the steep Highgate Hill is Highgate School, which Gerard Manley Hopkins attended and where for a brief period, soon after he arrived in London, T. S. Eliot taught "French, Latin, lower mathematics, drawing, swimming, geography, history, and baseball." A little to the south is a short street called The Grove, quiet and secluded though only a block from where the lorries grind in low gear up Highgate Hill; and in one of the row of semi-detached houses, each with its flowery front garden, lived a physician, James Gillman; and with Gillman, from 1816 to his death in 1834, lived Samuel Taylor Coleridge. (A century later, the occupant for some years was J. B. Priestley.) Coleridge's residence here inspired Carlyle's famous sentence, in his *Life of John Sterling:* "Coleridge sat on the brow of Highgate Hill, in those years, looking down on London and its smoke-tumult, like a sage escaped from the inanity of life's battle; attracting toward him the thoughts of innumerable brave souls still engaged there." He also attracted the brave souls in person, for Mr. Gillman's house was the scene of many interviews in which Coleridge held forth at immense, cloudy length on metaphysical subjects. Like Swinburne's, Coleridge's poetic muse was stifled in those latter years of voluntary protective custody, but his monologic genius was unaffected. His admiring listeners understood little of the message, but they were enthralled by the medium. The complex grandeur of his utterance seemed to guarantee the profundity of his thought. Together, though, if we are to believe Max Beerbohm's wicked caricature of "Coleridge, Table Talk-

---

* In this case, the references would be to Max Beerbohm's classic essay on his youthful pilgrimages to Swinburne in this house (the title is simply "No. 2 The Pines"; the essay appeared in *And Even Now*) , to almost equally entertaining pieces by A. C. Benson ("Theodore Watts-Dunton," published in *Life and Letters,* 1932) and E. V. Lucas ("At 'the Pines'," *New Statesman,* 1916) , and to E. F. Benson's vivacious pages on the Putney retreat in the book quoted earlier.

ing," they were very efficacious soporifics. Max shows five audi-
tors leaning against one another as they snore openmouthed, and
five more opposite them, with their heads on the table as the indefatigable Coleridge continues to discourse.

The generally dull expanses of north London are well worth
exploring in quest of plaques. To trace the successive later residences of Charles and Mary Lamb requires the better part of a
day and a fair amount of travel by bus and tube. The one nearest central London is Colebrook Cottage, Islington, where the
Lambs lived from 1823 to 1827, in the middle of which period he
retired from his clerkship at East India House. In a letter to his
friend, the Quaker poet and banker Bernard Barton, Lamb was
touchingly proud:

> When you come Londonward you will find me no longer in
> Covt Gard. I have a Cottage, in Colebrook row, Islington. A
> cottage, for it is detach'd; a white house, with 6 good rooms;
> the New River (rather elderly by this time) runs (if a mod-
> erate walking pace can be so termed) close to the foot of the
> house; and behind is a spacious garden, with vines (I assure
> you), pears, strawberries, parsnips, leeks, carrots, cabbages, to
> delight the heart of old Alcinous. You enter without passage
> into a cheerful dining room, all studded over and rough
> with old Books, and above is a lightsome Drawing room, 3
> windows, full of choice prints. I feel like a great Lord, never
> having had a house before.

A contemporary print bears out Lamb's celebration of the cottage's rustic charms. It shows a willow tree in the front garden, a
paling fence, and a boy fishing in the New River, which is represented as being only the width of a footpath distant from the
fence.

The so-called river was actually a canal built early in the
seventeenth century to convey water from the River Lea to the
City. Its sedate presence in front of his cottage was responsible
for one of the most diverting episodes in Lamb's life. Among his

friends was George Dyer, a classical scholar who might well have
served as the prototype of the absent-minded professor. Lamb describes him and his amiable eccentricities with great affection in
the essay "Amicus Redivivus." The essay recounts, with typical
Elian trimmings, the incident Lamb reported in a somewhat
more factual manner in a letter to Hazlitt's wife:

*You have seen our house. What I now tell you is literally
true. Yesterday week George Dyer called upon us, at one
o'clock* (bright noon day) *on his way to dine with Mrs.
Barbauld at Newington. He sat with Mary about half an
hour, and took leave. The maid saw him go out from her
kitchen window, but suddenly losing sight of him, ran up in
a fright to Mary. G.D., instead of keeping the slip that leads
to the gate, had deliberately, staff in hand, in broad open
day, marched into the New River. He had not his spectacles
on, and you know his absence. Who helped him out, they
can hardly tell; but between 'em they got him out, drenched
thro' and thro'. A mob collected by that time and accompanied him in. "Send for the Doctor!" they said: and a one-
eyed fellow, dirty and drunk, was fetched from the Public
House at the end, where it seems he lurks, for the sake of
picking up water practice, having formerly had a medal
from the Humane Society for some rescue. By his advice, the
patient was put between blankets; and when I came home at
four to dinner, I found G.D. a-bed, and raving, light-headed
with the brandy-and-water which the doctor had adminis-
tered. He sung, laughed, whimpered, screamed, babbled of
guardian angels, would get up and go home; but we kept
him there by force; and by next morning he departed sober,
and seems to have received no injury. All my friends are
open-mouthed about having paling before the river, but I
cannot see that, because a . . . lunatic chooses to walk into
a river with his eyes open at midday, I am any the more
likely to be drowned in it, coming home at midnight.*

The paling nevertheless was put up, as the old picture shows, and Lamb thus avoided George Dyer's mischance. But it is hard to reconstruct the scene today. Duncan Terrace, where Colebrook Cottage is situated, is a cheerless street not far from the roaring road junction which still bears the coaching-days designation of the Angel. The cottage, which in Lamb's time stood free, was later joined to a terrace on the south side; the whole row eventually became a slum tenement, and its appearance was not improved by the bombs it received during the Second World War, though Lamb's own house seems to have escaped. Immediately adjacent to the north is a ramshackle repair garage. Saddest of all, the New River has vanished. Some time after the Lambs moved away, its flow was terminated at reservoirs at Stoke Newington, some distance to the north, and its course is now recalled only by the name of the narrow parkway that covers its site, "New River Walk."

From the scene of George Dyer's immersion the Lambs moved to another, more rural, spot which also happened to abut on the New River. This was the squat white cottage, now called Clarendon House, at Enfield Chase, a residential community which still enjoys a half-country atmosphere, with inviting-looking houses, some eighteenth-century and some Victorian, facing on the stream. In 1833 the Lambs made their final move, somewhat closer to London, to lodge with the husband and wife who cared for Mary during her periods of insanity. Walden Cottage is near the Lower Edmonton railway bridge, only a few hundred yards from the busy Edmonton shopping center—a tiny brick cottage recessed behind an iron fence, with a frontage of no more than fifteen feet and squeezed between a modern yellow brick nursing home of the Sisters of Mercy on one side and a car park on the other. It was here that Lamb died the next year; he and Mary are buried in the churchyard nearby.

Perhaps the most important London literary site that is as yet unplaqued is 50 Albemarle Street, a few steps north of Piccadilly. This is the office of the venerable publishing firm of John Murray. As befits the dignity of its age and its list of distinguished writers, the house of Murray is averse to publicity. The modern inquirer's experience in identifying the house is precisely that of Hawthorne in September, 1855:

> *I walked through Albemarle-street for the purpose of look-ing at Murray's shop, but missed it entirely at my first inqui-sition. The street is one of hotels, principally, with only a few tradesmen's shops, and has a quiet, aristocratic aspect. On my return, down the other sidewalk, I did discover the famous publisher's locality, but merely by the name—"Mr. Murray"—engraved on a rather large brass plate, such as doc-tors use, on the door. There was no sign of a book, nor of its being a place of trade in any way; and I should have taken the house to be—if not a private residence—then a lawyer's office. I think it vulgar in "Mr. Murray" to be ashamed of his business.*

Today, on the contrary, the lack of a show window and the mod-est painted inscription by the door, "John Murray," strike one as erring, if at all, on the side of undue self-effacement; it is cer-tainly not to be attributed to embarrassment.

Within these unmarked eighteenth-century walls a great deal of honorable literary business has been transacted. It has been not unaccompanied by high drama, for in the front room on the first floor (the second, in American usage) was burned the manu-script of Byron's memoirs; only the covers are preserved. The room is kept much as it was then, when it was the private office of the firm's head. It is, in effect, a museum of Byroniana. Trea-sured here are Byron's surgical boots of dry, whitened leather, and a folding screen which Byron and Gentlemen Jackson, his boxing instructor, pasted over with montages of pin-up girls taken from fashion magazines of the time and newspaper clippings re-lating to prominent boxers. The latter seems a curious occupa-tion for a romantic poet, but screen-embellishment was a hobby long indulged in the nineteenth century; some thirty years later Jane Carlyle, who was distinctly not a Byronic type, likewise covered a screen with prints and engravings in more feminine taste. It is now in her bedroom in Cheyne Row. In the Murray front office also are kept packets of paper containing locks of hair from Byron's various mistresses, each endorsed in Byron's hand with the name of the lady and the date of the liaison, except for one which Byron identified only by year and place (Athens), confessing that he had forgotten her name.

The Murray offices are hung with portraits of some of the firm's other famous authors as well as of a few who published under other imprints, and in the basement are preserved the firm's archives, which have as yet been explored only in part by students of nineteenth-century literary and publishing history. But it should be added that although the house of Murray has long been favorably known for its hospitality to serious scholars desiring to use its records, 50 Albemarle Street is still a business concern, and it therefore is not open to the public. Possibly that is why its literary significance is not advertised by a plaque.

The eye that is peeled for markers is conditioned to respond to literary names, and these it sometimes finds in unexpected contexts. Some years ago, for example, there was a shop just off Ludgate Circus whose display window contained an assortment of ladies' hosiery and undergarments; its name was the Jane Eyre, and it has now been supplanted by a Wimpy hamburger bar. In Leadenhall Street, in the City, there is the firm of Dombey and Son, custom clothiers; in Wardour Street, Soho, is the Henry James Institute of Hairdressing (has it ever enrolled a student named Daisy Miller?) ; and in Maddox Street, Mayfair, one finds the shop of Squire Western and Son, Ltd., genteel tailors.

*Blake's cottage, Felpham, Sussex*

§●‚§●‚§●‚

# 10

# *Field Work*

IN THE EIGHTEENTH CENTURY, when some people had unlimited
money and singular notions of grandiosity, there was a fad for
building follies, and hang the expense. A folly was any kind of
extravagant, conspicuously useless structure; the most celebrated
example of the genre was Horace Walpole's pseudo-Gothic pile
at Strawberry Hill. Toward the end of the century a wealthy
eccentric named William Beckford determined to build his own
folly-to-end-all-follies on a site in rural Wiltshire. From childhood, Beckford had been obsessed with towers, a peculiarity inherited from his father. Beckford's tower fixation is reflected in
the opening pages of his "Arabian tale" *Vathek* (1786) in which
the hero, a caliph with large ideas, mounts such an edifice (1600
steps) to conduct astrological rites and incidentally to feel himself lord of all he surveys. And so, over a period of twenty-two
years, Beckford built Fonthill Abbey, a monstrous assemblage of
transepts, chapels, arcades, galleries and every other adjunct of a
combination monastery and baronial hall, the whole being dominated by a three-hundred-foot tower that was the most prominent landmark within a radius of over sixty miles. (The ground
level of the abbey was five hundred feet higher than the spire of

Salisbury Cathedral.)

One of Beckford's manifold eccentricities was his passion for building in a hurry; much of the abbey was constructed on a round-the-clock schedule, the night shift working by torchlight. If the term had been current in the first decades of the nineteenth century, there would have been special fitness in calling it a crash program, for crash the tower did, before the dinner hour on December 21, 1825. By that time Beckford was no longer present to appreciate the inadvisability of erecting a high tower on impracticably narrow underpinnings, for his extravagance in building Fonthill Abbey and stocking it with a great collection of books and *objets d'art* had forced him to retire to more modest quarters near Bath, where, however, he built a second tower from which to gaze across at the first. But the sudden disappearance of the latter soon made the former superfluous, and the abbey itself was demolished in later years.

In search of the site of Beckford's vanished folly, I drove to the "Fonthill Estate," a cluster of subdivisions being prepared for real estate activity, not far from the Marquess of Bath's magnificent house at Longleat. Passing through the stately arch whose construction Beckford himself supervised, I covered miles of roads without finding any trace of the abbey. Finally emerging upon a main highway, I stopped for lunch at the Beckford Arms Inn and there fell into conversation with a tweedy type who turned out, as most of them do, to be a retired colonel. A self-acknowledged authority on the Fonthill neighborhood, he had, he said, definitely planned to write a book on Beckford and his spectacular hobbies until he learned that such books already existed. (How often does one hear this story! Britain abounds with men and women, more sanguine than well informed, who are bent upon writing books about the historical and literary highlights of their neighborhood. They are always surprised to hear that what they propose to do has already been done, perhaps several times over, extensively and authoritatively. It is, I suppose, a mark of the devoted amateur that in his enthusiasm he never considers the possibility of someone's having long since anticipated his bright idea.)

Anyway, after we had finished our sandwiches and pints the Colonel volunteered to show me where the abbey was. He climbed into his car, a colossal Jaguar saloon, and I climbed into mine, a Lilliputian Austin 7, and, gunning his motor, he proceeded to lead me a merry chase through rutted lanes into the heart of the woodland. Finally I caught up with him as he stopped beside a clearing in the midst of which stood a single tower adjoining a small lodge. The tower was, of course, not the calamitous one but a more modest (and better engineered) associate; the lodge, the Colonel said, was occupied by a resident woodman. Even the foundations of Beckford's fairy palace have disappeared. There is, indeed, some doubt that, in the haste with which they were obliged to work, Beckford's builders bothered to install them. But the site is marked by a great rectangle of grass which is kept cut, while beyond, the woodland and hay lots encroach. The Colonel and I stood there for a while, each occupied with suitable reflections on the vanity of human megalomania. "I really do think a very interesting book could be written about Beckford," he said as I thanked him and we shook hands. He then piloted me hell for leather away from this silent vacancy where once a half-mad Wiltshire Kubla Khan had reared a Gothic pleasure dome.

The search for literary sites is the best excuse I know for unlimited, unsystematic exploration of the English countryside. Although the routes to a few of the better-known ones are signposted and some houses, thanks to the energy of local authorities or groups of enthusiasts, bear markers, most have to be discovered by sheer ingenuity and tenacity. Sometimes the people one would expect to be most knowledgeable aren't. Helpful as they are in other respects, the police are not to be relied upon as repositories of information on literary locales. I remember an amusing episode when two stalwart young members of the Dorset County Constabulary, consulted at their substation at Wool, after much searching of their maps and memories had to confess they didn't know where Thomas Hardy's Max Gate was. I am not positive they knew who Thomas Hardy was, either.

There is good hunting in the west of England for places associated with the first great stirrings of romantic poetry. In the Quantock Hills north of Taunton, Coleridge and Wordsworth lived close together in 1797–98. The cottage Coleridge then occupied is not hard to locate: it is a small, tile-roofed, stucco house abutting directly on the road in the village of Nether Stowey. This was the birthplace of "The Rime of the Ancient Mariner" and the first part of "Christabel." Within Coleridgean walking distance across country, but accessible by car only by way of a long, vagrant, desperately cratered road that poses a mortal peril to automotive apparatus, is Alfoxden, the commodious home of the Wordsworths at the same time. A low-slung two-story farmhouse whose native, Wordsworthian plainness is interrupted by an incongruous classic portico over the entryway, Alfoxden is now a hotel. Its white walls set off by ivy and climbing pink roses, it is surrounded by sloping fields and pastures, some dedicated to the comfort of the establishment's riding horses. Through the trees in good weather one can see, miles away, the waters of the Bristol Channel. It is country which one can well believe inspired the poetry of *Lyrical Ballads*.

It was here, too, that Wordsworth and Coleridge, neither of whose characters or lives was particularly humorous, were involved in a seriocomic episode deriving from the jumpy state of English nerves at the time of the war with revolutionary France. Coleridge and William and Dorothy Wordsworth were strangers to Somerset, and as such they were regarded with much suspicion. As the result of gossip among former servants at Alfoxden, a local doctor wrote to the Home Secretary about "a very suspicious business concerning an emigrant family" who now resided there:

> *The Master of the house has no wife with him, but only a woman who passes for his Sister. The man has Camp Stools*

*which he and his visitors take with them when they go about*
*the country upon their nocturnal or diurnal excursions and*
*have also a Portfolio in which they enter their observations*
*which they have been heard to say were almost finished.*
*They have been heard to say they should be rewarded for*
*them, and were very attentive to the River near them. . . .*
*These people may* possibly *be under-agents to some princi-*
*pal in Bristol.*

The nature-loving trio attracted attention for a variety of other reasons. They inquired of the natives whether the brook was navigable to the sea, they indulged in such un-English habits as washing and mending clothes on Sunday and spending most of the night on or near the tops of hills, two of them (the Wordsworths) spoke with foreign (i.e., north country) accents, and one—Dorothy—had a "gypsy tan" which easily identified her as a Frenchwoman.

Actually, the three were guilty on all counts, as their letters substantiate. All, that is, but the obvious inference so easily drawn from their appearance and odd activities. Drawing that inference, the Home Office sent a detective named Walsh on a counter-espionage mission. Coleridge later declared that Walsh hid behind sand dunes listening to him and Wordsworth talking about "Spy Nozy" (Spinoza), which the eavesdropper presumably took to allude to his mission and his ripe nose. In his reports back to London, Walsh discounted the rumor that the three under surveillance were foreigners; but, relaying the opinion of the Stowey innkeeper that "they are people that will do as much harm as all the French can do," "I think," he wrote, "this will turn out no French affair but a mischiefuous [sic] gang of disaffected Englishmen." Walsh continued to keep tabs on their comings and goings, including the number and character of the people the Wordsworths entertained at dinner—his official reports thus adding a modicum to our knowledge of Wordsworthian biography for this period. But finally he decided he was wast-

ing his time on a mare's nest and left Coleridge and the Wordsworths to their unconventional, but evidently not indictable,
pursuits.

Memories of this incident inevitably come to mind when one
visits the tiny thoroughfare called Blake's Lane at Felpham, a
seaside village in Sussex, near Chichester. Here, in a thatched
cottage which is still standing and occupied, William Blake lived
between 1800 and 1803 while he reworked *The Four Zoas* and
wrote the first draft of *Milton*. In the vegetable garden in front
of the cottage, Blake recorded, he once saw a fairy funeral, and
here too he conversed with Moses and the prophets, Homer,
Dante, and Milton. A much more palpable apparition in this
same garden got him into trouble toward the end of his visit. A
gardener working there invited a passerby, one Private Scholfield
of the First Dragoons, who was billeted at the Fox Inn fifty yards
away, to pitch in and help him. Blake, happening by, counter-
manded the invitation and, in the poet's words, "desired him as
politely as was possible to go out of the Garden, he made me an
impertinent answer . . . then threatened to knock out my Eyes
. . . it affronted my foolish pride." Blake propelled him, still
cursing, back down the lane to the inn, where the offended soldier was reinforced by a comrade-in-arms until the landlord
thrust both inside. Scholfield's subsequent deposition claimed
that in the course of the brief fray Blake had "uttered seditious
and treasonable expressions, such as 'D—n the king, d—n all his
subjects, d—n his soldiers, they are all slaves; when Bonaparte
comes, it will be cut-throat for cut-throat, and the weakest must
go to the wall; I will help him; etc. etc.' " On the strength of this
accusation Blake was charged with high treason and tried at the
Chichester Assizes.

It is good to be able to record that he was acquitted. But he
might not have been so lucky if his prosecutors had been as aware
as we are today of the true extent of Blake's political radicalism.
He was protected by the obscurity of both his person and his
poetry: the authorities seem to have regarded him as a harmless

eccentric, and of the few who read his poems, even fewer comprehended their inflammatory message. Shelley, on the other hand— a considerably younger man—enjoyed no such immunity. He denounced with fervid explicitness the evils of existing political and social institutions, and found himself repeatedly in trouble on that account. One of the prime documents in his case is *Queen Mab,* a youthful blast against "statecraft." The guidebooks say it was written at the house where he was born, Field Place, near Horsham, Sussex. Since not many places with Shelleyan connections remain, I sought it out. It was not easily located. Finally I enlisted the help of a pair of municipal dustmen, who were emptying garbage cans along the road. Not wishing to complicate matters, I did not mention the poet Shelley or the poem *Queen Mab:* I merely asked for Field Place. The garbage rustlers paused in their labors to point out a gateway down the road. There being no one at the lodge to whom I could apply for admission, I ventured up the straight road through the grounds and stole a picture of the house. If the present occupants, at breakfast, saw my intrusion they failed to raise an alarm. On the basis of this hasty inspection, all I can report is that the Shelleys were indeed (as the biographers assure us) a prosperous family to have owned so much land and so adequate a house. It is not the sort of setting in which one would expect revolutionism to have been bred or a subversive poem like *Queen Mab* to have been composed. As a matter of fact, it was written in Wales.

Other sites associated with Shelley have to do with his troubled posthumous fame rather than with the early kindling of his radical zeal. Sir Percy Florence, his son by his second wife, Mary Wollstonecraft Godwin, married a formidable lady who made a career of wrapping her father-in-law's fame in a thick Victorian cocoon of respectability. In addition to seeking to control all biographical writing about Shelley (she had a virtually unbeatable advantage, because most of his personal papers were in her and her husband's possession), she commissioned what she deemed appropriate monuments to his memory. The most famous was a close replica of Michelangelo's *Pietà* representing—with execrable taste, considering Shelley's atheistic views—the dead poet being held, Christ-like, in the arms of his wife. She intended to have it erected in the church she and Sir Percy patronized near their home, Boscombe Manor, on the south coast near Bournemouth. But the vicar declined to receive it, and so to see it one must travel a few miles farther on to the priory church at Christchurch. It is worth a visit, especially if one knows its history. Adjoining the pietà with its revised cast of characters is a brass tablet to Sir Percy Florence Shelley, who died in 1889. It is possible to find special significance in the fact that the inscription carefully specifies that he was the son of the poet "by Mary Wollstonecraft Shelley." The family entertained a morbid retrospective hostility toward Shelley's first wife, the girlish Harriet Westbrook. Some of their heaviest artillery was leveled against writers who attempted to make a case for the much maligned Harriet, at the expense, naturally, of her successor, Sir Percy's mother. It was indispensable, therefore, to leave posterity under no misapprehension on the matter. Sir Percy was "Mary Wollstonecraft's" son, not Harriet's; he was therefore respectable. It is possibly significant that Mary's name is not given in full: it was Mary Wollstonecraft *Godwin*. But because William Godwin, her father, was a notorious freethinker as well as a political radical, the name obviously had to be suppressed.

Unchastened by her experience with the pietà, in 1891 Lady Shelley commissioned a second monument to the poet, which she intended to have placed over his grave in the Protestant Cemetery in Rome. But again she ran into opposition, this time from the daughter of the old adventurer Edward Trelawny, who had been a close friend of Shelley during the poet's last days and who, after his death in 1881, had been buried by Shelley's side. The daughter maintained that the plot was owned by her father and that the original marker was not to be disturbed; furthermore, she argued with considerable cogency, the monument was so big that it would spill over from Shelley's grave onto Trelawny's.

The issue was submitted to Lord Dufferin, the British ambassador to Rome, and again Lady Shelley lost. She then offered the monument to University College, Oxford, from which the undergraduate Shelley had been expelled for issuing an earnest pamphlet arguing "the necessity of atheism." This administrative decision had long weighed upon the conscience of University College, and its authorities seized with almost unseemly haste the opportunity to make amends. The amends were not unequivocal, as anyone will realize who penetrates from the quadrangle of University College to the Shelley Memorial. There, in a hushed room washed in a dim religious light—one somehow has the feeling he is in a bathysphere—reposes a marble representation of the poet, even more naked than the one in the pietà, lying more or less on his side. At University College, Ariel has been transformed into something resembling a beached flounder. (Neither this representation nor the earlier takes account of the fact that when Shelley's body was washed up from the Gulf of Spezzia it was in a regrettably damaged condition which, as much as the Italian health laws, required its immediate cremation.)

As a restorative after this gloomy encounter, I recommend a quick walk to the nearby precincts of Merton College, which houses one of the most entertaining, as it is among the least known, literary exhibits in Britain. Max Beerbohm was a student here, and Merton is proud of it. Sixpence admits you to the Max Beerbohm Room, whose walls are lined with unpublished caricatures, a number dating from the years when he used his pencil for disrespectful purposes during lectures and examinations. There are even two drawings transferred bodily from the walls of the room he occupied. Also on display are a number of books from Sir Max's library which show his irrepressible pen or pencil at work on the title pages. The examples of inspired defacement on display include one of Kipling depicted as a "Kilroy was here" figure, a copy of *Eminent Victorians* with a caricature of Lytton Strachey, and one of Strachey's *Queen Victoria* with a more elaborate (and impious) drawing and the words "Queen Victoria" heavily embellished in blue and gold. The whole collection of vintage Beerbohm caricatures and title page improvisations, most of them unpublished, repays an hour of anyone's time. In the Ashmolean Museum at Oxford, incidentally, are still more Beerbohm originals, including some of his best-known drawings.

At least two other permanent exhibitions dedicated to English literary men deserve mention. One has to do with Hardy. His birthplace at the hamlet of Higher Bockhampton, Dorset, a thatched cottage straight out of a colored calendar, is open to visitors who survive the exceedingly rough lane leading to it, but it retains nothing of personal interest. The home he occupied in his mature years, Max Gate, hides behind hedges on the Wareham road just east of Dorchester, overlooked by a modern housing development with television antennas and picture windows —an intrusion which Hardy, who fiercely guarded his privacy, would not have liked. Max Gate, however, is not open for inspection. The closest one can get to the novelist is at the Dorset County Museum in Dorchester, and a pleasing discovery it is. Even apart from its Hardy interest, the museum deserves to be visited. Erected in 1883, one of the first provincial buildings to be designed specifically for general museum purposes, it quite evidently is the result of many decades' prideful collecting and preservation on the part of Dorset men and women. Its galleries have a rich collection of antiquities and "bygones" (domestic artifacts) —iron fire backs, costumes, samplers, police truncheons, reeves' staves, glass jugs, and other relics evocative of old Dorsetshire. But the literary visitor is drawn above all to the Thomas Hardy Room, a valuable (and, like the rest of the museum, intelligently annotated) collection of photographs, portraits, testimonials—including the Freedom of Dorchester and the Order of Merit—, a model clipper ship John Masefield made for Hardy, and important manuscripts, among them the heavily corrected *Dynasts* and *The Mayor of Casterbridge*. At one end of the room, behind a plate glass window, is Hardy's reconstructed study, with his books on the shelves, his Oxford D.Litt. gown thrown carelessly over a chair, his cello and violin in a corner, and two desks at which he wrote many of his books. Some may feel that the effect is too patently calculated; a poet-novelist should not be contemplated under glass. And they may be right. But if Hardy cannot be represented by the preserved spontaneity of Shaw's Corner, one would rather have this artfully arranged showcase than nothing at all.

The recently established Tennyson collection at the Usher Art Gallery in Lincoln, although lacking a reconstructed study, is even richer in personal memorabilia than the Hardy Room at Dorchester. Here a considerable portion of the Tennysoniana that remained in the family is displayed under the auspices of the poet's grandson and biographer, Sir Charles Tennyson, who has designated this place as the headquarters of Tennyson scholarship. Here are manuscript letters, corrected proofs, many books from the poet's library, playbills and other material relating to his stage productions, family photographs. We are brought closest to Tennyson the man, perhaps, by his black sombrero, the certificate of his laureateship (and the laurel wreath itself), his pipes, cigar cases, and penknives, the medicine droppers used in his last illness, and the notice of his death, signed by the attending doctors, that was nailed to the door at Aldworth on October 6, 1892.

*Tennyson's birthplace: The Rectory, Somersby, Lincolnshire*

ॐॐॐ

---

## 11

---

# Browning and Tennyson

As is probably apparent by now, I have a special interest in finding the locales associated with nineteenth-century English writers. The Victorian age in particular is my professional bread and butter, a fact which provides an open-ended excuse for traveling widely in search of pertinent Victorian literary settings. Naturally, the period's two greatest poets, Browning and Tennyson, have demanded to be traced here and there. Now that this series of errands is substantially completed, I have been struck by the markedly varying degrees of reward that such projects offer. To the student of the man and his works, there is comparatively little profit in hunting the places Browning knew, but quite the opposite is true of Tennyson, as I propose to demonstrate.

The home of Browning's childhood in Camberwell, then a rural suburb but now a decayed London neighborhood of factories and tenements overripe for urban renewal, has disappeared. At its address, 179 Southampton Row, the front portion of which is now occupied by a cycle maker's shop, a plaque so coated with South London grime as to be almost indecipherable says "Browning lived here." But this dreary row of houses was clearly built after his time. The plain nonconformist chapel which his mother attended and where he was baptized, just off busy Walworth Road in York Street (now renamed Browning Street), has become the workshop of "Stage-Decor Ltd.," evidently a firm of set builders for West End theaters: a secularization of which Browning, who had great youthful ambitions to be a dramatist, might well have approved.

At the address in Wimpole Street where he paid surreptitious visits to Elizabeth Barrett there is a blue plaque attesting that fact, but the present house replaces the one the Barretts occupied. The house Browning occupied upon his return from Italy after his wife's death is also gone now, but its later history deserves to be recorded. This residence, at 19 Warwick Crescent, Paddington, was one of a row of tall stucco houses that overlooked the confluence of the Regent's and Grand Junction canals at a place called "Little Venice." Here for the next quarter-century Browning lived and wrote many of his greatest poems, including *The Ring and the Book.* Events long after his death have given special meaning to one of those poems, "House" (1876), in which he decried the publicity that is a price of literary fame. The metaphor he used to describe the Victorian appetite for spicy morsels of gossip about celebrities' personal lives was that of a house damaged by an earthquake, which "stood gaping, nought to baulk/ Man's eye wherever he gazed or glanced."

> *The whole of the frontage shaven sheer,*
> *The inside gaped: exposed to day,*
> *Right and wrong and common and queer,*
> *Bare, as the palm of your hand, it lay.*

The inevitable crowd gathers in the street, delighting in the chance to inspect the domestic arrangements and private habits of the late owner:

> *"Odd tables and chairs for a man of wealth!*
> *What a parcel of musty old books about!*
> *He smoked,—no wonder he lost his health!*

*"I doubt if he bathed before he dressed.*
*A brasier?—the pagan, he burned perfumes!*
*You see it is proved, what the neighbours guessed:*
*His wife and himself had separate rooms."*

But Browning deplores such vulgar curiosity, and the rest of the short poem is a vigorous defense of the poet's right to privacy. He had no reason to anticipate that fifty years after his death, several of the houses immediately to the east of his in Warwick Crescent would be devastated to just the result he described, not by an earthquake but by Nazi bombers. Number 19, however, escaped intact: "enemy action," though by no intentional discrimination, spared Browning's house the fate of the others. The row was still standing, parts of it occupied and in good repair, the rest mere bombed-out shells, when I first visited it in 1958—the symbolism remained intact, Browning's privacy inviolate. But several years later all the houses were razed and a housing block erected on the site, and Browning's long residence there is now commemorated only by the name of the tiny island in the urban lake which his study overlooked.

Two years before he died, Browning moved to 29 DeVere Gardens, a street of five-story houses, now private hotels and clubs, leading off Kensington Road. Diagonally across from him lived Henry James, who was to find in Browning's dual personality—the man and the poet being rigorously kept in separate compartments—the *donnée* for his story "The Private Life." One wonders what courteous words the bearded old poet and the young American novelist exchanged when they happened to meet on the pavement.

But this is just about the sum of the rewards that a pursuit of Browning on English soil provides. For, apart from the glorious episode in Wimpole Street (the Brownings' ensuing marriage in the nearby St. Marylebone Church is recalled in a stained-glass window there), his whole life in England was uneventful and, as has often been remarked, oppressively conventional. And England figures very little in his poetry; nearly all of the poems we remember, as well as most that go unread, have Italian or other continental settings. With Tennyson, however, the case is quite different. To follow his progress from one locale to another is to understand, more vividly than would otherwise be possible, both the man and his poetry. Visiting the "homes and haunts" of the Laureate is not merely a sentimental journey in the hallowed Victorian fashion: it is a pilgrimage of discovery.

Some twenty years ago the biography of the poet by his grandson, Sir Charles Tennyson, threw much new light on the wretched circumstances of his early life which fed the melancholy that is perhaps the most characteristic strain in his poetry. He grew up in a country rectory at Somersby, Lincolnshire, whose domestic atmosphere was rendered oppressive by a father embittered by his early disinheritance from the family estate to which he had claim as the eldest son. During Tennyson's childhood, this sense of irremediable injustice drove the father to drink and fearful bursts of violence, and eventually to the verge of psychosis, if not beyond. To make things worse, his children inherited the Tennyson family's long tradition of black bile. Beneath their curiously un-English swarthiness coursed tainted blood, which later manifested itself in a series of personal tragedies. The physical setting in which Dr. Tennyson's sons and daughters grew up for the most part·simply intensified their innate morbidity, and it was in this indissoluble combination of spirit and outward circumstance that the springs of Tennyson's most personal poetic utterance lay. (Only a few years later, not too many miles to the north, a similar fusion of psychological stresses in an unhappy rectory set among the Yorkshire moors would produce a woman who wrote *Wuthering Heights*.)

Although there are abundant evidences elsewhere in his poetry of Tennyson's part-inherited, part-acquired melancholy, it finds its most poignant expression in *In Memoriam,* most of which was written after the young poet had left the neighborhood. Some of the most moving sections of that poem might well be called

"Somersby Revisited." They deal with various way stations in Tennyson's faltering progress from the emotional numbness and religious despair visited upon him by the sudden death of his Cambridge idol and prospective brother-in-law, Arthur Henry Hallam, toward a measure of serenity and hope. These way stations are not merely figurative; they have a physical habitation of a sort at the pinpoint on the large-scale map of Lincolnshire that is labeled Somersby.

The place is as remote today as it was when Tennyson was growing up there, a century and a half ago; one drives from the south across the "Holland Fen" section of the county, as flat as Nebraska, and then into the sparsely populated hills and heaths known as the Wolds. Somersby, found by carefully following the signposts at successive forks and intersections of the narrow, seldom-traveled roads, is merely a cluster of a few houses almost hidden among the ancient trees that especially stirred Tennyson's sense of the vastness of time. In their midst is the church from whose pulpit preached the elder Tennyson, who had never wanted to be a clergyman. It is a small church; together with the neighboring one of Bag Enderby, whose living the rector also held, in Tennyson's youth it served a population of less than a hundred. Today it is in sad disrepair. The rough gray stone of the walls and the stubby tower has been extensively but crudely mended with old brick and slapped-on mortar, and the entryway is screened with chicken wire to keep out vagrant birds. In the equally small and decrepit churchyard are moss-covered, crumbling tombstones, many of them tilted or broken—the very ones among which young Alfred would throw himself, wishing for death, after a particularly dreadful scene across the road at the Rectory.

The Rectory, a white two-story house with a steep tiled roof, lies behind a tall hedge fence. Alongside the entrance to the drive that curves by the doorway is a sign civilly but firmly denying admission. But there is no need to intrude upon the ghosts of the unhappy Tennyson family; the present setting is quite enough to recreate the mood in which the tall young man with the already deep-graven dark features ate out his soul in those years that preceded and followed the shock of Hallam's death. Ideally, the scene should be visited on a sultry, lowering August afternoon. Somewhere to the south there is occasional thunder, and Somersby itself sleeps in an unnatural stillness, not a leaf stirring in this shadowy lane in the midst of nowhere. The season is different in the poem, but the effect is the same:

> *Calm is the morn without a sound,*
>   *Calm as to suit a calmer grief,*
>   *And only thro' the faded leaf*
> *The chestnut pattering to the ground:*
>
> *Calm and deep peace on this high wold,*
>   *And on these dews that drench the furze,*
>   *And all the silvery gossamers*
> *That twinkle into green and gold:*
>
> *Calm and still light on yon great plain*
>   *That sweeps with all its autumn bowers,*
>   *And crowded farms and lessening towers,*
> *To mingle with the bounding main:*
>
> *Calm and deep peace in this wide air,*
>   *These leaves that redden to the fall;*
>   *And in my heart, if calm at all,*
> *If any calm, a calm despair . . .*

Yes: this is where Tennyson learned the calmness that does not comfort, the despair that paralyzes rather than moves.

Behind the old Rectory is the wide lawn where, several years after Hallam's death, the Tennyson family, including the daughter to whom Hallam had been affianced, gathered according to custom in the long slow evening that followed a summer day such as this.

> *By night we linger'd on the lawn,*
>   *For underfoot the herb was dry;*

*And genial warmth; and o'er the sky*
  *The silvery haze of summer drawn;*

*And calm that let the tapers burn*
  *Unwavering: not a cricket chirr'd;*
  *The brook alone far-off was heard,*
*And on the board the fluttering urn:*

*And bats went around in fragrant skies,*
  *And wheel'd or lit the filmy shapes*
  *That haunt the dusk, with ermine capes*
*And woolly breasts and beaded eyes;*

*While now we sang old songs that peal'd*
  *From knoll to knoll, where, couch'd at ease,*
  *The white kine glimmer'd, and the trees*
*Laid their dark arms about the field.*

As he goes on to narrate, Tennyson withdrew from the company, went to his room and once more read the packet of letters that were his sole remaining physical bond with Hallam:

*So word by word, and line by line,*
  *The dead man touch'd me from the past,*
  *And all at once it seem'd at last*
*The living soul was flash'd on mine . . .*

In this climactic mystical experience of the poem, Tennyson found a resolution of his doubt and despair, and in the morning the Somersby landscape seemed to reflect his fresh sense of renewal.

*. . . East and West, without a breath,*
  *Mixt their dim lights, like life and death,*
*To broaden into boundless day.*

In earlier stages of his tortured reaction to Hallam's death, Tennyson had had other night visions. In his imagination he had followed the progress of Hallam's body from Vienna,

where he died, across the Mediterranean and around the
Iberian peninsula to the West Country town of Clevedon, where
he was buried. In section LXVII of *In Memoriam* he recounts
the final experience in this series of visions:

> *When on my bed the moonlight falls,*
> *I know that in thy place of rest*
> *By that broad water of the west,*
> *There comes a glory on the walls:*
>
> *Thy marble bright in dark appears,*
> *As slowly steals a silver flame*
> *Along the letters of thy name,*
> *And o'er the number of thy years.*
>
> *The mystic glory swims away:*
> *From off my bed the moonlight dies;*
> *And closing eaves of wearied eyes*
> *I sleep till dusk is dipt in gray:*
>
> *And then I know the mist is drawn*
> *A lucid veil from coast to coast,*
> *And in the dark church like a ghost*
> *Thy tablet glimmers to the dawn.*

As Tennyson traveled from Somersby to Clevedon in imagination, so we travel in actuality. The town of Clevedon itself is not
far from Bristol, and one whose anticipation of it has been
formed from Tennyson's verses is unprepared for what he finds.
Far from being remote and desolate, it is quite large, with road
upon road of villas, shopping streets, park promenades high
above Severn Mouth, resort hotels, and caravan (camp trailer)
sites. The parish church is somewhat removed from the town.
Standing on a promontory and surrounded in part by fields bris-
tling with nettles, it overlooks the Severn, just as Tennyson describes it in the poem. The heavy gray stone church, several times
as large as that at Somersby, has been elaborately restored since
Hallam was buried there, but his family's monuments remain

prominent, and on the wall of the south transept is the very tablet Tennyson saw in his mystic dream:

> *To the memory of Arthur Henry Hallam of Trinity College, Cambridge B.A. eldest son of Henry Hallam Esquire and of Julia Maria his Wife, Daughter of Sir Abraham Elton Bart of Clevedon Court who was snatched away by sudden death at Vienna on September 15th 1833 in the 23rd year of his age.*

> *And now in this obscure and solitary church repose the mortal remains of one too early lost for public fame, but already conspicuous among his contemporaries for the brightness of his genius, the depth of his understanding, the nobleness of his disposition, the fervour of his piety, and the purity of his life.*

> VALE DULCISSIME VALE DILECTISSIME DESIDERATISSIME REQUIESCAS IN PACE PATER AC MATER HIC POSTHAC REQUIESCAMUS TECUM USQUE AD TUBAM

Like Edward King, Keats, and Clough, the subjects of the other three great English elegies, Arthur Henry Hallam is infinitely better honored by the poem of a bereaved friend than by the starched phrases of the memorial, whose counterparts—clichés, however sincerely meant—are found in every church in the kingdom.

In the waters below Clevedon church, it is useful to note while we are in the vicinity, occurs a phenomenon that lends extra appropriateness to the description, in section XIX of *In Memoriam,* of the poet's expression of grief being stifled by the tears he cannot shed:

> *The Danube to the Severn gave*
> *The darken'd heart that beat no more;*
> *They laid him by the pleasant shore,*
> *And in the hearing of the wave.*

*There twice a day the Severn fills;*
*The salt sea-water passes by,*
*And hushes half the babbling Wye,*
*And makes a silence in the hills.*

*The Wye is hush'd nor moved along,*
*And hush'd my deepest grief of all,*
*When fill'd with tears that cannot fall,*
*I brim with sorrow drowning song.*

*The tide flows down again, the wave again*
*Is vocal in its wooded walls;*
*My deeper anguish also falls*
*And I can speak a little then.*

On its face, the image describes the process of the tide in any successively narrowing series of waterways. But in the specific context of the Bristol Channel, Severn, and Wye it has intensified meaning, because here the ordinary tidal action sometimes is accompanied by a "bore" or tidal wave, a moving wall of water which further inhibits the normal seaward flow of the rivers. Tennyson's analogy is thus enriched by the implicit local reference: a not invaluable insight into a detail of the artistry of *In Memoriam* which might be overlooked if one did not linger in the vicinity of Clevedon and happen to learn of the bore.

The year *In Memoriam* was published (1850), Tennyson succeeded Wordsworth in the laureateship and was married to the lady to whom he had been engaged for twelve years. His future prosperity was assured after years of misgivings and indirection. Three years later, he and his wife settled in a capacious house called Farringford, on the western tip of the Isle of Wight. It is worth following them there for the sake of acquaintance with the setting in which Tennyson first flourished as a national celebrity. The Isle of Wight had already become a popular summer resort; now, in addition to its more ordinary allurements, it boasted the living presence of a Poet Laureate whose verses were household words throughout the realm, quoted from every pulpit, in

every newspaper and magazine, and at every fireside. And so
Tennyson became a tourist attraction. According to contemporary accounts, hosts of trippers—Papa, Mama, and all the family
—made excursions to the vicinity of Farringford in hope of seeing the Laureate on his solitary walks, busy (no doubt) compos-
ing an immortal poem. Some, especially bold, went up to the
house and tried to gain admission, a privilege restricted, as they
soon discovered, to Tennyson's numerous friends, the literary and
public men of London and Oxford. The poet, always a preter-
naturally shy man, loathed the intrusion of strangers, and it is
said that when he did encounter them, he swept by without a
glance; but if in their delicacy they affected not to notice him, he
would stop, look back, and silently execrate them for their neglect. Whether such stories are true or not, they are faithful to
the man's spirit, which was at once complicated and simple.

The Isle of Wight is still a popular resort, and in the summer
one can easily understand why Tennyson favored its green landscape and equable climate. One way to approach Farringford is
by foot from the yachting town of Yarmouth. A public path leads
across ripened wheatfields and along the leeward side of barn-
yards, coming out near Freshwater church. Then the route is
along country roads sporadically lined with rows of cheap bunga-
lows and late Victorian semi-detached villas. Farringford stands
in the midst of lawns and flower gardens, with plenty of room for
croquet and sunning in deck chairs. It is now an expensive hotel;
and, the management's brochure adds, Tennyson's study, where
he smoked his strong tobacco and talked with his friends into the
late hours, has been converted into a television lounge. What the
crusty speaker of "Locksley Hall Sixty Years After," railing
against all manifestations of modernism in the 1880's, would say
to that does not bear pondering. Literary "Zolaism," democracy,
money-greed, and all the other fruits of so-called progress were
bad enough, but the idea of his home giving hospitality in de-
generate latter days to American situation comedies flanked by
commercials for soap powder would move him to almost inarticu-

late rage. Nor, for that matter, would Tennyson in all likelihood approve of making a hotel out of the first home of his married life and laureateship. But it is good to know that in the neighborhood remembrance of the genius who once lived there is by no means faded. At a crossroads near Farringford, for example, there is a smaller, definitely more commonplace hotel. It is called— inevitably—Locksley Hall.

The Tennysons lived at Farringford (conveniently close to the Queen, who had a summer home at Osborne, just across the island) for fourteen years. But unlike Victoria, as the poet once told her, he could not have a sentry at his gates, and the privacy she enjoyed as a matter of course became less and less his. To escape from the constant annoyance of sightseers and favor-beggers, he and his wife prospected for a site which would give them the utmost solitude. In 1867 they found it on the southern slope of Blackdown, several miles from the Surrey town of Haslemere. Although not excessively distant from London, it was far enough from the madding crowd to satisfy the most reclusive temper. There Tennyson built what was to be his last home, Aldworth. In his remaining years he was never again troubled by tourists.

One can understand why, because a century later Aldworth is still exactly as Tennyson's friend Richard Monckton Milnes, Lord Houghton, described it: "a most inaccessible site, with every comfort he can require, and every discomfort to all who approach him." Blackdown itself is owned by the National Trust, and therefore is preserved in its natural wildness, which is considerable. The road up its slope, posted as "Tennyson's Lane," is steep and winding, bordered with thick growths of bracken and heather. The determined motorist who defies the preliminary PRIVATE sign at the lane leading across the ridge to Aldworth does so at his own risk. One who did found himself at a dead end, before a gate with the legend, incapable of misinterpretation, THESE GROUNDS ARE STRICTLY PRIVATE. THE PUBLIC ARE NOT ALLOWED. An addendum warned of disagreeable dogs at large in the vicinity. Turning the car around as a precaution in case a hasty getaway was required, the interloper clambered about the dense vegetation hoping for a camera angle, but the house itself remained hidden somewhere down the lane, behind a grove of pine trees. Then, just as advertised, the watchdogs began to bay; this was Surrey, not Devon where Dartmoor is located, but their tones were Baskervillian. Under such circumstances, one does not wait for meat-starved beasts to materialize; one jumps into the car and decamps, with a spatter of gravel from beneath the wheels. But it was satisfactory to have learned, beyond any possibility of doubt, that if impregnable privacy was what Tennyson longed for, privacy is what he got; and it was what His Highness the Gaekwar of Baroda, the fabulously rich and high-living Indian prince who occupied the premises from 1920 to 1947, enjoyed in turn. The fleeing motorist, once he had regained the broad highway and had time for reflection, found it fitting that Tennyson, official poetic celebrant of the glories of the Empire, should have left the solitude he prized so highly as a fortuitous legacy to an Indian potentate who would eventually become disemployed.

. . . So this chapter, as originally written, ended. But intelligence lately received forbids leaving it at that, however satisfactorily melodramatic, not to say symbolic, such a conclusion may be. The ferocious privacy at Aldworth has now been tempered, and placid Victorian ceremonialism once again invokes the spirit of its builder, his fame, and his age. "The Poet's house at Aldworth," reports the October, 1967, issue of the *Tennyson Research Bulletin,* published by the Tennyson Society at Lincoln, "was the scene of a most appropriate and charming ceremony in June of this year. Members of the Society were the guests of Mr. and Mrs. W. T. Suren, the present owners of the house, and the occasion was the unveiling of a bust of Tennyson by the present Lord Tennyson. Sited in the grounds, the bust is basically a copy of the original work by Thomas Woolner the original of which is at Lincoln. . . ."

How reassuring to learn that so little, after all, has changed! Tennyson—to borrow words he used of Hallam—"O'erlookest the tumult from afar, / And smilest, knowing all is well."

*Sir Richard Burton's tomb, Mortlake, Surrey*

## 12

# *Cemetery Haunting*

ON THE NIGHT of February 10, 1862, Dante Gabriel Rossetti found his wife Elizabeth—"Lizzie" or "Guggums" as she was known to her husband's artist friends—dying from an overdose of laudanum. It was a tragic end to a short, troubled life which had seen the slender lady of the long red-gold hair, initially a London shop assistant, become the Pre-Raphaelite painters' reigning model and then, after a long engagement to her indecisive and not wholly faithful lover, Rossetti's wife. A week later, after an inquest had resulted in a verdict of accidental death (we are now quite sure she killed herself), Lizzie was buried at Highgate Cemetery, in the plot of her husband's father, a doughty old Dante scholar and political exile from Italy. Beneath her luxuriant hair, as if to mark a total and irrevocable break with the past and no doubt also as a dramatic token of his remorse as a negligent husband, the painter thrust the unpublished manuscript of the poems he had written in the past several years.

There it remained for seven years. Then, urged by his friends as well as by his own desire to attain a second fame, Rossetti instituted the legal proceedings necessary for his wife's body to be exhumed and the manuscript retrieved. When these were concluded, there followed one of the most macabre scenes in English literary history. In the darkness of an early October evening, a bonfire casting flickering shadows over the adjacent tombstones and vegetation, Rossetti's friend Charles Augustus Howell and witnesses from the Home Office watched workmen uncover the coffin. When it was opened, Lizzie's hair proved to be as magnificent as ever; it had continued to grow after death. And from beneath her hair the grim-faced men drew the discolored manuscript of her husband's poems, which an attending doctor took away to disinfect and dry out, and which, with additions, became Rossetti's published *Poems* of 1870.

The site of so grisly a transaction deserves to be inspected; and Highgate Cemetery, by its very nature, is warranted to convert what begins as a mere visit into an Adventure. As has been noted, Highgate is a region of steep streets not far from central London, but once inside the cemetery, one might as well be a thousand miles away. A genial gravedigger-cum-caretaker, upon being applied to, agrees to conduct the explorer to "the Rossetti," as the site is known in local terminology. The route leads through a jungle in which man's memorializing efforts have been almost nullified by nature. Highgate Cemetery represents what would result if the accumulated monuments of Westminster Abbey were transferred, in their full marmoreal extravagance, to the Amazonian rain forest. Although the guide maintains that the lush growth is systematically eliminated during the winter by the use of billhooks and wholesale burning, one cannot believe it has been curbed for years. Thick "cuckoo grass" rises to a height of four or five feet, and one is not disposed to doubt the guide's claim, based upon much experience in digging, that the roots go down nine feet. Trees, saplings, wild shrubs, weeds, all the rank vegetation that a weeping English climate can bring forth, swallow up every tombstone that does not front directly on a path. And there are few paths, and the plots are so crammed together they seem almost piled upon one another; the Victorian company that founded and developed this gothic Garden of Memory squeezed revenue out of every inch of space. To reach "the Rossetti" requires plunging from the path through the brambles and burrs and hip-high undergrowth and tough, ground-clinging vines that constantly trip up the explorer fresh from the London pavements. A machete is not ordinarily part of one's traveling equipment in England, but it would come in handy here.*

Finally the spot is reached. The elder Rossettis' tombstone is upright and the inscription still plain: it commemorates the Neapolitan scholar-exile (d. 1854) and his wife (d. 1886) as well as William Michael, their younger son—Dante Gabriel's junior by a year—who died in 1919, "having seen the realisation of Italian unity." Leaning against its face at a forty-five degree angle is another stone, much weathered and only partly decipherable. This was the one that was moved in the course of that lurid night-scene; it marks the grave of both the ill-starred Guggums and her sister-in-law, Christina Rossetti, who died in 1894. (Dante Gabriel himself is buried at Birchington, in Kent.) The whilom artist's model and the saintly spinster-poet must make uneasy grave-fellows. . . .

After his exertions, the explorer feels as James Bruce must have felt when he stood at the source of the Blue Nile. But the end is not yet. The guide, proud of the variety and eminence of his defunct charges, strikes out anew with his guest and eventually arrives at a path of sorts which allows single-file traffic through the stone-and-vegetation wilderness. Of considerably more interest to him than "the Rossetti" is the elevated brown sarcophagus bearing the prominent lettering, MRS. HENRY WOOD: here rests the prolific best-selling Victorian novelist. Mr. Henry Wood no doubt is also within, but it is his wife who gets her

---

* The ill-kemptness of Highgate evidently is of long standing and wide notoriety. I have seen complaints about the lamentable condition of George Eliot's grave dating from 1905 and 1930. There is a fine picture of an overgrown precinct of the cemetery in Pritchett and Hofer's *London Perceived* (facing p. 85); and in the recent Penguin guide to London architecture among the untrodden ways, *Nairn's London* (1966), Ian Nairn has some justifiably acerb remarks on the subject.

name in lights, so to speak. Only a stone's—or elephant tusk's—throw distant is the final stand of Mr. Wombwell, the celebrated "menagerist" of the same era. In another region ("Beware the tigers," one comments with nervous facetiousness, whereupon the guide matter-of-factly replies that there *are* foxes around) is a single horizontal slab, virtually invisible until one is right upon it, marking Mrs. Charles Dickens and several of her children. Her husband is in the Abbey; poor Kate, whom he cast from his bed and board in 1858, is commemorated just about as obscurely as can be conceived—and seemingly nobody is troubled to keep her grave free of the encroaching weeds and saplings. On the other hand, the Galsworthy family plot (John himself was cremated and his ashes scattered over the South Downs) is meticulously tended and surrounded by well-trimmed box hedges: a striking bit of dignity and order in this grotesque chaos of death, oblivion, neglect, and natural exuberance.

Across precipitous Swain's Lane from the older portion of the cemetery is a newer part, not quite as wild; the term, though, is merely relative, and here means that the vegetable growth has not reached true wilderness stature. This part of Highgate is the one which appears in the papers whenever an important delegation from a Communist country is in town, because laying a wreath on Karl Marx's grave is always *de rigueur*. The monument cannot be missed, because it faces on a main path, is bulkily, amorphously monolithic, and is surmounted by a heroic-sized bust of the man who wrote *Das Kapital* in the British Museum a few miles to the south. Whatever else may be said about it, Marx's memorial is utterly unlike any other in Highgate Cemetery.

"The Marx" serves as a point of reference for finding several graves of literary significance in the immediate vicinity; it is much more useful, and assuredly less inappropriate, than the one employed by the cemetery attendants, which is a statue of Christ. For in this little pocket of Highgate rest several distinguished nineteenth-century secularists. Two hundred feet from Marx is

George Eliot, who moved far from her youthful piety to embrace a rationalist "religion of humanity." The inscription on her obelisk reads, "Of those immortal dead who live again in minds made better by her presence," and she is called both George Eliot and Mary Ann Cross (her married name in her last years.)

Equidistant from Marx is another proponent of Victorian rationalism, Herbert Spencer. And closer to George Eliot—no more than twenty-five feet away—are buried two other men to whose names the explorer, coming upon them by accident, instantly responds: George Jacob Holyoake, the political radical and freethinker, whose bust faces her tomb, and Henry Crabb Robinson, the man-about-London whose voluminous diary is full of intimate accounts of the major English literary figures throughout the whole first half of the century. Though wholly fortuitous, there is much suitability in Robinson's being here. He first met George Eliot in 1851, before she began her career as novelist, when he recorded that despite her being the translator of that bible of the skeptically inclined, Strauss' *Leben Jesu*, "there was something about her which pleased me much both in look and voice." Nine years later he lunched with her and wrote in his diary: "She has quite won on me . . . I began a course of instruction on Wordsworth's poetry, repeated to her what I could by heart, and in the evening . . . I devoted several hours to the making out of a list of those of Wordsworth's poems which I thought a beginner ought to read. She will buy his works." Robinson could not have foreseen that Wordsworth, to whom he thus belatedly introduced her, would become George Eliot's favorite poet or that *Adam Bede* would subsequently be praised for its transplantation of Wordsworth's philosophy of nature into fiction. I do not know whether George Eliot was aware she would be buried so close to "old Crabb" (he died in 1867, she thirteen years later), but her debt to him would have inclined her to approve. How Robinson himself, a man of conventional opinions, would have regarded the variously heterodox company that eventually joined him—George Eliot apart—can only be a matter for speculation.

The one London cemetery which boasts an incidence of literary remains as great as Highgate's is Kensal Green. Like Highgate, it is a product of Victorian private enterprise. When the yards of old London parish churches could not accommodate any more bodies—revolting conditions such as those described in *Bleak House* led to the closing of many churchyards on urgent sanitary grounds—venture capital found new and profitable employment in laying out big commercial cemeteries in what were then the city's outskirts. Kensal Green is kept in better repair than Highgate, though the grass and nettles get pretty thick away from the paths; but to do his field work with satisfaction even in this relatively domesticated environment the researcher needs strong legs, plenty of time, and limitless tenacity.

These sloping acres in a run-down district of northwest London are presided over by a cluster of giant gas storage tanks to the south, and beyond the walls in the same direction is an unseen but busy railway line; Highgate has at least the advantage of being more in touch with nature. At the entrance lodge, the gatekeeper will lend a copy of an old printed list of famous decedents interred here, whose names on one side are keyed to a simplified plot-map on the other. They include, besides the superior literary eminences to whose tombs one's ambition particularly runs, the sensation novelists William Harrison Ainsworth and Captain Mayne Reid; the admired early nineteenth-century tenor John Braham, who figures in Byron's letters among other places; Charles Blondin, the French tightrope walker who traversed Niagara many times, adding such embroideries to the basic feat as going across blindfold, wheeling a barrow, walking on stilts, and carrying a man on his back; Michael Balfe, the composer of *The Bohemian Girl* and other operas; the great engineers the Brunels, previously mentioned; the *Punch* cartoonist John Leech; and John Forster, Dickens' friend and biographer and a man both ubiquitous and influential in Victorian literary circles.

Because there are no markers to identify the various sections shown on the map—none, at any rate, that are immediately visible—the trick is, first, to orient oneself by the curve of the paths and other topographical clues and then, when one's approximate bearings are fixed, to try to zero in on the particular grave in question. Some offer little difficulty; the price is merely that of much walking among the thousands upon thousands of piously inscribed monuments, some tilting, some broken, some overgrown, some restrained in their sentiments and some representing, in choice of phrase and design, Victorian taste at its abysmal worst. Thackeray's tomb is the simplest of all: a plain stone box topped by a flat slab and surrounded by a rusty iron railing, the inscription noting only that William Makepeace Thackeray and Anne Carmichael-Smyth, his mother by her first marriage, lie here. The most elaborate tombstone memorializing a literary man is that of Thomas Hood, who died in poverty. This imposing monument of polished pink granite, surmounted by a heroic-size bronze bust, was "erected by public subscription, 1854"—nine years after Hood's death. Lest posterity suffer any doubt why a tubercular hack journalist and occasional poet should have been honored so ostentatiously, the Victorians lettered on the stone's base the epitaph Hood himself devised: "He sang 'The Song of the Shirt.' " Small comfort to him that he did; poor punning Hood has it grander in death than he ever had it in life.

Not far away from him is buried Leigh Hunt, also commemorated by a stout shaft (of light gray granite this time) topped by a white marble bust whose portrayal of its subject as a kind of judicious Ariel attempts to identify him as one who belonged to the romantic generation of poets yet was blessed with unromantic common sense. The inscription contains no mention of his close association with Byron and Shelley, or of his services—more valuable than his poetry—to the arts of criticism and the informal essay. Instead, the Victorians' estimate of him is contained in the quotation from "Abou Ben Adhem" on the pedestal: "Write me as one that loves his fellow-men." Much is to be learned of the shifting grounds of literary fame from the engraved terms various generations select to characterize their dead authors.

With Hunt is buried his alcoholic wife Marianne, whose slatternly housekeeping scandalized Jane Carlyle and whose brood of children Byron once feelingly described as "dirtier and more mischievous than Yahoos." One of those children, Thornton, is also buried here, along with *his* wife. The proprieties are thereby better observed than they were in life, because in the 1850's the Thornton Hunts belonged to a close-knit circle of London journalists and artists, including the editor and scientific writer George Henry Lewes and the portrait painter Samuel Laurence, who entertained advanced ideas on the relation of the sexes. Thus it came about that Thornton won the peculiar distinction of being the father, not once but twice, of a pair of children born within a few months or weeks of each other. The concurrent mothers, on both occasions, were Mrs. Thornton Hunt and Mrs. George Henry Lewes. It was the latter's participation in this liberal arrangement that in due course provided her husband with a rationalization of sorts for living with George Eliot. Such achievements as enabling a cuckolded husband to become the extralegal spouse of a great novelist are not likely to be preserved on Kensal Green tombstones, but awareness of them adds piquancy to one's graveyard meditations.

Similar reflections are available when one pauses before a stone cross standing determinedly upright in a region of Kensal Green where the numerous crosses seem to have a special propensity for leaning every which way. "IN MEMORY OF WILKIE COLLINS," says the inscription, "AUTHOR OF 'THE WOMAN IN WHITE' AND OTHER WORKS OF FICTION": a rather blatant piece of commercialism, it may well be thought—as if Collins' publisher paid for the stone and copied the words from one of his advertisements. But this marker is more interesting for what it omits. The suppressed fact is that the grave also contains the body of Caroline Graves, Collins' mistress, with whom he shared a house for many years and who died six years after him. According to Kenneth Robinson, the novelist's best biographer, after Caroline's burial here the plot was tended by one Martha Rudd, her replacement in Collins' household while Caroline was temporarily married to another and herself the mother of three illegitimate children by the consolable Collins. Deeds of piety sometimes are enacted in odd circumstances.

But enough of the "irregular connections," as the Victorians would have called them, about which the stones in Kensal Green are understandably silent. The last objective of an afternoon spent visiting the tombs of writers is Trollope, whose whereabouts long elude the best-laid plans and patient diligence of the cemetery searcher. The little map, examined and cross-examined, assures one that the location is right; but where is Trollope's grave? After repeated trips up and down the relevant paths, and into the thick and treacherously pitted stretches of grass between, it is still unlocated. The closing hour approaches, and the invisible peak-hour commuter trains rattle past beyond the wall, draining London's wage earners off to the suburbs; still no Trollope. But just as he is about to be abandoned as a bad job, one more trip through the area that has already had saturation coverage, and there he is. His grave is a low one, and the white-paint inscription on one of the slanting slabs that comprise its top has been completely hidden from view by a thick wild bush that has grown up alongside. Drastic reduction of Kensal Green plant growth is needed before photographic proof of one's triumph can be obtained. But there is substantial pleasure to be had in heading back along the noisy, grimy Harrow Road after returning the precious old map to the caretaker—the satisfaction of an afternoon's mission well accomplished.

It's impossible, of course, to generalize about the condition of cemeteries that hold objects of literary interest. Some are as tangled and neglected as Highgate; some, especially those which are still receptive to new arrivals, are well maintained. There is for example the lovely little churchyard in the village of Laleham,

on the western outskirts of London not far from the light manu-
facturing and market-gardening town of Staines, where Matthew
Arnold and his wife are buried, flanked by their several children.
But no advertisement here: Arnold's sole distinction, if we are to
infer his fame from the stone, is that he was "Eldest Son of the
Late Thomas Arnold, D.D., Headmaster of Rugby School."
Nothing of "Dover Beach," "The Scholar-Gypsy," or *Essays in
Criticism*. It is fitting enough that Arnold should be buried here,
for he was born in this village. Yet, as one who has always entertained certain reservations about the way he conducted his cultural mission to the Philistines, I have sometimes regretted that
he did not find his resting place at Rugby, his home during most
of his youth—where the parish church is named St. Matthew the
Evangelist.

The churchyard at Edmonton, in London's northern reaches,
is rank with grass and weeds, and some of the stones are crumbling. The marker over the tomb of Charles and Mary Lamb,
with memorial verses by Henry Francis Cary, the translator of
Dante, is better preserved, but it can be located in the un-
trimmed vegetation only after the visitor wanders inside the
church, where an aproned and slippered parishioner who is busy
dusting the pews and shining the brass obligingly gives directions. Why, one wonders, if vicars can find lady volunteers to
keep the interiors of churches reasonably neat, cannot they round
up a few male communicants to operate outside with pruning
shears, scythe, and lawn mower? England owes that much to its
illustrious dead—and to the Americans who come in respectful
search of them.

By all odds the most extraordinary literary tomb in London, if
not in the whole of Britain, is Sir Richard Burton's, in the Roman Catholic churchyard of St. Mary Magdalene at Mortlake, a
western suburb. The road which the churchyard adjoins is split
up the middle by a busy line of British Railways, Southern Region, and the tomb itself is overlooked by a row of cheap working-
class houses just across the street—a locale that is the very defini-

tion of English prosaicness. The tomb, built of native English marble, has the form of an Arab tent, twelve feet square and eighteen feet high. Running frieze-like across the front is a row of Islamic stars and crescents, but in the middle, surmounting what was originally the carved tent-flap entrance to the tiny chapel within but is now cemented shut, is a crucifix. This massive reminiscence of the burning Arabian sands squatting in a dreary West London suburb, a bizarre mélange of the pagan and the Papist, was the inspiration of Burton's redoubtable wife and the scandal of all who deemed the great explorer, anthropologist, master of forty languages and dialects, and translator of *The Arabian Nights*—and an agnostic to boot—deserving of a more suitable memorial.

In locating Roman Catholic cemeteries, which in England are more obscure than their more numerous and ancient Anglican neighbors, one often needs the help of a knowledgeable passer-by, typically a middle-aged lady with a shopping bag who goes out of her way to conduct the American pilgrim to the desired site. This was true at Mortlake and again in the south coast town of Lymington, where I had come in quest of Coventry Patmore. I have long cherished against this mid-Victorian poet a dislike as irrational and implacable as the hostility which Mr. F's Aunt entertained for the unoffending Arthur Clennam. The reason, such as it is, is that I regard Patmore's poem *The Angel in the House,* that once hugely popular celebration of the chaste and spiritual joys of marriage, as in fact a cover-up—sublimation, if one wishes to be more charitable—for Patmore's baser nature, which found secret gratification in his avid perusal of pornography. I happen not to be enthralled by this kind of Priapian religiosity, the use of domesticated Mariolatry as a front for erotic obsession: it borders on the hypocritical. And so, when I read in a biography of Patmore that his grave was marked by an obelisk, I was evilly delighted. All I desired beyond this was ocular verification. At Lymington I had much trouble finding the Roman Catholic church he patronized, and when I did—it proved to be entirely hemmed in by buildings at the foot of the busy High Street—I discovered there were no graves nearby. Liberated from my perplexity by the usual kindly lady, I then drove to the residential heights overlooking the town, where I found a modern cemetery, a portion of which was set aside for Catholics. Yes, Patmore was there. His grave is not set apart from those of other local Popish decedents, but it is distinguished, to my great satisfaction, by a thoroughly phallic obelisk. The stony emblem is only ten feet or so high, and I had hoped to find it as towering as Cleopatra's Needle; but, as Mercutio says, 'tis enough, 'twill serve.

Some uncomprehending people tend to disparage this kind of literary field work as a mild form of necrophilia, and once in a while the patient, while not concurring in the specific diagnosis, has his own misgivings. Some seven or eight years ago I visited the old churchyard at Chiswick for the sake of Hogarth's tomb and its inscription of verses written by David Garrick. The time was about noon or one o'clock. When I emerged from the churchyard and was walking through one of the adjacent lanes on my way back to the bus line, I was confronted with the sight of two Nazi stormtroopers in full uniform coming smartly toward me. This is it, I thought: one cemetery too many has driven me off my rocker. The Hitlerites marched past without a glance, not even so much as a *Sieg heil*. Torn between concern for my sanity and my conscientious duty to alert the police—or Military Intelligence—I continued shakily on my way. And then, not too soon, I passed a building, noticed a sign, and was reassured. It was a film studio, and the Nazis were obviously actors heading to the pub for lunch.

Not all of the illustrious dead are to be discovered in consecrated ground; not all of them, indeed, are even buried. The most accessible of the latter is Jeremy Bentham, father of utilitarianism and in a very important sense one of the law-givers of the Victorian age, though he died before Victoria came to the throne. Old Jeremy's ideas do not sit well with most moderns;

the rigorous, humorless nonsense of the Benthamite "calculus of pleasure and pain" with its elaborate arithmetical apparatus for making moral or legislative decisions, the Benthamite rejection of such humane values as the arts, all the fallacies and blindnesses and intellectual grittiness comprehended in the philosophic system that was to redeem society forever—for these enthusiasms, which he transmitted to such followers as James and John Stuart Mill and thus to the Victorian spirit at large, we find it hard to forgive him.

Yet whatever his crotchets, and they were many, Jeremy Bentham was an amiable, disinterested friend of mankind. His lifelong philanthropy found its final expression in his will, which directed that after his death his body be dissected by his friend, the pioneer "sanitary reformer" Dr. Southwood Smith, for whatever value the resulting knowledge might have. Smith performed this friendly last service in 1832, after which, still in pursuance of Bentham's wishes, the philosopher's bones were deposited at University College, the constituent of the University of London which had recently been founded by a group of Benthamites and other liberal intellectuals as a secular alternative to the old universities.

And there he is today. When you apply at the barrier at the university library, an attendant after procuring the necessary key leads you to the end of a corridor, where stands a dark wooden cabinet, the size of a pair of telephone booths, inscribed in golden letters JEREMY BENTHAM. After this is opened, a second, older cabinet is also unlocked, an electric light is switched on— and you are literally in the presence of the great utilitarian. He sits in a chair that was his in life, and in his own clothes, dark coat, nankeen trousers, broad-brimmed straw hat, and white ruffled neckcloth; his hands are folded over the knob of his cane, and his waxen face bespeaks measureless benevolence. The basis of the composition may be his skeleton, but the effect on the beholder is simply that of a quite realistic waxwork such as may be seen in quantity only a mile or so away, at Madame Tussaud's.

Bentham's actual head was not reunited with his skeleton after
the post-mortem; it is preserved in a separate box kept nearby,
but it is not available for public scrutiny. A photograph reveals
it to be shrunken. (There is a story—is it true?—that every
year, at the dinner marking the anniversary of the founding of
University College, Jeremy is removed from his silent telephone
booth and placed at the head of the table: a skeleton at the feast
in the strictest literal sense.)

It used to be said that Laurence Sterne also came under the
dissector's knife, though in his case not by prearrangement. He
was interred in 1768 in a plot owned by the church of St. George,
Hanover Square—a site, some distance from the church itself,
used as an annex to the parish's original burial ground. Not long
afterwards, the contemporary story went, grave robbers dug up
the body and sold it to Cambridge University for the usual edu-
cative purposes; but the professor in charge recognized the author
of *Tristram Shandy* and had him returned to his resting place.
Appended to the legend was the assertion that Sterne's skull was
retained as an exhibit in the university's anatomical museum. But
the ironic fitness ("Alas, poor Yorick!"—Yorick, of course, was
Sterne's pseudonym in *A Sentimental Journey* as well as the
name of Hamlet *père's* court jester) is just too neat; it had occurred to more than one of Sterne's obituarists. This story too is
in all probability apocryphal.

Whether or not Sterne's dust continued to moulder in London,
I wanted at least to view the site of his grave. According to his
modern biographers, about 1780 two fellow-Masons erected a
slab against the wall of the cemetery, stating that near that spot
(the location was no more exact) Sterne was buried. The five-acre
burial ground was said to lie behind the late-Victorian Chapel of
the Ascension in the Bayswater Road, only about three hundred
yards west of Marble Arch. Several times I went to the location
but was regularly unsuccessful in my attempt to find, let alone
gain access to, the burial ground. The chapel proved to be a
bombed-out ruin, with trees growing inside the shell and even an

ambitious sapling or two sprouting from the broken cornice. Between it and the street lay a plot of grass ending in a high wall, and into the wall was set a padlocked iron gate. Although I canvassed the surrounding streets, I could find no other means of entry to the burial ground, which was itself invisible from the Bayswater Road. The last time I was there, I touched a button inset in the gatepost which evidently was connected with a bell in a cottage adjoining the ruined chapel to the west. I saw the window curtains stir in response and knew I was under surveillance, but nobody came out to learn what I wanted. I turned away in despair once again. Sterne's grave continued to elude me.

The next day, a Sunday, I surmised the reason why I was not welcome: the people inside the cottage may well have mistaken me for a reporter. For the front page of the *Observer* contained a three-column article captioned THE GRAVEYARD THAT FETCHED A MILLION. It related the fourteen-year-long struggle of a churchwarden of St. George's, Hanover Square, to overcome the complicated legal obstacles in the way of selling off the property, which had not been used for burials for more than a century and which happens to be in a neighborhood of London where real estate values are extremely high. At last he had won his fight. The five acres were sold to a non-profit housing society, and the Church of England was £950,000 richer.

I am glad for the Church of England (and I hope, for one thing, that a good portion of that windfall has been channeled toward the repair of some needy cathedrals: see the following pages). But that doesn't alter the fact that I never saw Sterne's grave.

*The Great Octagon, Ely Cathedral*

---

## 13

---

# Mark 11:15

THE TEXT FOR this brief homily is taken from the revised legend on an alms box in the restored London church of St. James, Piccadilly. It originally read: "The poor need your help." But over the first two words has been pasted the eloquent monosyllable "We"—that is, the church itself. Everywhere in the domain of the Archbishops of Canterbury and York the traditional poor box has given way to ecclesiastical ticket offices and scare-head posters appealing for contributions.

Nothing in the following burst of ill temper should be construed as suggesting I am unaware of the ever-tightening financial bind that afflicts all English churches, most painfully, of course, the cathedrals. Nobody who can read can escape the knowledge, for at the entrance to every cathedral the pressing need for more money to "repair and restore the fabric" is spelled out in bold figures of pounds sterling. Nor can anybody deny that the need is genuine. The financial stringencies through which the nation has passed for many decades, the deleterious effect of climate and polluted air upon the ancient stone, and the mounting cost of such monumental repairs, all conspire to make the present situation critical. Hence the appeals, typified by that at Ely (which is in even worse condition than most cathedrals) : a program of urgent repairs, which cost over £60,000, has now been completed; but "these operations have shown up other grave defects which must be dealt with in the order of their urgency. . . . This year's programme of repairs [to the west porch] will cost not less than £12,000." *Please* give.—The sum is modest compared with the figures posted in other cathedrals. But all deans and chapters lead lives of quiet economic desperation.

The current appeals are backstopped by the frequent testimony which tablets on the walls bear to the liberality of other ages. The evidence they provide of the value then receivable from a modest expenditure must sadden every hard-pressed bishop. A tablet in the nave at Ely, for instance, reads: "1676. Roger Clopton Rector of Downham Gave two hundred pounds By which the greatest Part of the Nave of this Church was Paved." And at Winchester, on walls not far from the tablets commemorating the valor of the Hampshire regiments in several modern wars, are longer ones, ledger pages in stone and brass, giving statistics of the major reconstruction work done on the building at the end of the nineteenth century and the beginning of the twentieth, with precise statements of the cost expressed in proud, undevalued British money.

I concede that it is a little unreasonable to be offended by the constant intrusion of account-book mentality and values in the sublime realm of tracery and fan vaulting. After all, there is venerable precedent for it. The great medievalist G. G. Coulton reminds us that between 1229 and 1367 alone, English bishops found it necessary to issue eleven separate injunctions against the holding of markets in churchyards and churches themselves. "Bishop after bishop had thundered in vain . . . against those who 'turned the house of prayer into a den of thieves.' " A bishop in 1560 suggested that the old (pre-Fire) St. Paul's was, among other things, a virtual all-purpose financial exchange: "The south alley [aisle] for Popery and usury, the north for simony, and the horse-fair in the midst for all kinds of bargains, meetings, brawlings, murders, conspiracies, and the font for ordinary payments of money, as well known to all men as the beggar knows his bush." Under Cromwell, shops were set up in the portico.

Even when outright commercialism was frowned upon within the sacred walls, it was slipped in through the side door, in the guise of piety. In the north transept of Southwark Cathedral, London, is a colorful monument to Lyonell Lockyer, a pharmacist who died in 1670 at the age of seventy-two. This estimable citizen is shown resting on one elbow, in the seventeenth-century mode of sepulchral repose, sumptuously attired in robe and full wig. The epitaph is inclined to praise the product more than the person:

> *Here Lockyer lies interr'd, enough; his name*
> *Speakes one hath few competitors in fame;*
> *A name, soe Great, soe Generalle may scorne*
> *Inscriptions w$^{ch}$ doe vulgar tombs adorne:*
> *A diminution tis, to write in verse*
> *His eulogies, w$^{ch}$ moste mens mouthes rehearse.*
> *His virtues & his* PILLS *are soe well known,*
> *That envy can't confine them under stone,*
> *But they'll survive his dust and not expire*
> *Till all things else at th'universall fire.*
> *This verse is lost, his* PILL *Embalmes him safe*
> *To future times without an Epitaph.*

Age, if nothing else, exempts such ecclesiastically tolerated commercial messages from the general censure. One does not begrudge old Lockyer whatever additional revenue his heirs and assigns may have collected as a result of this posthumous plug.

But still—! The guidebook- and postcard-stalls found at the rear of every cathedral except Coventry (where they are relegated to a separate adjacent shop, as at Westminster Abbey) are innocuous enough, though I did find unseemly the haste with

which the attendants at St. Patrick's, Dublin, set up their tables
of printed ware and color slides while the last notes of the morning service were still echoing—this directly beneath the memorials to Dean Swift and his Stella. One may buy or one may not.
Restricting freedom of movement, however, is another thing.
The visitor has to pay to go up, into the tower or the dome, as at
St. Paul's, and he has to pay to go down, into the crypt. In
Westminster Abbey the whole east end, containing the principal
historical and architectural grandeurs—the royal chapels, the
sanctuary, the central shrine of Edward the Confessor, the
chapels of the saints Edmund, Nicholas, Paul, and John the
Baptist—is out of bounds to the casual stroller: two shillings,
please. (Inflation note: Hawthorne was charged sixpence in
1855.) And to magnify the crassness of the system, at the entrance
to this magnificent region sits a verger operating a genuine movie-
theater ticket dispenser, from whose brass slot, when money has
changed hands and the mechanism is activated, spits a tongue of
ordinary tickets. This is a more sophisticated arrangement than
can be found in provincial cathedrals, where the roll of tickets to
the undercroft where sleep the happy dead is out in the open and
the attendant tears segments from it by hand, as if he were selling trips on a Ferris wheel.

Again a concession: things are worse on the Continent. Not
only do some cathedrals reserve certain of their treasures, in the
English mode, for the sight of those who pay (at Ghent the
charge to see the Van Eycks' "Mystic Lamb" is five francs) : sometimes, as at St. Bavo's Church in Haarlem and Roskilde Cathedral near Copenhagen, one cannot even enter the building without paying. But the great English churches also charged
admission at one time. In 1823 Charles Lamb found himself
"excluded; turned out, like a dog, or some profane person, into
the common street" because, the choral service being over, visitors were not allowed to stay in Westminster Abbey except upon
payment of a fee. In the October *London Magazine,* in the course
of an open "Letter to Robert Southey, Esq." (this portion was

reprinted under the title "The Tombs in the Abbey" in the *Last Essays of Elia*), Lamb begged Southey to campaign against the outrage "till the doors of Westminster Abbey be no longer closed against the decent, though low-in-purse, enthusiast, or blameless devotee, who must commit an injury against his family economy, if he would be indulged with a bare admission within its walls." "In no part of our beloved Abbey now," he declared, "can a person find entrance (out of service time) under the sum of *two shillings.*" Nor, Lamb continued, was the practice confined to the Abbey. "A respected friend of ours, during his late visit to the metropolis, presented himself for admission to St. Paul's. At the same time a decently clothed man, with as decent a wife, and child, were bargaining for the same indulgence. The price was only twopence each person. The poor but decent man hesitated, desirous to go on; but there were three of them, and he turned away reluctantly. Perhaps he wished to have seen the tomb of Nelson. Perhaps the Interior of the Cathedral was his object. But in the state of his finances, even sixpence might reasonably seem too much. Tell the Aristocracy of the country," he implored Southey; " . . . instruct them of what value these insignificant pieces of money, these minims to their sight, may be to their humbler brethren. Shame these Sellers out of the Temple!"

Well, they were not shamed. Public opinion forced them to move their money boxes from the portal, which was of course an improvement; but they simply set up shop at other locations. At St. Paul's, for example, the principal feature of the crypt is accessible only to those who pay sixpence to descend to the lower regions: the Duke of Wellington's incredible funeral car, an eighteen-ton monstrosity with the grace of a Sherman tank, twenty-seven feet long, ten wide, and seventeen high, all black except for the names of the Duke's famous victories encircled by gilt laurel wreaths, a riot of allegory and funereal pomp so heavy it broke through the street during the procession.

At the Abbey, in addition to the two-shilling charge for admission to the sanctuary and chapels, there are separate fees to view the waxworks (the lifelike effigies once carried in the funeral processions of royalty: like the funeral car, they are worth the price of admission) and to enter the chapter house. For the latter sixpence one is lent a pair of filthy flannel slippers to fit over his shoes, so as to protect the seven-hundred-year-old tiles laid into the floor.

Elsewhere, the reserved specialty may be brasses. At Ely, a keen amateur of brass-rubbing may, "on payment of fees stated to the verger on duty," rub to his heart's content a brass dating from 1554 or 1614 for ten shillings, or one dating merely from 1845 at half price. At Norwich, indulgence of one's hobby or sentiment comes cheaper: permission to sketch or photograph Edith Cavell's grave costs but three-and-six.

In view of this widespread and unabashed zeal for cashing in on the tourist trade, even if sanctified by the near-hopeless aim to make ends meet in a penurious age, I find the symbolism at Chester very satisfying. There, the local Barclay's bank is built right against the wall of the cathedral. No armored car is required to transfer the day's take to safe secular hands.

There is irony, too, in the fact that every cathedral has one or two chapels set aside for rest, prayer, and meditation—small refuges dedicated to serving what, in the beginning, was the sole and exalted purpose of the whole building. Now that cathedrals are vast museums, echoing to the tramp of tourist shoes and the clink of extra-attraction shillings, spirituality is restricted to a few side areas. No admission fee is charged at these chapels, but attached to a column there is usually a box which will accept free-will offerings.

*The Cotswolds, near Broadway, Worcestershire*

§◗§◗§◗

---

## 14

---

# Driving in England

UNQUESTIONABLY the best way to see England is by car. Motoring
makes possible a wholly flexible schedule, amenable to every con-
tingency and whim; you can linger when you want, change your
plan at every tempting signpost if you wish. It is far preferable to
any pre-packaged, regimented coach tour—so, at least, must be
the opinion of anyone who subscribes, as I do, to the forthright
sentiment of the diarist John Byng, writing in 1787: "box'd up
in a stinking coach, dependent on the hours and guidance of
others, submitting to miserable associates, and obliged to hear
their nonsense, is great wretchedness!"

It is true that one can still use trains to advantage in England.
On the main railway lines the service is excellent, far superior to
anything America now possesses. The trains are frequent, fast,
and comfortable, and many English people use them for distance
traveling. But, as in America, hundreds of miles of branch lines
have been abandoned in the past few years, so that if you go by
rail to the chief cities and towns, you still have the problem of
getting on from there to the outlying village church, manor
house, literary site, or whatever other place you seek. Buses ply
nearly every road, even in the remotest country, and like other

forms of local transportation, they have the advantage of bring-
ing the tourist into the midst of the nation's daily life; you
mingle with the shoppers, schoolgirls, laborers who ride the bus
every day, and, if camera-less, find yourself unobtrusively assimilated into the scene. But bus service is often infrequent and on
some days, on some rural routes, it simply doesn't exist. It is
better on market days (but you have to know when they occur in
the various towns) and worse on early closing days (ditto). You
can waste much valuable time, too often at a shelterless stop in
the countryside during a heavy shower, if you depend on buses to
move about.

The expense of hiring a car is not great (petrol is priced high,
but you get an imperial gallon for your shillings) ; rental cars are
available in all cities; and the roads are beautifully maintained
—a tradition stemming, perhaps, from the early and mid-
nineteenth century, when work on the roads, chiefly stone-
breaking, was a prerequisite for relief among the able-bodied
unemployed. It was not for nothing that the ingenious John
Loudon McAdam became surveyor-general of metropolitan
roads in 1827. If you seek his monument, consult any road map.
The petrol companies supply excellent ones, sufficiently detailed
for any tourist; a set of five or six covers the whole of England,
Scotland, and Wales, but each part costs a shilling. No free maps,
as in America. But as a compensatory bonus, English roads are
innocent of billboards.

Despite the horror expressed by stay-at-homes who have never
done it—"that driving on the wrong side of the road!"—driving
in England isn't really difficult. Anybody who is about to venture
for the first time into English traffic is well advised, however, to
ask the rental agency to provide him with a "pilot"—a member
of the staff—who can drive him out of the central city and then
supervise him for a little while after he takes the wheel. The
traffic of any large English city can intimidate even the most
experienced American driver if he must accustom himself at the
same time to the driver's seat being on the right and the controls

in equally alien positions, and, what is just as bad, if he must summon up from the dim distant past the art of using a manual gearshift; most British cars don't have automatic transmissions. I admire the temerity of any American driver whose first experience of driving in England some fine summer morning is up London's Arlington Street, alongside the Ritz (behind which my favorite rental agency has one of its West End garages), and into bus-choked Piccadilly, where he has the Hobson's choice of heading toward the maelstrom of Hyde Park Corner in one direction and the clogged narrowness of Piccadilly Circle and its tributary streets in the other. It's a test that separates the professionals from the dilettantes.

But once the strangeness of car and custom has worn off and you are sailing along a suburban "clearway" (arterial thoroughfare: parking strictly banned, sometimes limited access), it's as if you have been driving an English car on English roads all your life. It is surprising how quickly the lifelong habit of driving on the right can be reversed. When everybody else is driving on the left, after the first half-hour or so it seems the most natural thing in the world for you to do too. The rule is simplicity itself: Stay to the *left* except when passing; pass to the *right*. When signs refer to the "near side," remember that's the *left;* the terminology of horse transport dies hard in a country like England. The one maneuver that is likely to revive your American reflexes, with possibly interesting consequences, is the right turn, across oncoming traffic. For some reason, when the turn is completed the instinct is to go to the right side of the new road. Don't. Repeat to yourself, every time you make such a turn, "Turn right . . . but stay *left*."

Roads are always clearly and uniformly marked. If you remain normally alert, there is little danger of making a wrong turn or overshooting the place where you should have turned. Except on the few motorways and the more numerous "dual carriageways" (four-lane divided highways) speed cannot be maintained to American standards. Most main roads are only two lanes wide, without broad shoulders, and in the country many roads are but the width of a single car, with ditches and high hedges on both sides. I know a portion of Devon, in fact, where byroads leading to the sea are nothing more than perpetually dark lanes snaking like tunnels between faces of rock supplemented by overarching hedgerows and trees. (Admittedly, this is one point in favor of seeing some parts of the country by local bus: the landscape behind the hedges is visible only to passengers on the top deck.)

On the whole, the motorist who is out to experience the English scene with the greatest comfort should consider shun-piking as often as the map permits. The secondary roads, designated by the prefix B before the number, are as well maintained as the chief, or A-prefixed, routes. They are not necessarily the shortest routes between two points, but they offer fewer hazards. They carry far less traffic, including lorries; because there are fewer oncoming cars, it is easier to pass cyclists with safety. Even though they are usually more circuitous and narrower than the A-routes, in the long run they really demand less of the driver. And they are certainly to be recommended as the most intimate way of seeing the real England.

Unlike their continental neighbors, the British don't have facilities for working the speed demon out of their souls along protracted straightaways. It is perhaps to this frustration that they owe their penchant for taking chances; if they can't really speed very long at a time, they can behave as if they wanted to. They weave in and out of traffic with a fine recklessness that appalls the American; they are more given to passing on hills, it seems, than they are to passing on a straight road; and blind curves seem to rouse the same sporting instinct that led the outnumbered R.A.F. to take on the Luftwaffe in 1940. They can hardly be blamed, for there is a greater proportion of slow-moving vehicles on their roads than on American, one reason being that the British do not scrap their moribund cars until they fall apart. A second reason is that there are more slow drivers on the roads. Watching them behind the wheel, the elderly in particular, one receives the impression that the British are self-conscious about being drivers, as if the motor car were an amusing novelty that no really sensible person should take seriously. Their attitude is a curious mixture of distrust, self-consciousness, even embarrassment. Their posture contains elements of both off-handedness and severe concentration.

Perhaps the relation between man and car in Britain is epitomized by the fact that some men wear leather gloves to drive, even in high summer—as if they were holding reins. And, come to think of it, the men who pilot the fleets of excursion coaches which are always on the go in England customarily wear smocks that are the lineal descendants of the Edwardians' motoring dusters. But this aura of anachronism is not limited to cars; it applies, I think, to all machinery. The ordinary Britons one sees in some relation to an engine—a hotel maid with her vacuum cleaner (which she invariably calls a "Hoover"), a construction worker with his pneumatic drill—look uneasy, and treat their labor-saving appliances with a certain apologetic gingerliness. Although the Industrial Revolution was born in this country, the inhabitants clearly have not come to terms with it two centuries later. Besoms rather than any more efficient contrivances, such as brooms, are still standard equipment in parks and gardens.

That is why English bicyclists strike one as more truly belonging to the landscape than do their compatriots behind the wheel of a car. But however authentically indigenous they may be, they are also road hazards, sedately pedaling along with never a backward look, let alone a mirror, and taking their ample share of the road as if they owned it. (After all, if priority of possession is nine-tenths of the law, they do.) Bicycles are becoming less numerous in Britain as small cars and motorcycles come within the reach of more people. But there are still plenty of cyclists around—elderly clergymen and laborers with clips around their trousered ankles, and middle-aged and more-than-middle-aged women in village and country—and if you sometimes think cycles really are vanishing from the English scene, you should get caught in the hordes of them that emerge from factories at lunch-time or at the end of the day.

Neither in town nor in country is sufficient provision made for off-street parking. (In some places, such as Oxford and Cambridge, finding overnight parking is harder than earning a first-class degree in *literae humaniores*.) Consequently there is a great deal of random parking in the traffic lanes of streets and highways: evidently the practice is entirely lawful. This is even greater a hazard, perhaps, than the prevalence of cyclists. Between the two, the driver is forced to leave his proper lane many times oftener than in the United States.

British traffic engineering has lagged far behind that in America and on the Continent. Most important intersections in the country and often in metropolitan areas are of the kind known in America as traffic circles and in Britain as "roundabouts." They are useful in that they can show young American drivers how things were back home in the 1930's. The basic rule in navigating them is that traffic entering the circle must yield to traffic which is already inside.

There are relatively few cloverleaves or other such sophistications. Nor are there roadside rest areas in the American style; the closest approach to these are "lay-bys," which are simply extra paved widths of road where cars and lorries can pull off and park. Petrol stations are not nearly as numerous along the roads as in America, and only in the past few years have they begun to offer the facilities the American motorist takes for granted.

As for food on the road—well, the less said, the better. There is no English equivalent of Howard Johnson's, more's the pity; whatever reservations one may have about the chain restaurant in the United States, there are plenty of English occasions when one would be glad to settle for even a respectable drive-in. The highway traveler finds, in general, only roadside inns, which may or may not serve snacks or full meals, which may or may not be sufficiently inviting to enter, and which in any case are open only at certain hours; places—the word is chosen with care—

which offer lunches and teas in the larger towns; and, on a few main routes, lorry drivers' "caffs," which are no more luxurious than the typical American truck stops and beyond question offer no hope of the superior cup of coffee the latter are reputed to supply.

One also has the option of eating alfresco, as many motorists and cyclists do. The hours of eleven and four see the roads suddenly depleted of through traffic; virtually all right-thinking English drivers pull their bundle-laden cars or family-size motorcycles toward the verge (not necessarily all the way off the road, as the American motorist would desire, but a little farther from the center line than when they are in motion) and extract from somewhere in the mass of impedimenta all the proper components of a tailgate tea—folding chairs, table, kettle, portable stove, teacups, cutlery, parcels from the chain grocer, even a morning paper or two. And there, in sybaritic comfort, repose the family from mumbling Granny to mewling infant, replenishing the inner man and savoring the delights of nature. The gentle rain may fall and passing cars may swerve to avoid this poor man's *fête champêtre,* but the happy holidayers are enjoying their life and hard-won leisure the way custom dictates. On the whole, if he does not care for this kind of improvisation, the pampered American motorist is well advised not to get hungry while driving in England. Even if he does have an occasional pang, the limited alternatives at his disposal to alleviate it would suggest he'd better bear it until he can acquire a proper high tea or dinner at the end of the day.

While accumulating considerably less than half or even a third of the mileage an American is in the habit of piling up on a single cross-country day, the exploratory driver in England can cover an extraordinary variety of locales between breakfast and early dinner. In a day of unhurried motoring it is possible to drive through or touch upon as many as seven English counties, as I have done, using Oxford as my base: Oxfordshire, Warwickshire, Worcestershire, Gloucestershire, Wiltshire, Berkshire,

Somerset—a noble array. Similarly, one can start off in the morning from a spa hotel in Derbyshire, cross the Pennines (which resemble the terrain of West Virginia) , burst out into high rolling moors with grazing sheep herds and views of great distances, thread through the industrial periphery of Manchester and Liverpool at the lunch hour, and arrive in good time for tea at a town in the Lake District, where descendants of Wordsworth's philosophical peasants still cultivate their farmland in sight of the Irish Sea.

But in the interests of realism it is necessary to add that there can be, and are, frustrating delays. The weather is not a major hazard, at least in summer; the occasional downpours, though so torrential as to reduce visibility almost to zero, don't slow down traffic on the country highways. The efficiently educated American driver, however, feels himself an oddity when he drives in heavy rain with headlights on and no native motorist bothers to do so. The English have a curious aversion to turning them on even at night, in the towns at any rate. A few years ago a provincial city required the use of headlights, and considerable surprise was expressed when the night mortality rate sharply decreased. In matters like these, the British are dedicated empiricists. A Bristol policeman in a well-worn patrol car once flagged me down for innocently running a series of stop signs. "Me heart was in me mouth," he said after forgiveness was induced by the "Visitor to Britain" sticker on my windscreen; and by way of conversation—and to impress upon me that stop signs mean business—he went on to explain that they are not installed at a city intersection, in Bristol anyway, unless and until there has been at least one fatal accident there.

It is wise to avoid the late-afternoon rush hour in towns of any size. The local drivers have all the advantage: they know the geography and the customs of the road, such as when and where to change lanes in anticipation of a turn and how to avoid long delays at busy junctions where there are no traffic lights. Coping with swarms of home-bound cars and cycles in the narrow, winding streets of a strange town, while looking at the same time for a hotel whose location is completely unknown, does not contribute to the holiday mood. Half an hour of driving in an English town between five and six p.m. is more nerve-racking than a whole day on the open road.

In the industrial regions the highways are totally inadequate for the volume of heavy traffic they must bear. On the tortuous road between Leeds and Manchester, for example, one is usually fated to crawl for many miles behind lumbering, diesel-smoking lorries, through landscape, in addition, which neither soothes the eye nor brings peace to the spirit. Moreover, although bypasses are being built as fast as the national economy allows, many towns still have to route all traffic through their constricted business quarters. Rain or shine, in the country centers—the market, cathedral, and county towns, the last-named being the capitals of miniature states, if English shires can be so called—traffic jams can be relied upon throughout the day. Apart from such obvious explanations as the layout, or more precisely the unplanned development, of the main streets centuries before motor traffic was dreamed of, the principal reason for the continuous daytime congestion of town streets is the lack of refrigeration in a great many homes. Housewives have to shop for food several times as often as Americans do, and because there are as yet very few shopping centers on the outskirts, women in quest of a lovely bit of mutton gravitate to the town center in red-cheeked, scarf-covered, stringbag-toting crowds. The cycles, cars, and buses that bring still more of them in from the outlying areas clog the labyrinthine streets that are seldom more than two British-made cars wide. And because the sidewalks are proportionately narrow, much of the pedestrian traffic spills into the roadway. Here and there along the curb, light vans are parked in the line of traffic, despite "No Standing" signs, while their drivers make deliveries to the shops. So while at the town's main intersection, unseen because still a devious quarter-mile away, a policeman impartially adjudicates the claims of the clots and streams of traffic that

converge on him from several directions and the tall buses pant
as their motors idle and their drivers seize the occasion to clean
their fingernails with matchsticks, the touring motorist abides his
frustration and waits also. He would be well advised to improve
each such shining quarter-hour by studying his map and preparing to look sharp at the next turning, where a sign suddenly
revealed by a momentary break in traffic may dictate a drastic
change of course.

Among the nation's most dependable traffic jams, at any time
of day, is that in Salisbury, whose topography seems especially
well designed to inhibit movement. This crush is one of the most
venerable in England; Dickens described it in *Martin Chuzzlewit*
(1844), and, allowing for the superficial changes wrought by the
passing of more than a century, it is still recognizable from his
pages. In certain other towns, however, the traffic-clog periodically undergoes a change of venue, in the manner of the celebrated permanent floating crap game in *Guys and Dolls*. There
used to be a monumental daily backup in the main road of
Tonbridge, Kent; indeed, the line of traffic immobilized from
end to end of the shopping district was one of the finest in the
kingdom. The last time I approached it, fully prepared to inch
along for a half-hour or so, it wasn't there; a sign diverted
through traffic along peripheral streets. But my regret, such as it
was, for my old acquaintance was short-lived. In a minute or so,
following directions, I reached the end of a new queue, caused by
the intersection of the "diversion" road with the highway it re-
joined. The new jam, though relocated, turned out to have all
the splendor of the old. But it was nice to have some different
scenery to contemplate as I waited. Perhaps it was for the sole
sake of variety that the authorities moved their bottleneck;
certainly they were governed by no discernible principle of traffic
engineering.

English traffic jams do have this advantage to the curious
traveler: they enforce upon him a leisured, and therefore a
minute and critical, inspection of the scene. No quick succession,

now, of old churches, hedgerows, lodges at the gates of country places, thatched cottages, and crossroad inns, such as constitute the montage of a thirty-mile-an-hour traversal of the countryside. Esthetically speaking, what one sees when caught in a queue may not be worth close inspection (a dour, run-down semi-detached house, built in the worst style favored in 1875, with a scraggly excuse for a front garden and a damp-stained "bed and breakfast" sign in the window, for example). But it's undeniably a typical manifestation of the country one has come to examine— the natives have to live with it—and no less picturesque than an American gas station erected in the reign of Herbert Hoover. Still, it is regrettable that no traffic jam ever occurs in clear view of the west front of a cathedral. How convenient and forgivable a bottleneck would be at Wells, where one could use the time to study at leisure those marvelous rows of three hundred medieval figures which form a sculptural gallery of sacred and profane history!

Anyway, whether moving or stationary, the traveler sees England best from his car. And if his nerves are accustomed to American competitive driving, he has nothing to fear in England. He will, in fact, feel quite at home as he returns to London from a fortnight in the smiling countryside. Let him approach the metropolis from the south at the rush hour, through Mitcham, Tooting, Balham, Clapham, and intermediate congestions, and his sense of having been here before will never be stronger.

*Pub signs*

$9.9.9.$

---

## 15

---

# Bed, Breakfast, Beer,
# and Britannia

I

AFTER A protracted postwar period when the quality of English hotel accommodations was rather too austere for American comfort, conditions have much improved. In London and a number of the provincial cities, especially where there is a steady expense-account trade, there now are hotels designed to foster in the American traveler the illusion that he is back in Kansas City. Some, indeed, chiefly in London's West End, are owned and operated by American chains. Others belong to British chains or holding companies. The Ind Coope brewing people, for example, own a number of provincial hotels, as does the J. Arthur Rank film and television combine. The glossiest specimens boast a well-appointed private bath attached to every bedroom (a luxury found in very few English hotels built before the Second World War), and the bedrooms themselves are adequately furnished, even to the television set in the corner. In general, the bathing and sleeping accommodations in such new hostelries are indistinguishable from those at Howard Johnson's Motor Lodges and Holiday Inns.

Some British hotels enable you to eat your cake and have it too: you enjoy the animal comforts of the decadent present, but the past is right outside your window. At the modernized Eastgate Hotel in Lincoln, for example, some bedrooms overlook the magnificent flying buttresses of the cathedral, and in the forecourt, a dozen steps away from the car park, is a carefully fenced excavation where is exposed and preserved a fragment of the Roman wall. The new Wessex Hotel at Winchester, a fortunate acquisition in a town which desperately needed a decent hotel, is built in the very shadow of the cathedral. And at the high-rise Five Bridges in Gateshead, part of the cluster of heavy manufacturing towns centering in Newcastle, you can throw back the curtains of your cheerful modern room in the morning and find yourself surveying the grimy industrial northeast just as people saw it a century and more ago: a panorama of old workers' tenements, stretching up hill and down as far as you can see, their countless bunches of chimney pots pouring forth smoke and their every aspect bespeaking the monotony and resignation which must envelop the lives of these families as they did their great-grandparents'. And when you look in another direction you see stacks belching still more smoke to befoul the Northumbrian air—the evil "Storm-Cloud" which Ruskin found emblematic of modern industrial society. If you open your window, your nose is assaulted by the pungent fumes of burning coke and coal, and it, too, is back in the Victorian era, when cities like Newcastle forged the sinews of the British Empire and multiplied human misery at home. And then you close the window and go down to an excellent twentieth-century breakfast.

For those who prefer a less emphatically contemporary atmosphere inside their hotels, Britain offers plenty of choice, a choice that involves a delicate balancing of values, solid comforts on the one hand and intangible flavor on the other. Certainly one should stay at least once in a monument to English luxury living as it was known in the earlier part of the century, before two world wars, the depression of the thirties, and the austerity of the fifties and sixties made it an anachronism. In such hotels as the Queen's in Cheltenham—probably the best surviving specimens of the genre are in the watering places and seaside resorts— bygone opulence still puts on a brave face. The public rooms are large, the palms are potted, the attendants are in full fig, and the rates are fully as high as those at a hotel built five years ago. It is easy to understand why: these stately Victorian and Edwardian edifices with their lofty ceilings and ample stairwells are monstrously inefficient. No doubt a formidable percentage of the revenue must be earmarked for largely wasted heating and for maintaining square-footage whose space/patron ratio is so out of kilter that it would make an American hotelier weep. Such modernization as has been accomplished has been largely confined to the public areas, and the bedrooms remain essentially as they were forty years ago. Unless one has an insatiable desire to live back in the years of the Eternal Garden Party, these whited relics of past glory are best avoided once they have been sampled.

But at least they offer space and dignity, attributes which cannot be found in any of the more modest hotels that abound in, say, London's Bloomsbury, Bayswater, and South Kensington, and in the provincial towns. About all they have to recommend them is their cheapness, and there's not really as much difference as one might imagine between their rates and those of more comfortable establishments. They are usually small places, sometimes created by throwing together several houses in neighborhoods which once were upper middle-class residential districts. Because their proprietors seldom have the resources to effect any major improvements beyond repainting and installing a slightly less hesitant lift, they usually are shabby and dark. Their carpets are threadbare and the drapes, if you happen to brush against them, prove to be laden with dust. They have few private baths, and the ones you share with the other people on your floor preserve the plumbing that was modish when Asquith was prime minister, even to the pull-chain. Their bedrooms normally are supplied with well-worn, unmatched furniture that is offensive to the eye and unreceptive to the body—beds, chairs, and tables of no style at all, or of styles too plainly belonging to the misbegotten interim between late-Victorian antiquity and post-Churchillian modernity. Freestanding wardrobes, clumsily occupying precious floor space, do duty as closets.

Almost worst of all (and this, I am afraid, is true of the great majority of English hotels, excepting only the most modern or most thoroughly modernized), the illumination in the bedrooms is feeble and inconvenient. If there is a lamp anywhere near the bed, it contains no more than a twenty-five-watt bulb. If there is a lamp at the head of the bed, it probably doesn't work. More often the lighting comes from a fringed artifact of the *Chu-Chin-Chow* epoch dangling on a frayed wire from the center of the ceiling, or from rickety bridge lamps whose use the management discourages by putting them in the most inconvenient spots and, to make sure, loosening the wires or socket. If you like to read in your bedroom, you'd better bring your own equipment.

Moreover, the stairwells of small hotels always have a heavy odor of cooking; and English cooking smells worse than that of other nations. And late in the evening you can smell tomorrow morning's toast being forehandedly burnt in the kitchen.

In many such establishments, which constitute the most numerous type of English hotels, heat is another problem, for each bedroom may be served only by an electric heater or a gas grate which must be kept alive by the periodic insertion of shillings. To the American who regards well-maintained body heat as a normal concomitant of health, the chilliness of English bedrooms, especially in the country, poses a real problem. In the course of a tour I made after the present book was contracted for, to re-survey some of the ground I proposed to discuss, I spent a night in the "annexe" of a country inn not far from Cambridge. Though it was clean enough—most British hotels are—it had no amenities, not even a chair to sit in. The season was mid-May, and East Anglia at night was wretchedly cold. As I deposited my clothes in the oversized wardrobe my teeth chattered and my frame shivered, and I began to wonder whether being discovered a frozen coroner's case in the morning was not an excessive price to pay for authenticating a book. Only when I turned back the down-filled comforter, which, thick though it was, would not have kept me alive overnight, did I discover that Americanization had penetrated even into the English village: underneath the comforter was an electric blanket. Even though it was totally unexpected, it was not wholly alien to the sometimes inexplicable spirit of English innkeeping, for it covered only one half of the double bed. Being alone, I did not have to cope with the problem of who would sleep on the frigid side. In the upshot, the blanket cozily saw me through the night. But memory of the bone-chilling cold from which it had rescued me was still so vivid in the morning that when I wrote up my notes I understandably dated them "19 March" instead of "19 May."

It cannot be denied that, whatever their deficiencies, these minimal-comfort hotels and inns thrust the visitor into the intimate midst of British life-away-from-home. The natives seem to like them, not necessarily because they are cheaper by a few shillings but because, well, they've been around for a long time, it has always been part of the pattern of English life to stay at them, and anyway, what's the matter with them? So this is where respectable English of modest means stay when they come up to London from Devonshire or Northamptonshire or go to the seaside on holiday, and where expatriate families make their headquarters when they are on hard-earned leave from some tropical or antipodean land that once belonged to the Empire. One overhears a great deal of sociological interest concerning contemporary British attitudes and habits of thought, both domestic and overseas, as the people at the next table chat on, undismayed by the beige-flavored meal that is set before them by the underpaid waiter in his frayed uniform.

There is Dickensian entertainment sometimes in the silent

drama of the letter-board at the small hotel's reception desk, where one can observe the flow of correspondence to and from shadowy people. Once I was bemused by a missive addressed to one Mrs. Gubbins, which remained affixed to the board day after day. I waited with much anticipation for it to be collected, so that I could see what a real Mrs. Gubbins looked like. But before she materialized my stay at the hotel terminated (an event unlamented except for this fragment of unfinished business), and I still wonder whether the too perfectly named lady—undoubtedly middle-aged, dowdy, and fattish—may not have been a product of the letter writer's imagination, no more substantial than Sairy Gamp's Mrs. Harris.

One great advantage the tourist enjoys because of Britain's relatively short distances is the easy accessibility of hotels in country towns. Some people prefer for this reason to take each night as it comes, relishing not knowing where they will stay until they are there. But this is too chancy—the English would say "dicey"—for me. Theoretically it is true that if one is disappointed at a certain place there's usually another town or two a few miles away, but its inn may be full also, and although in a pinch there are nearly always crossroad pubs that have a room or two for overnight stays, as well as "bed and breakfast" places which used to be known in the United States as tourist homes, the comforts available at such establishments may be little more than Spartan. It is best, therefore, to telephone ahead. Hotels that belong to one of the chains will call other members for you, but you must pay the toll charge.

In choosing hotels one has the aid of the British automobile clubs' guidebooks, which rate them somewhat in the fashion of the AAA touring guide. But I have found their criteria of acceptability considerably more liberal than the American, and many a country inn that displays the RAC or AA sign and is favorably mentioned in the printed guides proves to be unsatisfactory on one ground or another. In America it would be damned with faint praise as "best available in the vicinity." Probably the best way to find basically agreeable hotel accommodations on the road is to rely wherever possible upon Trust Houses. (These should not be confused with the National Trust, which, as has been mentioned, is an organization dedicated to acquiring and preserving historic buildings and sites. The two have no connection.) The Trust House chain owns two hundred hotels and inns of every size, age, and description throughout Britain. Its policy is to maintain the individual personality of each house, whether it is the big Edwardian-elegant Randolph in Oxford or a ten-room former coaching stop, built in the seventeenth century, in Wiltshire. But the central company lays down standards of quality and practice to which each landlord must adhere, so that regardless of the elaborateness or modesty of the house, the traveler can be reasonably sure of cleanliness, decent food and service, and whatever level of comfort the scale of the place affords. I have acquired the habit of associating Trust Houses with the faint odor of fresh paint, which I think is a recommendation.

Especially in the country, English hotels are not merely a series of *pieds-à-terre* between adventures; they are an indispensable part of the English adventure itself. The floors of old inns sometimes slope precipitously, to the initial alarm of the guest until he realizes that they have been out of plumb for several hundred years and the building hasn't collapsed yet. Sometimes the walls slant too. The lintels often are so low as to deliver the American of average height a sharp crack on the head if he fails to heed where he is going. And, what with the remodeling and unsystematic enlargements that have taken place over the centuries, many hotels have features of the maze at Hampton Court. "There are long corridors," as Hawthorne writes, "an intricate arrangement of passages, and up-and-down meandering of staircases amid which it would be no marvel to encounter some forgotten guest who had gone astray a hundred years ago, and was still seeking for his bedroom while the rest of his generation were in their graves. There is no exaggerating the confusion of mind that seizes upon a stranger in the bewildering geography of a great old-fashioned English inn."

To the hazard of losing one's way in these erratic halls hung with old engravings and oil paintings of local interest may be added the occasional circumstance that the bedroom lies one or two steps lower than the corridor by which it is reached, a fact that the guest does well to bear in mind if he wants to avoid a sprained ankle. And in the famous Mitre Inn at Oxford, a labyrinth if there ever was one, at least one W.C. serves also as a fire exit, and is so marked.

At another old Oxford inn, the Golden Cross, a narrow wagon and coach entrance leads from the busy Cornmarket into an enclosed yard where, with the traffic noises suddenly cut off, it is easily possible to imagine oneself back in the sixteenth century. An even better place to reconstruct the setting in which the first Elizabethan plays were produced is the half-timbered New Inn at Gloucester. ("New" indeed! It was built about 1450, by a monk of the Abbey of St. Peter, to accommodate pilgrims to the shrine of Edward II in what was then the abbey church and is now Gloucester Cathedral.) Although I have seen no evidence that the London-based acting companies which often visited Glouces-ter actually used this innyard, it is easy to envision their doing so. They would have erected a "scaffold" (platform) at one end, and on the well-worn cobblestones the earliest denizens of the pit would have crowded to watch the show, while their betters looked on in comfort from the surrounding galleries which gave access to the bedrooms. The New Inn is an even more compli-cated structure than the Mitre, and some of its carefully pre-served features, such as the massive ceiling beams, affirm its great age. Unfortunately its picturesqueness has been exploited for all it's worth. Most of the ground-floor space, including what were originally the stables and other outbuildings, has been converted into no fewer than a dozen distinctively decorated "bars," more than half of which are devoted to drink rather than to food. Notwithstanding the contrived quaintness of the place, it de-serves a visit, for beneath the twentieth-century commercial veneer the basic structure retains its fifteenth-century character.

An inn of even greater antiquity which has more successfully resisted vulgarization is the frequently pictured George and Pilgrims at Glastonbury. This also originated as a primitive motel for pilgrims, in this case visitors to the nearby abbey, now in eloquent ruins, with its legendary associations with Joseph of Arimathea. Its stone façade and gateway remain as they were in the time of Edward IV, and though the interior has been reasonably modernized, the medieval flavor is retained in the use of the word                   on the doors of the W.C.'s. The lattice-windowed room which now serves as one of the lounges is also part of the original fabric. It has an affectionate place in my memory because I discovered there, some ten years ago, the refreshing quality of gin and bitter lime. Unlike bitter lemon, which has become as popular a mixer in America as in Britain, bitter lime seems not to have caught on; in fact, barmen in pubs now hardly even recognize the term. This is a pity.

"To one who has been long in city pent"—Keats's words are apropos enough, because he was a lover of inns and wrote part of *Endymion* at one, the still-flourishing Burford Bridge Hotel in Surrey, not far from George Meredith's home at Box Hill—there is nothing more restorative than a night in a quiet, well-kept English country inn, where the fragrance of the adjacent fields and woods floats into one's room. I think of the Brambletye Inn at Forest Row, near East Grinstead in Sussex, outside which, though the village is less than forty miles from London, cows moo and roosters crow. That it figures in the Sherlock Holmes story of Black Peter is merely an incidental dividend. I think too of the Red Lion at Grantchester, whose dining room has on one side a mural reminding one of Rupert Brooke's celebration of the village and on the other side French doors leading into a garden from which one can strike along the public footpath through the pastures and across the stiles to Cambridge, just as Brooke often did.

So far as I know, there is no definitive guide to English hotels

with literary associations, but there should be. It is not hard to
dispense with the ones which, on grounds firm or tenuous, claim
patronage by virtue of Mr. Pickwick's having stayed there, because so many others have more solid literary ties. There is, for
example, the Pheasant Inn near Winterslow, on the London-
Salisbury road, where Hazlitt often stayed and wrote between
1818 and 1828. It was known simply as "The Hut" in his time.
The Lion in Shrewsbury, a Trust House with a Tudor core and
eighteenth-century additions, greets the wayfarer with a neatly
printed broadside which states, among other facts, that De Quincey once slept in the assembly room when every other room was
occupied, and that Dickens stayed here with "Phiz," his illustra-
tor, and wrote his daughter appreciatively of the "strangest little
rooms," the windows bulging out over the street, and the "little
open gallery with plants in it." Paganini conducted two concerts
here, and in this same assembly room a generation later Jenny
Lind sang. Evidently it is not known at the Lion that Hawthorne
and his family were guests on September 4–6, 1855. Hawthorne
was delighted by Shrewsbury, "the finest old town that I have
seen, . . . retaining more of the stately and quaint old houses"
than any other he had visited—a judgment I had reached independently, years before I encountered his long, appreciative description of Shrewsbury. Of all the towns I know, Shrewsbury,
with its twisting and sometimes hilly streets, old churches, and
unusual number of half-timbered shops and houses, comes closest
to the American's specification of what an old English town
should look like. I recommend to the present landlord of the
Lion, for future promotional use, Hawthorne's forthright decla-
ration, "I never knew such pleasant walking as in old streets like
those of Shrewsbury."

I have especially grateful memories of two nights spent in Dorchester at the Antelope, whose name and tradition, if not the
actual building, are five centuries old. It had recently been re-
decorated, and my room was immaculate, spacious, and equipped
with a radio; I remember drowsily listening to a broadcast of the

Wimbledon tennis match and then going downstairs to a good
dinner of fried Dorset ham. Later I read that exactly a century
earlier, the minor Victorian poet William Allingham had
stopped here. "Rooms not good," he wrote in his diary (I was
pleased to know first-hand that they had much improved in a
hundred years), but he added that the hotel did "produce a pint
of good port at dinner," which, in view of the fact that his
companion was Tennyson, was a not unimportant consideration.
Neither poet, refilling his glass, could have known, because
Hardy had not yet revealed it, that thirty years earlier Lucetta
Le Sueur, in *The Mayor of Casterbridge,* was aboard the Bristol
coach which changed horses in this very innyard: she had made
an appointment with Henchard that she did not keep.

Neither of these literary associations was called to my attention
when I was in the hotel, a dereliction, perhaps, on the part of the
management. I know, however, of one London hotel which has
good reason for overlooking its accidental role in literary history.
It is today, as it was in the moment of its unsolicited notoriety, a
most respectable establishment; it stands on the corner of Sloane
and Pont Streets and caters to a clientele of unblemished repute.
I have stayed there myself more than once. But nowhere on the
premises, understandably, can one find a framed copy of John
Betjeman's lines:

> *A thump, and a murmur of voices—*
>   *("Oh why must they make such a din?")*
> *As the door of the bedroom swung open*
>   *And* TWO PLAIN CLOTHES *POLICEMEN came in:*
>
> *"Mr. Woilde, we 'ave come for tew take yew*
>   *Where felons and criminals dwell:*
> *We must ask yew tew leave with us quoietly*
>   *For this* IS *the Cadogan Hotel."*

The room, according to the records, was Number 58. Mine was
53. A near miss.

II

Within modern memory, English food has oftener been dis-
paraged than praised. But if Britain is not yet, and perhaps
never will be, a gastronome's paradise, the chances of finding a
decent meal are considerably better than they were ten years ago.
This is not to say they are as good as in other countries; it merely
means that things have been looking up recently. The subject is
a delicate one, demanding judicious rather than enthusiastic
treatment. In what follows, I do not wish to discourage the
reader who, in Dr. Johnson's words, "seldom thinks with more
earnestness of anything than he does of his dinner." I merely
would suggest that in England there are more dependable and
more easily accessible delights than those of the stomach.

This working principle would, I think, be accepted by all who
have sat down to meals in English hotels and restaurants over a
fair length of time. But of course the specifics are another matter:
*chacun à son dégoût.* My disrelish for the sloppy, tasteless sub-
stances that provide the official climax to a truly indigenous English meal—trifle, flan, pudding, or whatever they call those flac-
cid concoctions—is not, I am aware, shared by some people whose
palates I respect. On the other hand, my honest passion for a
breakfast brace of oily kippers would doubtless revolt every
American of the sort who fears that he will be unable to obtain
his customary cornflakes so far from home. (His apprehension is
groundless. Some of the standard American breakfast cereals are
always available, though not the innumerable variations on the
theme which issue from Battle Creek, and in addition there is
real porridge, such as figures in the old nursery rhymes.) To my
own taste, there is no better way to launch a busy English day
than with kippers and plenty of tea and buttered and marma-
laded toast. If kippers happen not to be on the card, sausages
and/or bacon with fried tomatoes are equally acceptable. A substantial breakfast is always advisable, because large-scale re-

fueling often cannot be accomplished until dinner. In the mean-
time, only fairly light lunches can be had at noon (see below),
and tea, involving cocktail-party-size sandwiches and buns and
sweet cakes, beginning at four o'clock. "High tea," a more elaborate meal, adds cold cuts of meat and salad.

Dinner is a rather iffy proposition. In London and the larger
towns ample selection is available, especially because of the
abundance of specialized places—seafood restaurants, Italian,
French, Chinese, and Indian establishments. Strictly British dining places tend to have less variety in their menus and less flavor
in their food. Although the much-deplored brussels sprout and its
congener, boiled cabbage, are not nearly as universal as the popular notion assumes, I find equal cause for depression when I
contemplate the choice of soups with which a native meal begins:
the thick or "brown" soup is too thick (it's glutenous, and it
*tastes* brown), and the thin soup is too thin (i.e., it's simply
flavored water). The meats are generally acceptable, if nothing
more, but outside the restaurants devoted to it, the seafood is
nothing remarkable; the plaice of which surrounding waters
have an apparently inexhaustible supply has no more taste than
the fish you extract from a supermarket freezer. But the taste of
food in general is not a matter of much concern to the British, as
witness their habit of thoroughly mashing together whatever soft
foods they have on their plate and conveying the resulting iden-
tityless mess mouthward on the back of their fork. This is probably no worse, however, than eating mushrooms, baked beans, or
spaghetti on toast. I have never seen it done, but the temptation
is available on certain eating-house bills of fare. Coffee is ordered
at one's own risk. For dessert, it is probably wisest to choose
either fresh fruit or an assortment of cheese. British ice cream is
nearly always pallid, and the designation of flavors is merely a
frivolity; whatever you order, it's still only faintly tinted vanilla.
I have already paid my respects to trifle.

In resort towns like Brighton, Eastbourne, and Great
Yarmouth—in fact, wherever there is a high concentration of

lower-middle- and working-class custom on holiday: at home they seldom eat out—so-called restaurants typically are pot-luck eateries, with menus as brief as they are stained and dog-eared, food as distasteful as it is badly prepared, cutlery as dubious as the china is chipped, surroundings as fly-blown as they are shabby, and service as fumbling as it is slow. Eating in such places is solely a reflex action, because both the sensuous and the nutritional values of the exercise are nil.

Although there is probably a higher incidence of such repellent holes-in-the-wall—greasy spoons in the quite literal sense—in the resorts, they are common everywhere. A modest cut above them, but available only for tea and sometimes for lunch as well, are the little tea shops operated by middle-aged women with or without husbands and by pairs of elderly spinsters with or without mustaches. Their atmosphere and quality vary widely; some are chintzy-picturesque, while others are plain to the point of despondency. Since there is no evident correlation between quality of food and tone of surroundings, one simply has to take one's chances. It is no good asking an inhabitant: the average Englishman's opinion of a decent place to eat has little in common with an American's.

Given this bleak situation, there is cause for temperate rejoicing in the fact that among the many manifestations of the reputed American takeover of Britain is the Wimpy Bar. This is a snack-bar chain, owned by the firm which also operates the numerous Lyons restaurants, and is not to be confused with the great English construction company which bears the same name. After an unauspicious beginning during which their staples, a small variety of hamburgers and milk shakes, were but pale and skimpy imitations of the American originals, the Wimpy Bars have improved in recent years, and in certain neighborhoods of London and in county towns they often prove to be lifesavers. They are still of uneven quality, and they assuredly will never figure in any Britannic Michelin guide, but—it is a terrible thing to have to say—they are better than eighty per cent of the eating establishments, of all qualities, that one runs across on an average day. This generalization includes several popular snack-bar and eating-house chains which, for reasons not unrelated to the English libel laws, I forbear specifying.

The success of the Wimpy operation, revealing as it did the true seriousness of the English plight, has resulted in the appearance of several chains of imitation American restaurants and pancake houses, including some whose names invoke the dubious assumption that Kentucky and Texas are tabernacles of the haute cuisine. They are bright, chromish places with big electric signs and piped music. Americans are often surprised by what passes for American specialties in these establishments, and the prices and the quality of the food are unpredictable.

In most towns and middle-sized cities, the larger hotels offer the best chance of finding a satisfactory full meal. In fact, the most encouraging aspect of the British dining situation is the proliferation of good hotel restaurants. In hotels like the Grand in Northampton and the Bull in Peterborough, I have found excellent meals, well served, at prices surprisingly lower than the London rates for their equivalents. And the dining rooms themselves are usually attractive enough; year by year, more of them are being renovated to add comfort and cheer.

I said "the *larger* hotels." There remain many smaller ones— the kind of places to which travelers on modest budgets naturally tend to gravitate and which are, as well, the principal hostelries in small towns—where all that can be said of the meals is that they may well contain proteins and carbohydrates. If the meals themselves, in aspect and flavor, do not put one off one's feed, the surroundings may. Here, in a pathetic attempt to preserve out-dated graces, the waiters are dressed in tails and there is ritual hocus-pocus with the table settings after one has decided on one's order. But the intended effect is much diminished by the fact that neither the cloth beneath the switched silverware nor the waiters' apparel is necessarily immaculate. The tailcoats are worn and soiled and need brushing, the linen that peeps above them should have gone to the laundry some time ago, and the shoes at the nether edge of the equally neglected trousers are cracked and unpolished. The wearers, moreover, often are specimens from whose over-oiled hair dandruff descends to besprinkle the shoulders of neo-Edwardian dignity. Among them are a fair number of Italian and German youths who work for a pittance in English hotels to gain experience for their prospective careers at home. Unless they look upon the practices they observe and participate in while in English employ as examples of how not to do it, the outlook for Italian and German hotels in the coming years is unpromising.

In many a hotel restaurant, including those that are commonly reputed to be the best in their respective towns, the whole atmosphere takes its cue from the scurfy waiters in outmoded fancy dress. I remember especially a well-recommended hotel in a cathedral town which may remain nameless. It is situated where the main line of the railway intersects one of the principal streets, and the chief occupation of the decorative waiters, which seriously affected their availability for their nominal purpose, was to open and close the windows every five minutes as shifting engines passed by, distributing their cinders on the adjoining tables. Despite the waiters' getup and the imposing height of the ceiling (one had to overlook the condition of the curtains in the railway-facing windows), the tone of the place was that of an ill-managed commercial travelers' hotel, with the morose guests dutifully downing their food, preferably with the merciful distraction of an evening paper propped against the cruet stand. It is easy to believe that it was in such restaurants that the renowned British stiff upper lip was conceived and nurtured. But perhaps no more fortitude is needed in a dining room like this than in that of a country inn, where on a summer day wasps buzz in from the garden to hover over one's meal: for the British have never heard of screens.

III

"What two ideas," demanded the early nineteenth-century clergyman and wit Sydney Smith, "are more inseparable than Beer and Britannia?" Right. The pub is one of England's most admired and beloved institutions, and nowhere else can the visitor come into more intimate and unstudied contact with English life and people than on what are officially called "licensed premises." America has nothing comparable. Like the Continent, she has lately seen the establishment of a few so-called pubs in city hotels and airports, but they are mere shadows without substance, coy imitations and nothing more. For the whole authenticity and unique effect of a pub depend on its being populated by a genuinely British clientele, a commodity not easily obtained in midtown Manhattan or at O'Hare Airport. The pub is one product of Britain that by its very nature cannot survive exportation.

The true pub is neither a bar-and-grill nor an old-fashioned saloon nor a cocktail lounge. (If cocktails are to be had at a pub, they are not to be trusted. The idea that the British cannot make a drinkable martini is an old wives' tale, and like some old wives' tales it is true.) The pub is, above all, a neighborhood social center. People go to it to foregather over glasses of beer: to exchange local gossip, to discuss the news in the day's paper, to argue cricket and football, to get warm—and, in any event, to fill a spot of leisure in the manner most conformable to the English spirit. The custom of dropping in at a pub is, I think, far more widespread, more ingrained in the Englishman's daily routine from attainment of legal age to senility, than any single American practice I can think of. Wipe out the Royal Oaks, the Globes, the Angels, the Cat and Fiddles, and you wipe out the heart of England.

The clientele of today's pub exemplifies the delicate balance between traditional class stratification and democracy that is the essence of modern British society. In the country, where there may be but one pub serving a fairly large area, everyone attends: the farmer, the laborer, the shopkeeper, the artisan, the school-master, sometimes even the parson. The closest American ana-logue would be the old-fashioned crossroads general store. Even in towns, where the patronage of each pub is more or less defined by its immediate neighborhood, it is heartwarming to observe the extent to which social differences are overlooked in the camara-derie at the bar or around the small tables to which people carry their pints to drink in reflective or conversational leisure.

Yet the physical layout of most English pubs retains vestiges of the old class consciousness, even though I believe they are disappearing as new houses are built and old ones remodeled. The typical pub is divided into at least two parts, served by the same bar and the one accessible from the other, though each has its separate outside entrance: the public and saloon bars. The basic distinction is a matter of furnishings and a penny or two in the price of a pint; but in most neighborhoods there is a degree of social difference as well. In the pubs near the British Museum, for example, the saloon bar is the province of intellectuals and the public bar the haunt of workingmen and of authors of chap-ters about English pubs taking refuge from the intellectuals. Un-less I have been unaware of the censoriousness or pity that a social error elicits from the initiate, it is not a grave solecism to drink at the wrong bar. Your choice depends on what kind of company you want to keep, and the company on either side of the partition is interesting enough. They are all foreigners as far as the visiting American is concerned.

Even though there inevitably are pubs so severely parochial in their patronage as to give the casual looker-in a sense of being an intruder, in most of those I have sampled both in London and in the country, the atmosphere is friendly enough, in the character-istic unaffected English way. In pubs, as everywhere else in Eng-land, the prime rule for the American to follow is not to force acquaintanceship; this may prove to be the cue for a withering frost. If one is not content merely to sit and sip and listen to the conversations going on around one, the most tactful way of probing for an opportunity to converse is to engage the landlord in innocuous chitchat about the weather or local points of interest. Then (at least I have found it so) the talk can turn to some of the quaint differences between English and American customs —the point being that not all the oddness is on one side. Most pub keepers have, for one reason or another, a lively interest in what the Yanks say and do, and what they think of things over here, and any normally diplomatic stranger can quite soon feel himself at home in a pub.

American women probably feel more comfortable in the saloon bar, although the public one is by no means an exclusively male domain. And at this point it should be noted that in Britain women of all social classes patronize pubs freely. I cherish my memory of the Plumbers' Arms, a cheerful establishment in a fashionable section of London, where, as I drank a pre-lunch pint, a succession of women from the neighborhood, who had been making the rounds of the greengrocer and butcher, dropped in for a glass of sherry and to pass the time of day with the landlord and their acquaintances from around the block. To judge from their appearance and manner, these ladies might well have been scheduled to attend a garden party at Buckingham Palace that afternoon, and their husbands might well have been barristers or Harley Street consultants. And their humbler sisters, in other neighborhoods, patronize their own "locals" just as unselfconsciously.

Many pubs, if their history is investigated sedulously enough, prove to have literary associations. The George and Vulture, hidden in a court in the City, is an ancient port of call whose chief distinction is that it figures in *Pickwick Papers*. On the edge of Belgravia is the Bag o' Nails, now patronized by business men and women from offices in the neighborhood as well as by the staff of Buckingham Palace; it is often mentioned in Victorian fiction, in Thackeray's "A Shabby Genteel Story," for example. The origin of its name, like those of many pubs, is something of a mystery: "Bacchanales"? The old Elephant and Castle, which gave its name to a busy road confluence in Southwark, is said to have begun as the "Infanta of Castile," honoring Eleanor, the queen of Edward I. The Bull and Mouth, a name found in Bloomsbury and elsewhere, is traced more or less reliably to "Boulogne Mouth," alluding to Boulogne Harbor, captured in the reign of Henry VIII.

An imaginative attempt to exploit the natural affinity between liquor and literature is that of the Whitbread brewing concern, which has dedicated two of the several London "theme" pubs it owns to literary figures. One, the Gilbert and Sullivan, is in John Adam Street, just off the Strand and virtually in the shadow of the Savoy Theatre. In addition to a series of dioramas over the bar, depicting scenes in the various operettas, it displays costumes, playbills, and other memorabilia of the fruitful but tempestuous collaboration. "Mr. D'Oyly Carte would be pleased, sir!": the remark, proffered by a passerby as I photographed the pub's exterior, would, I hope, reflect the impresario's opinion of this shrine. If his name itself is excluded from the signboard, his portrait receives equal billing.

The other Whitbread pub of literary interest, nearby in Northumberland Avenue, appropriately close to New Scotland Yard until the latter's recent move to the Victoria area, is the Sherlock Holmes, formerly the Hound of the Baskervilles. The latter name was predestined to be given to a tavern on the site of the old Northumberland Hotel, because it was in this hotel that Sir Henry Baskerville suffered the mysterious loss of two unmated shoes. Its walls covered with paper of a peculiar mauve shade which, judging from the frequency with which it is met in such locales, must have been especially made for pub use at the turn of the century, the Sherlock Holmes has some relics of the master in the bar itself: framed copies of the famous Sidney Paget illustrations, and a plaster cast of a footprint ("Mr. Holmes, they were the footprints of a gigantic hound!") But the main attraction is upstairs. Separated from the grill room by a plate glass window is the replica of the living room at 221B Baker Street which was one of the unexpected hits of the Festival of Britain in 1951. It is a shade too crowded—in such cramped quarters Holmes could not very well have indulged in pistol practice nor could he have scuffled in any comfort with a criminal he had just dramatically exposed—but it is, after all, no more packed with furniture and accessories than the reproduction of a typical Victorian parlor one sees in the London Museum. And it does contain a marvelous collection of Holmesian objects, the violin on which he scraped eerie melodies, the signed portrait of The Woman, the wax bust which Mrs. Hudson periodically got down on her hands and knees to move ("The Adventure of the Empty House"), the tobacco in the Persian slipper, the *Britannica* and the other books mentioned in the canon, the file of docketed scrapbooks, the deerstalker cap.

The décor of pubs runs a great gamut, from the glossy, efficient modern style (called "American" whether or not it is) to the unpretentious, darkened-wood late Victorian. Many a pub, particularly in the country, has not been significantly altered for sixty years. The framed prints on the wall, typically hung a little askew and bearing the stains of damp and sheer age; the anonymous oils of hunting scenes and domestic anecdote; the stained glass in the windows and the engraved and frosted glass of the partition that symbolically separates the hind from the squire; the scuffed benches and tables; the great beer pulls behind the bar, resembling the levers in old railroad switch towers that had to be pulled by main force—they are all part of an atmosphere that might best be called Edwardian-functional, old-fashioned without being in any sense antique. Such pubs have no more esthetic appeal and no more definable flavor than a well-worn shoe. But they serve their humble, simple purpose, and there is charm in their very lack of vanity.

Sometimes, however, one finds a pub which, whether or not it is intended to do so, speaks to the same tastes that respond to the colorful advertisements of the British Travel and Holiday Association. There is, for instance, the White Hart at Puckeridge, on the road from London to Cambridge: one remembers its low-ceilinged little private lounge with a big fireplace, a table made from a huge polished section of a log, and all available floor and wall space devoted to antiques, including an old music box that plays the perforated twenty-four-inch ancestor of the modern LP record. The aura of such places occasionally is too studied, although that of the White Hart did not strike me so; but strings of harness brasses, polished tankards, stuffed birds under glass, samplers, warming pans, browned pictures of mustached cricket teams, coaching horns, and ranks of churchwarden pipes, whatever the motive behind their collection and display in places devoted to commerce, are certainly authentic accessories of the English scene.

Most pubs in both city and country provide food at lunchtime and some do so in the evening as well. The London establishments with a heavy midday trade have separate snack bars, where an attendant compiles sandwiches direct from a large joint of beef or ham, or from containers of crab meat or other fillings; in addition to this buffet-style service, some have table service, with full hot or cold lunches. The more modest pubs, besides affording a small selection of wrapped meat pies and sausage rolls originating, possibly several days ago, in some distant factory, are equipped with a landlord's wife or daughter who upon request will repair to the kitchen and fix up a plate of freshly made sandwiches, complete with mustard and a sprig of watercress. These improvised lunches, absorbed along with their proper accompaniment of a mug of ale in the inglenook of a country inn when most of the customers have gone back to work and the landlord is free to chat, can provide some of the traveler's most affectionate memories of England.

There is one aspect of pub routine, however, to which the American can never wholly accustom himself, and which the British themselves deplore. I mean the hours during which licensed premises can be open for business. Although the exact times vary from place to place, in general pubs are open three and a half hours (11:30 to 3) in the middle of the day and then close until five-thirty. The arid hours that intervene in the afternoon pose a problem to the summer pedestrian who spends the day traipsing about in humid weather when the temperature may rise to the high seventies or even the eighties. Then, if ever, does he have a legitimate claim to refreshment; and it is at this precise time that the pubs are most inexorably locked. Or, what is worse, their doors remain invitingly open, for the sake of a wholesome airing, and they thus constitute, along with the mocking signs indicating their fidelity to the brewing satrapy of Truman, Charrington, or Younger, a mirage in the sun-bright English desert. The damp fragrance of beer wafts from the shaded interior, there are inviting tables and chairs in the patio outside, but the bar is, by the solemn statutes of the kingdom, unmanned. The only worse torture of this kind is to find oneself, perspired, footweary, and above all parched, in a dreary stretch of London tenement- or warehouse-land at four o'clock in the afternoon, and come upon a looming brewery itself, as odorous of malt as its frothy contents are inaccessible. So did Tantalus suffer by his ebbing lake.

I personally find no hardship, however, though many do, in the pubs' evening hours, which generally—there are some local variations—reach from five-thirty to eleven. This allows ample time for the humane purposes of the institution to be served, and toward the end of the stretch the smoke- and noise-levels could not well be further increased without discomfort. As the canonical hour nears, the landlord blinks the lights as a warning: Order up, ladies and gentlemen, it's your last chance. If you happen to be staying at a country inn, and are already half-asleep upstairs after a long day on the road, there is pleasure in hearing the cheerful burst of sound below as the bar closes and the regulars echo their good-nights and start up their cars and motor scooters in the car park. To be awakened thus is fresh assurance that this is England, a land where certain venerable institutions and customs defy an age of swift and relentless change.

The names of pubs and country inns, along with the swinging signboards which illustrate them, are a fascinating study in themselves. In the country, the names of many inns have local significance. The sign of the Dundreary or Chatterley Arms is the customary tribute to the family which seemingly from time beyond recall has occupied the estate up the road, had at its disposal the living of the parish church (and sometimes, before the reforms of the nineteenth century, a Parliamentary seat), succored the poor with soup and blankets in time of agricultural distress, and occupied the magistrate's bench from which poachers and other malefactors were sentenced. If you would know who was the landed magnate before whom the tenants tugged their forelocks, read the sign of the nearest pub. Less frequently, country pubs are named for local events. There is a Piltdown Man in Sussex, for example—the beer it has on tap is unquestionably more genuine than the anthropological discovery it commemorates—and at Shepton Mallet, Somerset, is the Cannet's Grave, whose sign vividly records the summary justice visited upon a sheep-stealer. Local allusions are also found, though less often, in the cities. On Highgate Hill, London, there is, not surprisingly, a pub called the Whittington and Cat, for this was where, according to legend, a discouraged Dick Whittington heard the bells that recalled him to town and eventual dignity as Lord Mayor.

The indispensable requirement for all pub names which originated, as most of them did, in times when few wayfarers could read, was that they be clearly representable by an image on a signboard. It is to Britain's former widespread illiteracy that we owe the indubitable picturesqueness of inn nomenclature. In the country (and often in cities, too: evidence that urban sprawl has swallowed up what used to be villages) the names naturally tend toward husbandry and agriculture: the Lamb, the Bull, the Beehive, the Hen and Chickens, the Haycock, the Plough, the

Wheatsheaf. Occupational names—study of these, in connection with their locations, would be a profitable exercise for the social and economic historian—appear more frequently in town settings: the Drovers' Arms, the Railwaymen's Arms, the Watermen's Arms, the Bricklayers' Arms, the Masons' Arms, the Wheelwrights' Arms, the Carriers' Arms.

Then there are the patriotic-historical-ceremonial names: the Star and Garter (several inns so named are visible from the Thames between Hampton Court and Chelsea), the Marquis of Granby, the George and Dragon, the Rose and Crown, the Queen's Head, the Prince of Wales, the Nelson, the Wellington. And the mythical or outré: the Green Dragon, the Griffin, the Unicorn, the Swan with Two Heads, the Black Boy, the World Upside Down (offering a special opportunity to an inventive sign painter). Naturally, the naming of inns often takes a festive turn, with the Punch Bowl, the Jug and Bottle, the Jolly Farmer, and the Bunch of Grapes; and the natural relationship between conviviality and sport and popular entertainment is embodied in the Cricketers' Arms, the Bat and Ball, the Fox and Hounds, the Hoop, the Maypole, the Greyhound, the Fiddlers' Arms.

Finally, there are the many names which seem to have been chosen not for any overtones whatsoever but because they were so explicitly translatable into simple pictures: the Bell, the Feathers, the Seven Stars, the Rising Sun, the Peacock, the Anchor, the Bear, the Grenadier. And what a rich harvest one could make of inn names of all sorts from the pages of English literature! Dickens alone could supply some twenty-five, including the Three Jolly Bargemen, the Blue Dragon, the Pig and Tinder-box, the Jolly Sandboys, the Lightermen's Arms, the Nutmeg Grater, the Crooked Billet, the Magpie and Stump, the Black Lion, the Six Jolly Fellowship Porters, the Valiant Soldier, the Rainbow, the Three Cripples . . .

The imprint of inn signs on the modern English scene is all the more noticeable because the names have indelibly lent themselves to localities. One sees them on the destination signs of

London buses: Green Man, Mitre, Cricketer's Arms. Road maps of the Greater London area single out old-established pubs as the most easily identifiable landmarks (and the ones most likely to be known to the local inhabitants of whom one asks directions) : the Orange Tree at Friern Barnet, the Baker's Arms at Walthamstow, the Eagle at Wanstead, the Bald Hind at Chigwell, the Swan and Mitre at Bromley, the Robin Hood at Penge, the Old Tiger's Head at Lee Green.

Is it any wonder, given so evocative an anthology of names, that the American has so much affection for the English pub? How his heart leaps up, as he rides from London Airport toward the city, when he spots the first public house! So must that of every returning Englishman. There are many reasons, nomenclature being only one, why beer and Britannia are inseparable in Anglophilic sentiment. From my own congeries of memories I can disentangle one which there is good ground for believing is somewhat out of the ordinary. One warm evening in Tunbridge Wells, the regulars in a certain pub were copiously perspiring, the men in unaccustomed summer jackets, the women in equally unwonted sleeveless dresses. Although I made no complaint, when I returned to the bar to have my tall mug refilled, the barmaid, recognizing my nationality and therefore my supposed necessity, compassionately dropped two large ice cubes in my fresh beer.

*St. Martin's-in-the-Fields, London, from the portico of the National Gallery*

## 16

## Dimanche Anglais

*It was a Sunday evening in London, gloomy, close, and stale. Maddening church bells of all degrees of dissonance, sharp and flat, cracked and clear, fast and slow, made the brick-and-mortar echoes hideous. Melancholy streets, in a penitential garb of soot, steeped the souls of the people who were condemned to look at them out of windows, in dire despondency. In every thoroughfare, up almost every alley, and down almost every turning, some doleful bell was throbbing, jerking, tolling, as if the Plague were in the city and the dead-carts were going round. Everything was bolted and barred that could by possibility furnish relief to an overworked people. . . . Nothing to see but streets, streets, streets. Nothing to breathe but streets, streets, streets. Nothing to change the brooding mind, or raise it up. Nothing for the spent toiler to do, but to compare the monotony of his seventh day with the monotony of his six days, think what a weary life he led, and make the best of it—or the worst, according to the probabilities.*

THUS DICKENS IN 1857, in *Little Dorrit*. He had an inveterate hatred of Sabbatarianism, the neo-Puritan denial of pleasure on the Lord's Day which continental peoples have long regarded as among the most inexplicable aspects of the English character. Conditions have improved since his time, when a brief experiment in providing Sunday afternoon band concerts in the parks was summarily ended by a storm of protest from the pulpit, and when museums and art galleries remained resolutely locked. But the English Sunday still is a day set apart. One cannot help wondering if Dickens' last comment does not still apply. How much true pleasure does Sunday bring to the people whose well-accustomed if dull routine it uninvitedly interrupts every seven days?

In Chelsea and South Kensington and a hundred other London neighborhoods men are out in the street washing their cars and coming back from the newsvendors' Sabbath locations, preferably near churches, with the Sunday papers: the latter a ritual that has not changed for a century and a half, since the English masses first grew accustomed to being served juicy helpings of sensation (sex, crime, scandal in exalted places, political chicanery) on the only day of the week when they could afford a paper or had time to read it. The English Sunday press remains the most various in the world, ranging from the uninhibited vulgarity of the multimillion-circulation papers to the sophistication and workmanlike prose of the *Observer* and the *Sunday Times.*

The main thoroughfares leading out of London are noisy and odorous with the passage of countless cars and motorbikes, the latter divided somewhat unequally between those ridden tandem (by a speeding lover and his lass, or even husband and young wife) and those equipped with a sidecar, the badge of domesticity, family-laden and proceeding at a restrained pace. Tonight the seaside and the open spaces in the Home Counties will be littered with empty beer bottles, wrappers from iced lollies, crumpled cigarette packets, discarded paper plates and utensils, and thousands of tattered pages of Sunday papers, now cast to the winds. There will be traffic blocks in all the roads leading back to London.

In town, if the weather is fine, everybody who is left moves to the parks. A warm summer day finds the broad grassy acres of Hyde Park, Regent's Park, and every other one of London's "lungs" almost hidden beneath the hordes of deck chairs that have appeared from nowhere, their occupants continuing to expose their sun-starved skin long after it has acquired a nasty salmon color—an exercise marked by a certain desperation, so determined are Londoners to waste not a single precious ray of the unclouded sun. On Hampstead Heath as in Kensington Gardens, boys and men of all ages fly kites, swing cricket bats, and sail model boats in concrete basins (the one on Hampstead Heath, according to the official notice, is reserved for horses, but since horses are now in short supply, nobody minds the misappropriation). In bandstands in half a dozen parks in central London and beyond, bright-tunicked military bands offer potpourris from *My Fair Lady* and *Oklahoma!*—a form of innocent entertainment long *passé* in the States but still flourishing in Britain. Along the walks, people stroll, push prams, reprimand errant children, take snapshots, and cluster round the ice cream vendor.

Across the Thames from Chelsea, in Battersea Park, a boating lake, playing fields, tennis courts, and landscaped walks draw their thousands. But here the greatest crowd, drawing heavily on the multi-hued proletariat, is at the Fun Fair, another legacy of the Festival of Britain: a comprehensively planned amusement park, gay with red and yellow paint, containing all the usual garish American midway rides and booths but by no means devoid of British taste and wit. There are brilliant formal flower gardens with fountains playing, and a marvelous contraption designed by Osbert Lancaster, an anticipatory parody of constructional art in the 1960's—a crazy flying machine made of all kinds of unlikely odds and ends including oil lamps, children's sand spades, milk bottles, a dilapidated life-boat, and anything else that Lancaster happened to have around. Through the great old sycamores that line one of the roads winds a tree walk, a gangway suspended twenty or thirty feet above the ground; cunningly laid into the branches of the trees are models of birds and animals, an inn, a farmhouse, and even a few moving figures—the old Tunnel of Love idea now airborne.

Four or five miles away, at the Marble Arch corner of Hyde Park, Free Speech is going full blast. From a dozen podiums flow hoarse exhortation and philippic: the world's errors are being vehemently anatomized. A wiry little man in his late sixties, whose placard advises that he has been robbed of his invention by the War Office, harangues on many subjects, the common denominator of which is his persuasion that all Tories are liars and villains and that the country is in its present parlous condition because the Army, Navy, Air Force, police, press, and BBC are all controlled by Tories. All speakers—atheists, pacifists, African nationalists, vegetarians, homosexual law reformists alike—are subject to persistent, facetious heckling. Some of the hecklers are as regular in their attendance as the speakers themselves, and their repartee is as predictable as the speakers' arguments. Ideological opponents though they be, speaker and heckler work in harmony, the heckler anticipating and mimicking the speaker's pet phrases, the speaker for his part being ready with the expected squelcher. Here and there stand young policemen, in case—one gathers the possibility is remote—things get out of hand. It is to be hoped that their minds are far away, on such an uncomplicated subject as their girl friends, for example; otherwise, if they were attentive to this cacophony of fanaticism and dissent, their brains would addle. But the crowd is amiable, and if there is no deep thought at Speakers' Corner, neither are there any hard feelings. Nor is the entertainment confined to the makeshift platforms. Elsewhere in the crowd a gray-haired Salvation Army captain patiently leads a few bystanders in the singing of hymns; and a few feet away, in a space cleared by amused onlookers, two uninhibited women, sober, middle-aged, "respectably dressed" (as the Victorian phrase had it), and wearing National Health spectacles, foot it in a sedate dance of sorts as they sing pop songs from the twenties.

If the day is cold or rainy, the museums are the mecca. Sunday afternoon is no time for the art lover to visit the National Gallery. The pictures are obscured by the crowd, and in any case on a truly dark afternoon the lighting is insufficient. The Victoria and Albert, like the adjacent Science, Natural History, and Geology Museums, draws its thousands from the flats, bed-sitters, and private hotels in Kensington, and one's first sight of the crowd that surges in when the doors are opened suggests that it is as unsatisfactory a place to spend Sunday afternoon as the National Gallery or the Tate. But the V & A is a huge complex of exhibition halls, and the secret is that nearly all the Sunday clientele remains in the areas nearest the two entrances. It is there to kill time, not to explore. Walk to the remoter rooms, such as those displaying fine glass and porcelain, and you find they are as deserted as on a dull weekday.

Meanwhile the regions around the London railway stations are packed with haggard families returning from what is over-optimistically called a holiday. They swarm through the station and down into the Underground: men and women of all ages and conditions, as well as unkempt teenagers, bent almost double under knapsacks and bed rolls; 'arrassed 'Arries and their missuses and infant brood, loaded with all the numerous, miscellaneous, awkward, and sometimes irrelevant impedimenta of a family on 'oliday. Presumably, despite all the anxieties and irritations they have endured, down deep they have enjoyed every moment, and now are returning, refreshed, to their dismal tenements and their cottages along monotonous semi-suburban streets.

Show me a nation on the move and I'll show you its character. The corollary to which is, the worst side of a nation's character is brought out at the popular seaside resorts. Whether he stands in a safe coign of vantage in a London station as the weary mobs pour from the trains or strolls the esplanade at Eastbourne or Brighton, inspecting the compatriots who have succeeded them for the next week in the beachfront hotels and gloomy back-street lodging houses, the student of modern proletarian life observes all he needs to observe in order to make a judgment. In the towns by the sea, the ineffaceable English love of bright flowers in profusion is the most distinctive national characteristic, as it is the most agreeable. There is usually a "parade" facing the beach, well planted with flowers and shrubs, perhaps with a floral clock or other designs; and the municipal lampposts bear capacious plantings, with vines trailing down from the edge of the tubs. But in the more populous resorts, at least, the beach (which in England is often composed of sharp stones, not sand) presents the same spectacle as at Coney Island or Atlantic City—the same gruesome revealment on the part of those who should not undress except in strictest privacy, the same clutter of food, comic books, paperback novels, and newspapers, as well as a pile of extra clothing to be added or removed as the ever capricious sun and breeze require, and, except where barred by local fiat, a blaring transistor radio. Conveniently near are the amusement piers, the catchpenny games and souvenir kiosks, the fish-and-chips and cotton candy establishments that cater to the spend-thrift and sensual impulses of the British masses at their fun.

Not all holiday resorts are like this, however. Along the coasts of England are occasional modest towns which mostly serve the regional trade. Exmouth, for instance, a clean community ten miles southeast of Exeter, has a wide and genuinely sandy beach and resolutely excludes honky-tonks and all other possible magnets for the "undesirable element." Apart from the broad floral esplanade and the beach itself, there is nothing but a small aquarium, a miniature golf course, a heated swimming pool, and a few other decorous diversions. Across the estuary, the Devon hills roll their patches of fields and clumps of woods right down to the water.

In other old-fashioned resorts there are greens for bowling, on which, in the lingering sunlight of an early summer evening, one can behold elderly men in white flannels and elderly women in white skirts and hats gravely measuring the lay of the jack. It is a scene out of an Edwardian photograph album, and it will not be available much longer. More recognizably modern (though their origin can be traced to the development of the *char-à-banc* a century ago) are the coach tours that are offered to holidayers at most resorts, whether by the sea or inland, throughout England. Still suffering a serious deficiency of private cars as compared with the American per-capita supply, the British depend heavily upon motor coaches for their pleasure traveling. Coaches transport them in great numbers from their cities—London, Sheffield, Manchester, Birmingham, Leeds—to their holiday resorts, and no sooner are they there than they are tempted to take to the road again. Especially when rain discourages the carefree outdoor life they confidently came to enjoy, they have their choice of trips to various nearby castles, stately homes, scenic spots, and other desirable destinations. They will be kept under cover en route, at least; and maybe by the time they get there the sun will be out. But, rain or shine, there is always the delicious uncertainty of the Mystery Tour which is advertised to leave at 2 p.m.: where, oh where might it be going? With such modest ventures into the unknown is British holiday life spiced.

Back in the workaday towns, Sunday winds its slow length, On a rainy morning in Nottingham, depressed families wend their umbrellaed way to church, hoping that there will be something diverting on the telly after dinner. In the afternoon in Huddersfield and Halifax, young men in their Sunday clothes emerge from the frowning brown terraces and dutifully push prams along the sidewalks, where even on Sunday the air is heavy with the sulphurous smell of coal fires. At the bus stops wait queues of workmen in cloth caps and Pakistani women wrapped in saris. Outside the pubs other knots of men await the opening hour.

And in every city, from London on down, in the afternoons and evenings people pass Sunday as they pass it in every city in the world—going to the cinema, promenading the business

streets and pausing at shop window after shop window, admiring
the latest styles in clothing, the newest triumph of household-
appliance engineering, and doing dreamy mental arithmetic provoked by the advertised hire-purchase terms. Among them are a
number of hungry Americans, who have discovered that the
worst part of the *dimanche anglais* is the closing of the restaurants. Except in the hotels and in certain regions like Soho meals
are hard to find. Most of the restaurants one takes for granted
during the week because they are omnipresent, even some of the
Wimpy Bars and Lyons houses, are locked. It is possible to walk
for miles in London's most-traveled streets before finding a place
to eat. And oftener than not it is the restaurant with the dullest
food and the most brusque service that eventually proves to be
the only one open. This is one serious accompaniment to the
English Sabbath which Dickens overlooked, doubtless because
like most Englishmen he had a home where he could dine. The
mingled chime of bells on a London Sunday, to which he inex-
plicably objected, can be endured; indeed, heard at vesper time
in the Strand the counterpoint of peals is a positive delight. But
the famished visitor could wish that the ringers would settle for
one less change and substitute for it what Byron called "That all-
softening, overpowering knell,/The tocsin of the soul—the dinner bell."

*The Shambles, York*

# 17

# English Is What They Speak

*I said it in Hebrew—I said it in Dutch—*
*I said it in German and Greek;*
*But I wholly forgot (and it vexes me much)*
*That English is what you speak!*
                    —*Lewis Carroll,* The
                    Hunting of the Snark

ONE OF THE minor advantages of exploring England rather than
some other country is that the language difficulty is neither
wholly nonexistent, which would make things dull, nor very
formidable, which might make them awkward. Some introduc-
tions to Britain written for the benefit of Americans include
glossaries, but these seldom are required by people who have
read their share of English books. Biscuits, not crackers, are
served with cheese as a postlude to dinner (crackers is when an
Englishman goes mad, or, synonymously, *round the bend*). A
*geyser* (pronounced *gayzer* or *gizer,* with a long *i*) is the hot
water heater which is inoperative when you want to take a bath.
You *book,* which is to say reserve, your railway or theater seats, at
a *booking office,* which also sells just plain tickets. You seek, and

often receive, information at a desk marked *enquiries* (*inquiries* is often seen nowadays, but I much prefer the antique spelling) . You make *trunk* calls on the telephone, though "long distance" is beginning to appear; and when the operator cuts in to ask "Are you through?" she—or he—means, Have you got your party? not Are you finished? *Across the road* is usually heard instead of the American *across the street; the next turning* is our *next corner; straight on* is the British idiom for our *straight ahead.* Terms like these are, of course, easily acquired from everyday experience. It does not take long to discover that a *subway* is a pedestrian tunnel only, that a *service,* in transport vocabulary, is a route or line, sometimes with additional reference to a peculiarity of schedule (pronounced *shedule*) ; and that the *way out* signs which are prominently displayed on railway platforms are not descriptive of avant-garde fashions, habits, or notions, but are simply the lucid Anglo-Saxon way of saying *exit.* When you pick up your dry cleaning at the shop, do not be alarmed if the *assistant* (our *clerk*) asks you if she should put your suit or dress in a *shroud;* she simply means a plastic bag.

In nearly all cases, English variations from American usage— perhaps it would be more polite to say this the other way round —can easily be divined from context. There are just enough of them to give a little more flavor to the scene. Pronunciation, however, occasionally offers larger difficulties, because it is unpredictable. Slight shifts of accent—laboratree for example—are of little moment. But once one knows that family names like Cholmondeley (the most notorious example, I suppose: pron. Chumley), Marjoribanks (pron. Marchbanks), and Featherstonehaugh (pron.　　　?　　　) are onomastic snares and delusions, he is on the lookout for other traps. If he tries to apply either logic or learning to the problem of speaking the tongue as the natives speak it, however, he is a predestined loser.

I once went in search of Theobald's Park, a former sixteenth-century estate in Hertfordshire, on the northern edge of London. I wanted to see Christopher Wren's famous Temple Bar, the

Palladian gateway which marked the boundary between the Strand and Fleet Street, and therefore between Westminster and the City, until it was taken down as a traffic bottleneck in 1878 and re-erected at Theobald's Park. Now everyone with the slightest acquaintance with the history of English literature knows that there once was a Shakespearean editor named Lewis Theobald, whom Pope pilloried as the King of Dullness in *The Dunciad* after Theobald pointed out the defects in Pope's edition of Shakespeare. His name was pronounced "Tibbald," and Pope so wrote it: "There hapless Shakespeare, yet of Tibbald sore,/ Wished he had blotted for himself before." Therefore, when I sought directions at a bus stop in Walthams Cross from a man in London Transport uniform, I asked for Tibbald's Park. He was a pleasant man and a knowledgeable one; he told me he was preparing to become a guide on one of London Transport's sightseeing tours. But "Tibbald's" rang no bell with him. Finally, feeling like a tourist myself, I showed him my guidebook. "Oh, The-o-bald's Park!" he exclaimed. "Yes . . ." I obeyed his directions, which eventually delivered me, after a lengthy trudge along a muddy, gnat-infested country lane, to Temple Bar (it turned out to be in bad shape, partly boarded up and hedged about with barbed wire: a depressing sight). But I haven't yet got over the episode of the man at the bus stop. I devoted several years of my life to earning a Ph.D. so I would be able to pronounce words like Theobald to the satisfaction of the English. To have them reverse their immemorial custom and pronounce a name as spelled is, to my way of thinking, dirty cricket. The day will come when Meopham (pron. Mepp'm), Marylebone (pron. Marlybun), Beaulieu (pron. Bewley), Bicester (pron. Bister), Alnwick (pron. Annick), and Chiswick (pron. Chizzick) will be true to their appearance. It will be a black day for all who prize the sublime illogicality of the English tongue.

But all is not lost. There remains to the lover of linguistic odds and ends, for one thing, the genteelism of public admonitions. True, the lengthy lists of forbidden practices displayed at the entrances to the royal parks—St. James's, Hyde, Regent's Parks, Kensington Gardens—are couched in strict and explicit bureaucratic periods. (It is noteworthy, by the way, that the prohibitions do not cover the sport of love, which proceeds on the greensward as if the notice boards contained, instead, a garland of Elizabethan invitational lyrics.) But once inside the park, only the velvet tongue is heard: PLEASE KEEP TO THE PATH. At construction sites, instead of the stern command seen at their American counterparts, workers read: YOU ARE ADVISED TO WEAR A HELMET. The grammatical imperative is used as seldom as possible, and the substitution of the tactful suggestion seems, in general, to have good results. UNSUITABLE FOR MOTOR VEHICLES, declares a sign at the entrance to an unpromising-looking country lane. You are not prohibited from venturing your motor vehicle upon it, but you are deferentially counseled not to. Sometimes the plea is picturesque in execution as well as in phrasing; in the parking lots at country pubs I have seen, in graceful antique lettering, *Please Park Prettily*. When asked in so winning a fashion, you do. And because the habit of the English in enforcing everyday laws and recommending conduct is so markedly toward restraint and diplomacy, there is much shock value in deviations from the usual practice. When you approach a roundabout on a highway and are confronted by a huge martinet of a sign which roars REDUCE SPEED NOW, again, you do.

I suppose that it is this gentility of language which, more than anything else, distinguishes the British mode of public announcement from the American. The City of Westminster sanitation trucks, according to the lettering on their flanks, belong to the *Cleansing* Department. What a difference in elegance, not to say euphony, the addition of a single letter makes!

On the whole, English newspapers are no more restrained or circumlocutory in their prose than are American ones. But in at least one conspicuous circumstance their evasiveness is superb: that is, when it's a question of possible libel. Since the British, despite all their justifiably vaunted freedom of speech, have extremely strict libel laws, the press must treat criminal cases with almost ludicrous circumspection. In a news account of a murder, for instance, the writer may simply say that the police "would like to interview" a man seen in the neighborhood shortly before the deed who, they say with elegant understatement, "may be able to help them in their enquiries." Translated into American idiom, this means the police are pretty sure he done it.

The daily headline posters seen at every newsvendor's stall and sidewalk pitch are a study in themselves. Seemingly hand-lettered (but they are really mass produced at the plant and delivered with the latest edition), they say just enough to whet the curiosity. These posters are not an ideal way of keeping abreast of the day's news, but they are always a dependable guide to what the circulation department thinks will sell the papers. The finest poster I ever saw was lettered SIR WINSTON CHURCHILL: RUMOUR DENIED. What an ingenious way to move papers—by advertising what is frankly admitted, if the point is pressed, to be non-news, and yet stimulating the curiosity! I was not sufficiently intrigued by the (now denied) rumor to buy a paper and find out what it was, but I admired the sales dodge no end. Possibly the office functionary who devised the poster remembered the occasion, legendary in Fleet Street, when the *Star* issued a poster reading THE POPE: NO NEWS. The headline was strictly true, but the dull day at the Vatican sold many extra thousands of *Stars*.

On these posters, only six or eight words, at most, can be accommodated. To have maximum effect, they must be short and arresting. SENSATION is a bit too long, though it is sometimes seen. The best words for the purpose, I have concluded, contain just five letters. The most useful word is DRAMA, whether it refers to a fire rescue, an episode in court, a would-be suicide on a window ledge, a child temporarily lost or trapped, or some other relatively routine incident of metropolitan life. In addition to its connotation, DRAMA has the advantage of being cryptic: even when preceded by CHILD, RAIL, SEA, FIRE, COURT, or whatever, the special plot line goes unrevealed until one buys the paper. The legend, in other words, doesn't blow the gaff. Almost equally useful are such other five-letter words as CHAOS (as in RAIL CHAOS, which means some trains are delayed), SMASH, CRASH, BLAST, SHOCK (it is amazing how many shocks the British population survives in the course of a year), THEFT (as in JEWEL THEFT) and, of course, DEATH. To this list may be added CRISIS, because its two thin I's make it in effect a five-letter word. A sustained study of these posters could constitute an instructive lesson in economical writing reduced to its ultimate rudiments. You can't easily communicate in fewer words than they do—and it would be impossible to do so more dramatically. DRAMAtically.

Whatever else the English landscape, whether urban or rural, contains, its incidental signs always hold the promise of unexpected delight. In the gallery of the Victoria and Albert Museum which displays Raphael's cartoons for tapestries commissioned by Pope Leo X, performances of chamber music are sometimes held; hence the sign near the one door, CONCERT TOILETS: MEN AND WOMEN. A South Kensington fish restaurant, only a minute's walk from the museum, is THE CONTENTED SOLE. But its paronomasial resonance is feeble indeed when compared with the name of a restaurant housed in a barge moored in the Regent's Canal at the London Zoo, THE BARQUE AND BITE. In such an environment it would be possible, though not very likely, to see the sign NO TIPPING; but it is distinctly odd to see the same words on a large sign in what seems to be a completely irrelevant place in the countryside. The answer is that "no tipping" also means "no dumping." I have also seen, at the entrance to a rustic lane in Dorset, NO TANKS ALLOWED—disconcerting, to say the least, even if one hypothesizes that the area is used for army maneuvers, but not as disquieting as meeting, as I once did, a Royal Army baby tank itself bucketing down a country road, with a big red L sign (the standard notification that a learner is aboard) displayed fore and aft. Is the West Country particularly rich in note-downable signs? Certainly it is there that one finds my favorite of all English place names, the inimitable ITCHEN ABBAS;

and it is only in the vicinity of Taunton and Bridgwater that I have seen, in the windows of pubs, the legend—of disturbing sociological significance, however unremarkable otherwise—NO GYPSIES SERVED HERE. These placards were not improvised on the premises but printed: evidence that they could be bought at local shops or, perhaps, were supplied by the local "licensed victuallers' " (publicans') association.

Every connoisseur of the humors of language collects his own business directory from English signs and newspapers. His discoveries assure him, for one thing, that dramatists and novelists such as Ben Jonson, Smollett, and Dickens, who liked to christen their created figures with names especially appropriate to their characters or occupations, did not have to invent them; they simply copied from life. Near Chessington, Surrey, are the Digger Nurseries, and in the London suburb of Lewisham is a firm catering to another kind of nursery: G. Swaddling, prams, toys, and baby furniture. At Oxford a firm of plumbers and hot water-fixture installers is Cooke and Dowse. In London, on Clapham Common, there is a bookmaking office conducted by A. and P. Stallion. At York a dental surgeon is named F. Grindrod. Somewhere in East Anglia—I think in Cambridge or Peterborough—is a firm of solicitors named Honnybun and Son, who presumably would not advise in divorce or breach of promise cases. In Cornwall I have seen the vans of the Catchall Dairy Company, and nearer London, at Camberley, there is the firm of F. W. Greedy and Sons, undertakers—a circumstance which seems to confirm Jessica Mitford's dark view of the mortuary profession. On the A6 road between Lancaster and Kendal there is the unfortunately named Heaves Hotel. This is not, however, the Lancashire inn outside whose dining room is mounted a whole battery of machines vending indigestion remedies.

For some reason, English real estate agents, members of a grave and honorable profession, tend toward risible names. Projecting from windows of houses and flats in the poshest reaches of Belgravia one often sees the "to let" or "for sale" signs of Pay, Lord, and Ransom, the suitability of which might easily be verified by applying to the firm for the asking prices. It is at Exeter, if memory serves me, that one finds the firm of Giddy and Giddy, surveyors (i.e., appraisers) and estate agents. And on one page of advertisements in the London papers can be found a whole galaxy of firms whose styles undoubtedly have provoked much ribald humor: Gascoigne Pees, Balls and Balls, Fuller Horsey. To the facetiously inclined, dealing with real estate concerns must be fraught with hazard.

The simple entertainments of English signs and news items are endless. At Harrods department store we find a display of "Flowers Specially Designed for Homes with Central Heating": plastic, of course. And it is impossible not to wonder if these synthetic flora will be featured at the next meeting of the Beaconsfield Flower Arrangement Society, at which "Arrangement for the Home" will be discussed by Mrs. A. Gotobed . . .

*Mount St. Michael, near Penzance, Cornwall: the "guarded mount"
of Milton's* Lycidas

$\text{\large ৯ঌ৯ঌ৯ঌ}$

---

## 18

---

# Thundery Rain in Some Areas, with Sunny Intervals

ONCE EVERY YEAR, some time between the first of May and the
first of September, there is a day in the British Isles which is
known as "British Travel and Holiday Association Photography
Day." It dawns cloudless, and it remains cloudless throughout;
the sky is deep Mediterranean azure, the sunlight pours down,
and there is just enough breeze to stir the flowers, which are at
the height of their bloom, and just enough heat to encourage the
noonday patrons at every pub in town and country to carry their
mugs outdoors. During this euphoric day, professional photogra-
phers all over the island, descending on picturesque spots they
have long had in view for just such an occasion, snap color pictures like mad. The results will appear in the travel association's
advertisements and brochures for the whole ensuing year, and
millions of Americans, among others, will be tempted to believe
that Britain is indeed a place of incessant sunshine, where
healthy young men and women in expensive and immaculate
outdoor attire find unbroken happiness in exploring quaint out-
of-the-way villages, talking with the friendly natives, and ad-

miring the Horse and Waggon inn sign that projects from under the thick thatch of the roof.

When that jocund day is over and the regular procession of
Atlantic low-pressure areas ("depressions" in BBC terminology)
resumes its inexorable movement into their island, jolly Britons,
meeting on the street under their dripping umbrellas, will greet
each other, "That was a fine summer we had yesterday!" And if,
in addition to the rain, the weather is chilly, they will quip
"Merry Christmas"—as I have in fact heard them do, as the
torrents beat against the windows on the top of a country bus in
Kent on June 27. My records show that at noon on one July 28,
when the United States may well have been boiling in hundred-
degree heat, a trenchcoat was none too warm as I walked across
Tower Bridge under low menacing clouds, a piercing wind blow-
ing down the river. I can also testify that in the late afternoon of
a certain Sunday, August 24, I shiveringly fed sixpence into the
gas meter in a hotel room in Peebles, Scotland.

These latter are (unlike the Photography Day) facts. The
English weather in general is a fact. And on few unalterable facts
has more attempted humor been lavished; it is, in short, a stale
and unprofitable subject. I admit it into these pages only for the
sake of a few philosophical observations.

Thanks in part, perhaps, to the way the English themselves are
always deploring it, the horrendousness of their climate has been
exaggerated beyond its deserts. In the months during which most
Americans experience it, it does tend toward dampness. In fact,
rain can be very frequent. The first wave of summer visitors
arrives in the middle of June, which is Ascot week; and Ascot
week, as any Londoner will assure you, is always recognizable by
its heavy clouds, frequent showers, and wind—and when the
wind dies down the humidity soars. On the other hand, many
days every summer are truly Photography Days, when the only
clouds are high, white, fleecy ones that do nobody any harm but,
on the contrary, make one's pictures of the South Downs or Lake
Windermere all the lovelier. Furthermore, granted that the aver-

age rainfall in a given summer is fairly copious—this is, after all, an inseparable accompaniment to one's English experience. I have never been seriously or lengthily discommoded by rain. One obvious way to checkmate the weather is to keep one's plans flexible enough so that indoor explorations—churches, museums, ducal palaces—are reserved for inclement hours. *Carpe diem* when the sun shines. One can never be sure how long one's luck will last and so it is advisable to stay outdoors as much as one can.

To an American, the two deepest mysteries in Britain are cricket and the weather. They are mysteries of different types, however. Cricket, I am willing to believe, ultimately can be understood and appreciated, and in any event it is not made *unnecessarily* inscrutable by its commentators; such oddities as it possesses are inherent and unavoidable. The weather, however, in addition to being full of vagaries in the first place, is made more exasperating (and, if you can be disinterested about it, more fascinating) by the sublimely ambiguous formulas the forecasters use. They seem mortally afraid of going out on a limb, or perhaps of disappointing someone. Hence, the day, every day, is foreseen as being both bright and cloudy, dry and wet. A uniform meteorological state, steady rain, for instance, or simply "fair and warm," is evidently unthinkable, or at least undesirable. In the daily forecast there must be something for all tastes and to cover all contingencies. Joseph Wechsberg, in an informative *New Yorker* article some years ago on the London fog, remarked on the "on-the-one-hand-but-on-the-other-hand" stance the official weathermen assume when asked when a thick fog will lift. He quoted a newspaper as saying, with British understatement, "The Meteorological Office is less forthright about fog than about other weather." In view of the feats it performs with the latter, this is no mean achievement. And to compound the ambiguity, the prophecies sometimes don't agree. I have heard two television channels giving flatly contradictory forecasts within five minutes of each other.

But in fairness, it must be admitted that British weather is in truth capricious and variegated. No amount of scientific pre-analysis can cover its hourly whims, and it is likely that by such cautious, touching-all-bases divinations British officialdom is merely facing up to that fact. *Most* English days are dappled. Looking out the window at the breakfast hour, one's hotel waiter may confidently, and sincerely, predict a fine day. Three hours later, after completing an inspection of the local museum, one may emerge to find the rain pouring down and passersby dodging the water the buses splash up from the gutters. At that very moment, five miles away, the sun may be shining brightly, and in half an hour it may be shining here as well. A comforting, if possibly unsupportable, axiom is that most British rain falls in the shape of heavy showers and that a degree of good-humored patience and faith in native institutions will soon see one out on the sunny side. In any event, how could England's countryside be so lushly green, its flowers so gay and prodigally flourishing, if it were not frequently moistened? And where would Constable have been if he had not had so inexhaustible a supply of dark, lowering clouds to paint?

There is a reliable formula for the American visitor to use if he really wishes to outwit the weather. If the day dawns lead-colored and threatening and he is in a cathedral town, say, where the subjects for camera study are many, he will naturally yearn for constant sunshine and blue sky. Encouraged by what he has read in the preceding paragraph, he will bide his time, sure that in half an hour or so the great façade will be bathed in light. An hour passes, and the skies remain leaden. Despairing, he then takes his pictures, glum in the certainty they will not do justice to their subjects. As soon as he has finished the roll, the skies miraculously clear, the birds sing, and the sun adjusts itself perfectly to his recent needs. This happy circumstance will prevail until he is ready to photograph his next point of interest, at which time even more ominous clouds will again assemble, to be dispersed only by a repetition of the ritual.

The best weather-proofing the visitor to England can have is a sense of humor and a determination to overlook the darker days. Many sundials on English lawns bear the legend, "I count only the sunny hours." The English have learned to do so; to stay sane, they have had to. So can their visitors.

*The Mill, Magdalen College, Oxford*

---

## *19*

---

# *The Last of England*

The BOAC bus on its way to London Airport crawls through the noontime traffic of Earl's Court. A passenger's thoughts are governed by the title and spirit of Ford Madox Brown's touching picture, "The Last of England": a young man and wife aboard an emigrant ship, staring back, heavy with feeling, as the English coast disappears. When, if ever, will they see it again?

It's goodbye to England, to all the little touches that make her English. Goodbye to one's favorite ghost from the past, memorialized by a tablet in Norwich Cathedral: the charmingly named Osbert Parsley, *"musicae scientissimo,"* for fifty years in the sixteenth century a singing man in the cathedral. Goodbye to the morning pint bottles of milk on the doorstep of every London shop and office, where the tea interval (several times a day) was a venerable institution long before America dreamed up the coffee break. Goodbye—in this case, forever—to the commemorative names of London telephone exchanges, now being abolished in favor of anonymous number combinations, American style: POPE's Grove, MACaulay (the area served is Clapham, where the historian's family, along with other leaders of early nineteenth-century Evangelicalism, had their Zion), BYRON (at Harrow, where the poet went to school), ARNold, GULliver, KIPling, WORDs-worth, FLAXman, FRObisher, KELvin, GLAdstone. Goodbye to the sharp double stamp of leather heel on pavement as the solitary sentry at St. James's Palace about-faces at the limit of his brief patrol. Goodbye to that superlative sole *bonne femme* at Bentley's in Swallow Street, and to those sumptuous teas at Fortnum and Mason's. Goodbye to "God Save the Queen" played in the theater after the curtain has fallen and the standing audience chafes to be outside, competing for cabs or heading for the nearest pub before closing time. Goodbye to the wild New Forest ponies exercising their ancient proprietary rights by loitering on the main highway and cropping the grass in the front garden of the Lyndhurst station of the Hampshire Constabulary. Goodbye to the nasty-looking *chevaux de frise* that top the high walls enclosing the Oxford colleges—spikes, jagged pieces of metal, and (most conspicuously) a multitude of broken beer bottles embedded in the mortar. One would imagine them to be a fairly persuasive deterrent to convivial undergraduates bent on stealing back to their rooms after the gates are closed for the night.

And goodbye to that recurrent mystery of the English countryside which, for the sake of assuring the imagination free play, one never really wants solved—the mystery of what lies behind the stone walls or palings, backed by thick woodland, that stretch along the road for a quarter- or half-mile or even longer. The only break is at a road entrance guarded by a gatekeeper's lodge, usually an example of Victorian domestic architecture at its least inspired. Seldom is the place identified by a sign; evidently everybody who has any business knowing what it is, already knows. Whose estate, whose "park" is this—what lord's or earl's, what county family's which atones for lack of blue blood in ancientness of residence? What volumes of history are contained in the great house, unseen at the end of the long winding avenue of elms?—stories of advantageous intermarriages with other landowning families, of younger sons falling of wound or disease in Bengal, of enclosure programs and poaching episodes and charity to the poor tenantry, and politics and travels to London for the fashionable season . . . Bounded by those old walls, erected so many years ago by hands now dust in the parish churchyard, are the scenes of innumerable English novels. This is where it happened: the beguiling thought that every book-reading tourist carries with him as he passes yet another sequestered, many-acred seat of the aristocracy or landed gentry. Goodbye to all these for now, because they belong exclusively to the English soil and such few examples as America possesses are mere impertinent imitations.

Hawthorne once more: "England . . . comprehends so much, such a rich variety, within its little bounds. If England were all the world, it still would have been worthwhile for the Creator to have made it; and mankind would have had no cause to find fault with their abode—except that there is not room enough for so many as might be happy there."

But no, this will never do; not at this moment of imminent parting. To ease our going, let us resolutely look on the less engaging side of our subject. Notwithstanding Hawthorne (a man not ordinarily given to hyperbole, who momentarily sacrificed his customary realistic moderation in that last sentence) and notwithstanding John of Gaunt, too, in his dying speech in *Richard II,* England is not in fact an earthly Eden, a "demiparadise." It has a number of deficiencies, most of them no doubt unimportant in the long run, but serious enough to argue (at the moment) against the wish to remain on her soil forever.

For one thing, there is the incessant dampness, present in the ditches and the fields and inside the houses even when the sun is bright overhead. The soiled mackintosh is the uniform of a stoic people resignedly enduring their climatological lot. Nothing— when one is in a deliberately jaundiced mood—better symbolizes Britain than those shapeless brown macs, and, in the country, the gum boots the churls wear as they herd the cows, scythe the grass by the roadside, or clomp along the village street. Inside every English door is a well used array of wet-weather gear. The pervasive clamminess and muddiness is one of the least agreeable built-in qualities of English existence.

Indoors, the dankness often can be smelled. And in many public places such as Underground stations, the offense is compounded by the strong odor of the disinfectant which the British favor. Here no attempt is made to overlay the smell with an ersatz fragrance, pretending that a germ killer masquerading as *eau de lilac* is an adornment of life instead of a blunt sanitary measure.

In England the ear, too, is sometimes assailed, as by the stridency of the middle-class conversational voice when raised in an animated social group. Listen to six or eight well-bred men and women chattering away over tea or after-dinner coffee in a hotel lounge, and you will tolerate no more nonsense about Americans being loudmouthed.

And while Americans sufficiently love dogs, in Britain caninophilia is a national obsession. Walking dogs is a ritual that proceeds independently of weather, cataclysms, and the movements of the planets; they are led or carried everywhere, into department stores, fishmongers', greengrocers', buses, trains. Who can easily overlook the foul condition of the sidewalks in residential neighborhoods? Official signs deplore and threaten to punish dog owners' negligence, but they are universally disregarded.

Furthermore (let us be ruthlessly frank) there is nothing very attractive in the physical appearance of most English people belonging to what used to be called "the masses." "The English populace," wrote Henry James in 1877, "are as ill-dressed as their betters are well-dressed, and their garments have that sooty surface which has nothing in common with the continental costume of labour and privation. It is the hard prose of misery—an ugly and hopeless imitation of respectable attire." James goes on to speak of their "flushed, empurpled, eruptive masks" which are suggestive of "alcoholic action." The attributed reason may no longer be valid, but the observation itself certainly is. In a wholly different social environment than the one James knew, an environment indeed which he could not possibly have envisaged, where the standard of living among the commonalty has markedly improved and the benevolent institutions of the welfare state have alleviated some of the cruelest forms of misery, the rank and file of English people still are not very comely to look upon. It is not so much the empurpled, eruptive complexions of which James complained, nor their too often pinched, careworn features; these may be due to physiological and psychological causes which are not easily remediable. More distressing is their shabbiness of apparel. The women, most of them, exhibit an almost studied, defiant dowdiness that strikes most forcibly the observer from a country where women of all classes strive to be stylish, whether they succeed or not.

Nor is this a characteristic of the working class alone. One often sees in provincial towns examples of an English type as numerous as retired colonels: the gentlewoman-farmer, masculine and hard-bitten in mien, distinguished by bobbed gray hair, floppy hat which between wearings may serve her grandchildren in a football match, shapeless pullover and skirt, and battered brogans; seen in a tea shop on her weekly visit to town, she looks as if she would be more comfortable carrying a cattle prod than a handbag. English girls—christened above their station as Daphne, Cicely, Jennifer, or Valerie—seldom live up to the promise of their euphonious names; only in a few sections of London, for example, do you find many young women who are worth a second glance. The gawky, chlorotic adolescent schoolgirl in her straw boater and striped summer blazer, looking eternally beaten down and resentful, is matched in unattractiveness only by her pasty-faced male coevals, Simon, Jeremy, Clive, Anthony, and Basil. (It is easy to understand why the single quality in American teenagers which the English most notice and envy is their brimming robustness.)

Except for professional men and businessmen of the grade of superior shopkeeper and above, the average English male is poorly dressed. The workingman's apparel is a badge of his class:

cloth cap, worn jacket, sometimes a knotted neck scarf in lieu of collar and tie, and seediness written large over everything. His garb when at work is merely a more threadbare version of what he wears when at leisure. There is something significant, though I don't know quite what, in the fact that his working uniform, unlike that of American or continental workmen, is improvised from mufti, not specifically adapted to his occupation as, for instance, overalls are. Construction workers, railway crewmen, and laborers on the land typically dress in a rumpled, stained assortment of ordinary clothing which long since lost its last vestige of presentability. Thus bricklayers officiate on their scaffolds and street cleaners wield their brooms in shirtsleeves and unbuttoned, dirt-encaked serge waistcoats.

When I first knew England, I was inclined to attribute the general indifference to appearance, not only among the laboring and artisan population but in much of the middle class as well, to the lingering effects of the war and the ensuing years of economic deprivation. Now, in the light of Henry James's observation many decades earlier, I am not so sure. The temptation to believe that this negligence is an innate and ineradicable national characteristic is supported also by the sight of the dwellings the English build, whether in public ("council" or "corporation") housing projects for lower-income families or in privately undertaken ones for the middle class. The typical American low- or medium-priced building development is not, heaven knows, a thing of overwhelming beauty, but at least the architects and builders make a token gesture toward styling because it is expected. The houses of the ordinary English suburb, however, whether they were built in the twenties or the sixties, are utterly devoid of proportion or grace; squat, boxy, composed of stucco or red brick, tile roofs, and casement windows thrown together with no particular effect in mind, they are a characterless package which today can only be called Labour Party Tudor. And there is still the problem of the dresser backs! A generation ago, Miss Mary Ellen Chase in *This England,* one of the finest of

all American appreciations of the modern English scene, remarked that in nine out of every ten modern English dwellings
you pass, the front bedroom window is occupied by the back of a
dresser mirror, which, in addition to effectively cutting off the
light, hardly enhances the house's external appearance. Today,
all the resources of British architecture and interior design have
not succeeded in moving the dresser away from the front window. Perhaps the English like it where it is.

But disparagement must have a stop, and as the airport bus
passes the junction of the A30 to "Staines and the Southwest"
Hawthorne's words return: "England comprehends so much,
such a rich variety, within its little bounds." One's thoughts are
drawn to the sweet countryside the road will traverse on its long
westward progress: the dairy farmland of Hampshire, the swell-
ing, bolster-like downs of Wiltshire on whose slopes graze flocks
of sheep, the serene villages and fields of waving gray-green cereal
crops in Dorset, Somerset, and Devon. It is in this spectrum of
the southern counties, reaching say from Cornwall eastward all
the way past London to the Kent coast, that one finds the qualities of scene that can be called "quintessentially English." Despite the new housing estates and ribbon developments along the
main roads and the growth of light manufacturing near the
towns, the predominant memory one retains is of villages little
changed from the aspect they had a hundred, two hundred years
ago, with their clusters of thickly thatched roofs, cottage walls
covered with climbing roses, windows open to the summer air—
and half visible through the great old trees, the gray tower of the
ancient parish church in its plot of lichened and time-effaced
gravestones.

In one way, the true quintessence of English beauty, as Hawthorne suggested, lies in its sheer variety. Typically, the flavor
and scale of the countryside are lyric, not epic. Most truly "English," to me at least, are the ochre stone villages of the Cotswolds huddled together on the sides of hills or in the fertile green
valleys, and the compact domesticated ruralness of Oxfordshire,

Warwickshire, and the Home Counties—Surrey, Sussex, Kent, Hertfordshire, Essex—with their kitchen gardens and orchards, their fields and manor houses, their copses and threading byroads living side by side in comfortable contiguity. But any portion of the countryside south of a generously arced line drawn from the Wash to the mouth of the Severn (excluding Northamptonshire and Bedfordshire, which are merely tame) is likely to meet the book-bred American's specifications, for it includes Henry Fielding's western counties, George Eliot's Loamshire, Hardy's Wessex, George Meredith's Surrey, and the Oxfordshire of "Thyrsis" and "The Scholar-Gypsy." These settled regions, gently undulating for the most part, populous with towns and villages and every square foot of soil under cultivation, are by no means the whole of England, however. One thinks, as Hawthorne may have done, of the unexpected ruggedness of the Pennines and the Yorkshire moors, and above all of the Lake District, more descriptively called the Cumbrian Mountains, whose desolate distances, heights, and rushing mountain-fed streams suggest certain portions of the Wyoming tablelands. One may indeed wander lonely as a cloud for many unpopulated miles, but the way is often steep and stony. And at the other extreme there is the uncompromising, almost unnatural flatness of most of Lincolnshire and East Anglia, topography which seems to have been created by a gigantic road roller. For a country often called "miniature," England manages to embrace immense variety. No larger, along with Wales, than the state of Georgia, "this little land," as Emerson wrote, "stretches by an illusion to the dimensions of an empire. . . . To see England well needs a hundred years."

Yes: there is so much more to be seen, thinks the departing traveler; so much more to take its place alongside present cherished memories. The gorgeous Adam library at Kenwood, the eighteenth-century mansion on the edge of Hampstead Heath, once Lord Mansfield's country place and now a distinguished picture gallery; the tranquil deer park and water mill at Magdalen College, Oxford, too picturesque to be real, yet real they are; innumerable villages like Goudhurst in Kent, the plaster of its half-timbered walls glowing in the late afternoon sunshine; the York Castle Museum, richest of the numerous provincial social-history collections, with its recreated streets of well-stocked Victorian and Edwardian shops; John Gower's tomb at Southwark Cathedral, brilliantly colored in red, green, and gilt, with the poet's effigy-head resting on the three dreary books which won him his fame, the *Vox Clamantis,* the *Speculum Meditantis,* the *Confessio Amantis;* quiet cathedral closes, such as those at Salisbury, York, Durham, Lincoln, and Peterborough, with their insistent suggestions of Trollope. (What must it be like, in these later years of the twentieth century, to live in a Georgian house in the immense shadow of a medieval cathedral, where the wife of the master of the choir school parks her little car alongside an ancient wall lined with hollyhocks, and the decanal television antenna coexists with gray flying buttresses? If there is such a mental state as chronological schizophrenia, it surely must flourish in these precincts.)

And (despite the splenetic generalized remarks above), one can never erase from affectionate memory the charm, helpfulness, and good humor of individual English men and women of all classes: The manager of a branch bank in Berkeley Square proudly showing a new client the restored eighteenth-century decorations in this mansion owned for several generations by a collateral branch of Captain Bligh's family. The red-cheeked, middle-aged woman so often met in village lanes who, having given directions to a nearby site, always proves to have relatives in Philadelphia whom the inquirer perhaps knows. The Automobile Association road patrolmen in their khaki whipcord uniforms, saluting every car with an AA medallion on its front and ready to repair a tire or adjust a carburetor on the spot. And, of course, the policemen in town and country, disturbingly young nowadays, looking self-conscious and status-proud behind their helmet chin straps. Such a diversity of occupations and costumes: Black-gowned barristers, skimpy powdered wigs perched on their pates, holding curbstone post-mortems behind the Law Courts in the Strand (near an office building named Oyez House). Colorfully uniformed, service-ribboned doormen and bank messengers, middle-aged and beyond—retired noncommissioned officers of Her Majesty's armed forces who fill responsible civilian jobs as members of the élite Corps of Commissionaires. At Oxford, the morning when examination results are posted, exuberant young men, still in the requisite garb of gown, white tie, and stiff white collar, standing on convenient doorsteps in the High Street and —incredulous at their success—tossing off glasses of champagne rushed from the nearest off-license establishment, and in the intervals between libations eating juicy red strawberries, all to the amused admiration of knots of onlooking town youth.

The diversity of England is embodied even in its sounds. There are the cries of the hawkers whose booths and barrows crowd the Sunday morning marketplace in "Petticoat Lane," London—cries designed to sell jellied eels, lingerie, household wares, fruit, leather goods, bric-a-brac, cheap jewelry, novelty toys, almost anything that is portable and even faintly susceptible to purchase; one cannot resist the suspicion that Scotland Yard is often curious about the provenance of some of the variegated merchandise exposed here. There is the deferential peal of an ambulance bell in traffic, so subdued to American ears, so different from the raucous wonk-wonk of emergency vehicles on the Continent. There are the notes of a not quite professional brass band experimenting with "Jesu, Joy of Man's Desiring" in the nave of Worcester Cathedral. And there is the unmistakable, confident Englishness of Elgar's music filling the great reaches of the Royal Albert Hall during a summer prom concert, as English an institution as Elgar himself, where thousands of young people, having queued outside for hours, stand in the pit throughout the evening and thousands more stand, sit, lean, or lie three deep along the broad horseshoe of the gallery promenade at the top of the hall. Whatever its vocal animal spirits between numbers (the stage attendant lifting the lid of the grand piano is ritually greeted by lusty shouts of "Heave!") , when the orchestra plays, utter attention prevails: a remarkable evidence of the spell good music exerts over London's student youth. Sir Henry Wood, founder of the proms in 1895, upon whose bronze bust at the back of the orchestra shell a wreath is lowered during the festive evening that marks the end of each season, might well look upon his handiwork and find it good.

But if the essence of England—the eventually undefinable attraction it holds for so many Americans, no matter how well they have come to know it—is to be captured in a single vignette of sound, I propose what I once heard in London's Sloane Street: a street musician on a virtually deserted pavement, playing, not a banjo, not a cornet, not an excruciatingly screechy fiddle—but an alto recorder.

Such are the disordered fragments of impression and reminiscence that have coursed through one's mind on the way to the airport. Here is the Overseas Departure Building—

But no! Not the sadness of farewell but the fair promise of return must occupy the last page of a book devoted to the pleasures—and occasional asperities—of England. And so: a fresh Arrival. (In my beginning is my end.)

In northern France, the landscape has been vivid with Van Gogh colors, the reapers busy with their modern machinery under a golden sun. But as the Channel steamer *Invictus* nears the chalk cliffs of Dover, perfidious, dependable Albion sends English clouds out to meet her. And as the boat train, emerging from the tunnels cut into the cliffs, picks up speed for its nonstop run to Victoria station, the sky has settled into its customary ashen twilight hue. Under the grayness, the county of Kent with its odd-shaped oast houses where hops are dried, its orchards and Victorian-vintage country places and manicured greenswards of cricket grounds, prepares for another evening. Along the hedged country road that is about to dive underneath the railway line slowly pedals a policeman, his folded raincoat lashed to his bicycle's handlebars. Cars are beginning to pull into the parking areas alongside the inns with their hanging pictorial signs of Roses and Lions, Crowns and Roebucks, Turk's Heads and Dolphins. It is a placid scene, utterly uneventful, maybe even spiritless and dull; but it is England, and that is all that really counts. Somehow—somehow—you know you have come home again.